FUNDAMENTAL PRI

Land Law

AUSTRALIA
The Law Book Company
Brisbane • Sydney • Melbourne • Perth

CANADA
Carswell
Ottawa • Toronto • Calgary • Montreal • Vancouver

AGENTS:
Steimatzky's Agency Ltd., Tel Aviv;
N.M. Tripathi (Private) Ltd., Bombay;
Eastern Law House (Private) Ltd., Calcutta;
M.P.P. House, Bangalore;
Universal Book Traders, Delhi;
Aditya Books, Delhi;
MacMillan Shuppan KK, Tokyo;
Pakistan Law House, Karachi, Lahore

FUNDAMENTAL PRINCIPLES OF LAW

Land Law

by

Mark Thompson, LL.B (Leicester); LL.M. (Keele)
Professor of Law in the Newcastle Law School at the University of Newcastle upon Tyne

First Edition

LONDON
SWEET & MAXWELL
1995

Published in 1995 by
Sweet & Maxwell Limited
of South Quay Plaza,
183 Marsh Wall, London E14 9FT
Computerset by LBJ Enterprises Ltd.
Aldermaston and Chilcompton
Printed in England by Clays Ltd.,
St Ives plc.

A CIP catalogue record for this book
is available from the British Library

ISBN 0421 527102

No natural forests were destroyed to make this product only
farmed timber was used and re-planted.

Preface

Land Law is an immense and complicated area of law which affects many people in society. Different people may have different concerns about land. To take two examples, for some the principal concern is that they have secure accommodation: for others, their main interest is in the commercial value of the land. At times these different aspirations, and others, may conflict. One of the tasks of the law is to seek to accommodate these different aspirations.

Land law is, probably more than most other subjects, an area of law where regard must be had to its history in order to understand the basic principles. Yet these principles developed when social conditions were very different from those that currently pertain. Part of the fascination of Land Law is to see how the basic principles have been adapted to meet different circumstances and how different policy considerations have been afforded varying priority at different times. In this book, I hope to explain the basic principles in sufficient detail for the reader to see how the law has been able to adapt to modern social conditions and be stimulated to view Land Law as an important, relevant and developing subject and one which repays further study.

This book is not, and is not intended to be a comprehensive work. In keeping with the general ethos of the series, I have tried to avoid becoming immersed in the finer details of the subject but, instead, sought to concentrate on what I perceive to be the more important principles underlying the subject and the issues involved in the application of those princples. Necessarily this involves omitting important areas: in particular, there is no discussion of the important topics of the statutory regulation of land use, either by planning legislation or the legislative regime affecting housing in either the private or the public sector.

It remains for me to offer my heartfelt thanks to the staff at *Sweet & Maxwell* for their encouragement and help throughout the period when this book was being written and for their skill in the production of it. I am also grateful to them for relieving me of the burden of producing the tables and index.

M.P. Thompson
Newcastle upon Tyne

CONTENTS

TABLE OF CASES

TABLE OF STATUTES

CHAPTER ONE

The Scope of the Subject

Land is a valuable commodity within society. Its principal utility is, however, viewed in different ways by different people. For some, the main value of land is that it represents a home. This will frequently be the case with residential tenants, but will also be true of freeholders. Similarly, people who share the property with the legal owner of it will also be concerned that dealings with it do not prejudice their interests: they will be concerned that the house is not sold over their heads. While it is true that most owners of land will be concerned not only with security of accommodation, but also with the resale value of the land, for some people this is their principal concern. Land is seen principally as an investment or a security for a loan. In such circumstances, it is of considerable importance to them that it is as easy as possible to be able to realise the asset by selling it.

The essential point to make, at the outset, is that, because people have different outlooks on the utility of land, it is inevitable that these interests may conflict. Thus, the greater the protection that the law gives to residential security in land, the less easy it will be for that land to be sold. Therefore one of the tasks of the law is to seek to strike a balance between the competing expectations affecting the land.

The conflict of interest does not only arise between people whose main concern is residential security and those whose principal interest is in the land as a realisable commercial asset. For many years, there has been a desire by some families to preserve the land as an undivided unit to be passed from generation to generation. This desire, to keep land in the family, conflicts with the wider view of society that it is in the general public interest that land should not be permanently removed from the market place. Because there exists only a finite amount of land, the more one permits such inter-generational transfers to be secured, the less land there is available to be bought and sold. Accordingly, this ambition with regard to the land is regulated by legislation.

The wider interest of society in the means of ownership of land has a considerable impact on the development of the law. Thus, when some of the underlying rules governing land ownership were being developed, land was seen in a very different way from the way it is seen today. When modern Land Law started to develop, society was organised upon feudal lines. One's interest in land was very important in determining one's status in society. As times changed, land became to be viewed in more economic terms; as being a commercially disposable asset. Consequently, a good deal of the pre-existing structure had to be unravelled, in order to effect this change. Despite this unravelling, a good deal of the underlying structure of Land Law remained essentially intact and, in consequence, to understand today's law, it is frequently necessary to have regard to principles developed during different social conditions.

Similarly, as conditions and social needs change, new regimes have to be superimposed upon existing structures. This can take the form of imposing substantial statutory regulation on a system developed principally by the common law, as occurred in the rental sector with legislation known collectively as the Rent Acts, or by the introduction of wide scale regulation of land development by planning legislation. In these instances, the basic principles of the subject are left substantially unaltered but they are heavily affected by a statutory superstructure. In other cases, it may be that existing principles are not thought to be sufficiently adaptable to meet modern requirements, with the result that new structures need to be developed. A good example of this is the proposal to introduce a new system of landholding, known as commonhold.[1]

In addition to ownership of the land itself, there exist a wide range of rights that can exist in other people's land. Examples of such rights include a right to cross a neighbour's land or a right to prevent a neighbour from using his property for business purposes. Such rights can be extremely valuable. One of the main factors that adds to their value is that, in general, these rights are not personal to the parties who created them. Rather, whoever acquires the land that enjoys the benefit of the particular right also acquires the right. Conversely, the purchaser of the

---

[1] See (1987) Cmnd. 179 (the Aldridge Committee.)

other plot of land is constrained in the use to which he can put that land to by the existence of that right. The land is subject to the particular burden.

Owing largely to the physical nature of land, it is particularly suitable to accommodate a large number of different interests in it, those rights being enjoyed, at least potentially, by a considerable number of people. One of the main tasks of Land Law is to create a structure whereby these rights are secured while, at the same time, not impeding, unduly, the market in land. One of the tasks in studying Land Law is to assess how satisfactory the law is in accommodating the various interests and expectations that people may have in land. To do this, it is necessary to understand the principles upon which the subject is based.

REAL PROPERTY

Land is frequently referred to as real property. The origin of this is historical. The basis of the term lies in the form of action that was used to vindicate a right. If a person, X, was dispossessed of his land by Y, then X could bring an action to to recover the land, itself: the res. Consequently, the type of action that was brought was termed a real action and the property in respect of which a real action could be brought was termed real property. By way of contrast, in the case of certain other property, such as a horse, if a person was dispossessed of it, then the wrongdoer could either return the horse or pay damages, representing its value. Such an action was termed a personal action. Generally, all actions relating to land or to interests in land were real actions and those to other forms of property were termed personal actions. Hence the basic division in English Law is between real property and personal property.

At the time that this distinction developed, a person who held a lease of land could not recover the land by a real action, if he was dispossessed. This was because a lease was regarded as a commercial transaction and so outwith the feudal system of land holding. This changed in the fifteenth century but, by this time, it had become accepted that leaseholds were to be regarded as personal property. To modern eyes, this seems wholly unrealistic and leaseholds have long been regarded as part of the law of real property, although, technically, they are still referred to as chattels real.

The distinction between real and personal property formerly carried with it some important distinctions, mainly relating to the rules on intestacy. Nowadays, the modern tendency is to distinguish between land and other forms of property but the term, real property is still commonly used.

THE MEANING OF LAND

Land is defined by section 205(1)(ix) of the Law of Property Act 1925 to include land of any tenure, and mines and minerals, buildings or part of buildings (whether divided vertically or horizontally), corporeal hereditaments; a rent and and other incorporeal hereditaments and an easement, right, privilege, or benefiting, over, or derived from land.

It will suffice at this stage, without going into some of the terms used in the definition, to point out that the definition of land extends beyond the physical entity of land and buildings but includes, also, rights over land. In addition to this, one can also consider the position of the air above the land and the ground below the surface. It is a maxim of English Law that the owner of land is presumed "to own up to the sky and down to the centre of the earth."[2]

Put into context, this means that the owner of the land owned mines and minerals below it. This principle has since been modified by legislation so that, for example, coal and gas are now publicly owned[3] but remains intact for other purposes, so that valuable items found below the surface, unless they constitute treasure trove or gold and silver found in a mine which belongs to the Crown, prima facie belong to the owner of the land.

Of, perhaps, rather greater importance is the ownership of the airspace above the land. The result of this is that if an object such as an advertising hoarding projects into a landowner's airspace, this constitutes an actionable trespass.[4] This approach, which is, perhaps, limited to incursions below what is a reasonable height above the ground[5] and does not, generally, apply to aircraft[6] is potentially important, both in the context of construction work in populated areas and also to what are known as flying freeholds,[7] examples of which include freehold flats, where what is owned is, in essence, a block of space in the air enclosed by the building.

FIXTURES

A further important area in determining what constitutes land is the position of fixtures. These are items of property that were

---

[2] *Corbett v. Hill* (1870) L.R. 9 Eq. 671 at 673.
[3] Petroleum (Production) Act 1934, s.1; Coal Industry Nationalisation Act 1946; Coal Industry Act 1987, s.1.
[4] *Kelsen v. Imperial Tobacco Co. (of Great Britain and Ireland) Ltd* [1957] 2 K.B. 334.
[5] *Bernstein v. Skyviews & General Ltd* [1978] Q.B. 479.
[6] Civil Aviation Act 1982, s.76, replacing earlier legislation.
[7] For flying freeholds in Lincoln's Inn, see Lincoln's Inn Act 1860.

originally merely chattels but have been attached to the land in such a way that they become part of the land itself. This issue is principally important in two contexts. First, when a person has contracted to sell a house, the purchaser is, from the date of the contract entitled to have conveyed to him all fixtures, unless they have been excluded from the transaction by the contract.[8] As a result, the vendor may find himself committed to conveying property that he had not intended to include in the sale. Secondly, if a tenant attaches fixtures to the building then, at the end of the lease, the landlord is, subject to the tenant's right to remove certain fixtures, entitled to those fixtures.

Test for Fixtures

In determining whether a particular item is a fixture, the courts have regard to two factors: the degree of annexation and the purpose of annexation. The degree of annexation means, simply, how firmly the object is fixed to the land. The greater the degree of annexation, the greater the likelihood that the item will be held to be a fixture. Regard must be had, however, to the purpose of annexation. Some items cannot be properly enjoyed as chattels, unless they are fixed, in some way to the property. Thus in *Leigh v. Taylor*,[9] the issue was whether a valuable tapestry was a fixture or a fitting. While it was physically attached to the property it could be removed without undue difficulty or causing damage to the property. Moreover, given the nature of the object, it could not properly be enjoyed unless it was attached to a wall. Accordingly it was held not to be a fixture. Similarly, items that rest upon their own weight, such as statutes, are unlikely to be held to be fixtures.[10] On the other hand, if the purpose of the attachment is to improve the general design of the room, then the item is likely to be held to be a fixture.[11] A wise vendor will take no chances and deal with such matters in the contract of sale.

Tenant's Fixtures

As indicated above a tenant has, during the lease, and, in certain cases for a period after the termination of the lease, the right to remove certain fixtures. Were he not able to do so, this may discourage him from running a business to the best effect. The

[8] See, for example, *Phillips v. Lamdin* [1949] 2 K.B. 33. (An Adam door held to be a fixture).
[9] [1902] A.C. 157.
[10] See *Berkley v. Poulett* [1977] E.G.D. 754.
[11] See *Re Whaley* [1908] 1 Ch. 615.

types of fixtures that may be removed fall into three categories: trade fixtures, ornamental fixtures and agricultural fixtures.

An example of the first category occurred the right of the tenant in *Elliott v. Bishop*[12] to remove fittings of a public house. In the category of ornamental fixtures, a more narrow view is taken of what fixtures can be removed and is generally limited to items that can be removed intact and without damaging the property.[13] The position of agricultural fixtures is now governed by statute, the current provision being section 10 of the Agricultural Holdings Act 1986.

[12] (1854) 10 Exch. 496.
[13] *Spyer v. Phillipson* [1931] 2 Ch. 183.

CHAPTER TWO

The Doctrines of Estates and Tenure

It is a common, but erroneous, belief that individual people own land in this country. This misconception frequently does little actual harm but it can obscure a proper understanding of the theoretical underpinning of English Land Law. The reasons why it is technically inaccurate to speak of people actually owning land in this country are the doctrines of tenure and estates. While the first concept is historically interesting, but of little practical importance, it is true to say that a proper understanding of estates remains of contemporary significance.

TENURE

Prior to the Norman Conquest in 1066, there was in existence a rudimentary feudal structure in English society characterised by a system of strip farming. After the invasion, a more far-reaching and sophisticated regime was introduced. The King, by virtue of conquest, regarded the whole of England as belonging to him. This remains the case today, so that it is still true to say that all land in England and Wales, technically speaking, is owned by the Crown.

To reward his followers, the King made grants of land to the leading barons. These powerful individuals held their land directly from the King in return for the provision of services. The people who held directly from the Crown were termed tenants in chief, or tenants *in capite*.[1] The provision of services in

---

[1] These people were the subject of the Domesday Book.

return for the land was central to the system and was the origin of the doctrine of tenure. The word derives from the Latin, *tenere*, to hold, and indicated the terms upon which the land was held.

There were many forms of feudal service, these being divided into three main types: chivalry,[2] spiritual and socage (principally agricultural). These tenants, themselves, made grants of part of their lands to other people, who, in turn, held their land in return for the provision of feudal services for their lords. That person could, in turn, make grants of land to other people, again in return for the provision of feudal dues. This process, termed subinfeudation, enabled a feudal pyramid to be established. The King was at the apex, with the next rung down being occupied by the tenants in chief.

Among the consequences of this feudal structure was that of escheat. This doctrine, as originally developed meant that a person who committed a felony would lose his land to his superior lord. Similarly, if a tenant died without heirs, then the holding would be at an end and the land would revert, by escheat, to the superior lord.[3]

The existence of the feudal pyramid was, for a number of reasons, considered unsatisfactory. To prevent the continued practice of subinfeudation, the Statute Quia Emptores 1290 prohibited the creation of new tenures. This meant that, instead of further rungs in the pyramid being created, dispositions of the land acted as a transfer. The incoming tenant replaced the previous landholder. In addition, the exaction of feudal dues fell into desuetude and were initially replaced by the payment of money, known as quit rents, in their stead. These, too, after a time ceased to be collected and the feudal system started to decay.

As with any organic system that cannot grow or reproduce, the system of tenure started slowly, but surely, to decline. As it was impossible to create further rungs to the pyramid, movement occurred in the opposite direction. The number of feudal holdings shrank, with the result that, today, it is readily assumed that all land, which is not leasehold, is held directly from the Crown: we are all tenants in chief.

ESTATES

The doctrine of tenure explained the terms on which people held their land. The far more important doctrine of estates explains principally for what length of time the land is held.

[2] For some of the more outlandish forms of tenure, see Megarry's *Miscellany at Law*, pp. 154-157.
[3] For a modern example which, by a happy coincidence involved a property called The Phoenix, see *Re Lowe's* [1973] 1 W.L.R. 882.

What is an Estate?

If a person owns a car then, subject to the general law, there is no restriction on what the owner can do to it. He can drive it, sell it, give it away, destroy it or leave it by will. The restrictions imposed on the enjoyment of the car relate to matters such as the manner in which it is driven, or the condition of the driver when the driving takes place. Any restrictions are imposed by the law to safeguard the public interest. The "owner" of land has similar rights. Generally speaking, such a person can sell the land or give it away, either while still living or by will. The land can be built on or left to go to rack and ruin. As is true in the case of ownership of a car, however, there are also restrictions imposed upon how one uses land. These restrictions generally derive from the law of nuisance or from statutory provisions, such as planning regulations. As with the example of the car, these restrictions upon use are imposed to protect the public interest. Given the generally unfettered rights that exist with regard both to the car and to the land, a question that arises is why it is that one actually owns the car but, in the case of land, one does not actually own the land but, instead, owns an abstract entity known as an estate in land.

The principal reason for this is that, in the case of land, it is quite possible for various important rights of ownership to be divided among different people. It is, of course, true that, in the case of a car, this can also happen: car leasing arrangements being an obvious example. In the case of land, however, there is much greater scope for various rights associated with ownership to be divided between different people and so the structure of ownership needs to be sufficiently flexible to accommodate this. To a considerable extent, the doctrine of estates performs this role.

To give examples of the separation of various ownership rights, in the context of land, one can look at the right to possess. It is quite possible and, indeed, at one time it was relatively common, for the right to possess land to be ceded to another person for that person's lifetime. Because the person allowed into possession did not have total dominion over the property, his enjoyment of it being limited by the fact that his rights were limited to his lifetime, then, even ignoring the theoretical idea of ownership of estates in land, as opposed to ownership of the land, itself, it is evident that such a person could not be said to have all the rights of an owner. To give another example, a person may wish to limit the ability of another to leave property on death to people outside the range of the immediate family. Again, this desire could be accommodated by the use of estates.

Freehold Estates

Traditionally, estates are described in terms of time periods: the length of their duration; although a feature of freehold estates was also that that duration was uncertain at the outset. At common law, there were two estates: the fee simple and the life estate.

The fee simple. The word fee means that the estate was inheritable. Simple meant that the inheritability of the estate was not limited in any way. So, if a person owned a fee simple in land, it would pass, on his death, to any member of his family, however remote. It is, of course, inherently unlikely that a person will die without leaving any relatives. The prospect, therefore, of this estate terminating is extremely remote. Because it was inherently improbable that the original owner of the fee simple would die without heirs, if he sold his interest, then the duration of the purchaser's fee simple would be measured by the survival of his family. To relate the duration of the estate to the survival of the vendor's family would not have been practical. As will be seen, this is not so in the case of lesser estates.

To reflect the size of the estate, a person who owns a fee simple has the largest collection of ownership rights that it is possible to own with respect to a piece of land. It is the closest that it is possible to come to ownership of the land itself. Moreover, the persons hoping to inherit the land after the death of the fee simple owner do not have rights in the land during his lifetime. They have merely the hope, or *spes*, of succeeding to the land. They do not, therefore, have any right to restrict the use to which the fee simple owner puts the land.

Qualified fees simple. The fee simple described above is not qualified or cut down in any way. It is a fee simple absolute. A fee simple can, however, be cut down. For example, a person may be given a fee simple which is expressed to determine on a given event, such as " to A in fee simple or until he becomes a solicitor." In this event, the fee simple is a determinable one. While it is true, that the determining factor may never occur, it might do. If it does, A's interest will determine and some other person will become entitled to the land. That person, therefore has a contingent interest in the property.

A further example of a contingent interest would be one where a testator leaves land in his will, in fee simple, " to the first of his children to qualify as a barrister." At the time of his death, he may have had several children, none of whom, as yet, have satisfied the relevant condition. In these circumstances, the people who are potentially entitled to the property do not have a present interest in the property; they merely have a hope that one day they will become entitled to the land. If the condition is satisfied, however, the person who qualifies will become entitled to the land thereby ending the entitlement of another person.

In cases where interests of this nature are created, by the use of contingent estates, the nature of the contingencies may be rather more complex than that seen in the example given above. The result may be that it may not be known for a considerable period of time whether the contingency, or contingencies, will ever be satisfied. To avoid this uncertainty persisting for too long, the rule against perpetuities, the details of which are beyond the scope of this book,[4] operates to limit the time period during which these contingencies are permitted to operate.

The life estate. The second freehold estate recognised by the common law was the life estate. The duration of this estate is self-explanatory. A couple of points can be made, however, with regard to the estate. The principal right that the holder of a life estate, who is referred to as either the life tenant or the tenant for life, has is physically to possess and enjoy the land in his lifetime. Because his interest is limited, however, some restrictions had to be placed on the extent of that enjoyment. At the end of the life estate, another person would become entitled to enjoy the land. Unlike the situation where a person has a contingent interest in the property, in this case, it is certain that the condition of entitlement will be satisfied. The holder of the life interest is certain to die at some time and the person next entitled, or his heir, is bound to succeed to the property. This means that the person entitled upon the death of the life tenant has a present interest in the property; the only element of futurity is his right actually to possess the land. To reflect that person's existing right in the land, it would, therefore, be wrong if the use by the owner of the life estate was allowed to exhaust the value of the property. To circumvent this possibility, the doctrine of waste developed.

Waste. Technically, the doctrine of waste means a change in the use of the land. This may improve the land, ameliorating waste, or it may cause the land to deteriorate in quality. A person with a life estate was not generally liable for ameliorat-

---

[4] See Megarry's *Manual of the Law of Real Property* (7th ed.) Chap. 6; (1993) Law Com W.P. No. 133.

ing waste.[5] Nor, in general, was he liable for permissive waste: that is the natural deterioration of the property caused, for example, by the failure to repair buildings, or clean out a ditch.[6] On the other hand, he would be liable for voluntary waste: that is actively committing acts which reduce the quality of the property, such as the cutting of timber. Even if, as not infrequently occurred, the life tenant was expressly made unimpeachable, *i.e.* not liable, for such waste, he would nevertheless be liable if what he did effectively amounted to acts of devastation.[7]

The fee tail. The original two freehold estates did not meet the demand of some for a legal device which enabled land to be retained within the family over successive generations. To meet this demand, the Statute De Donis Conditionalibus 1285 ushered in a new estate, the fee tail. Tail derives from the French "taille", meaning cut down. The fee tail is a cut down version of the fee simple. Unlike the fee simple, which can be inherited by any relation of the deceased, the fee tail will pass only to lineal descendants.

The existence of this estate, which can be cut down still further, for example by limiting the inheritability to sons alone (a fee tail male), did much to prevent land from being transferred outside of the family. If, for example, A owned a fee tail in land and transferred it to B, then the fee tail would continue for as long as A continued to have lineal descendants. The family line of B would not be substituted for that of A. This estate, which is termed a base fee, reflects a general rule of property law, frequently described in the Latin maxim, *nemo dat quod non habet*: one cannot give what one has not got. Similarly, in the case of a life estate, if C, the owner of such an estate, transfers it to D, then D's interest in the land continues for as long as C lives. He has a tenancy *pur autre vie*: a tenancy for the life of another.

This general principle, which did not apply in the case of a fee simple, had an obviously inhibiting effect on the transferability of land, which was subject to such estates. This ran counter to another aspiration with regard to land: that it should be freely transferable. In order to facilitate this essentially fictitious legal devices of either a recovery or a fine, were invented to convert a fee tail into a fee simple. This process, known as barring the entail, produced different results, depending upon who actually

---

[5] *Doherty v. Allman* (1879) 3 App. Cas. 709.
[6] *Powys v. Blagrave* (1854) 4 De G. M. & G. 448.
[7] *Vane v. Lord Barnard* (1716) 2 Vern. 738.

sought to bar the entail. In essence, if done by the person in possession, a fee simple resulted and, if done by the person entitled to possession in the future, the outcome was the creation of a base fee. It is not necessary for present purposes to know the details of these procedures, which are now regulated by statute.[8] The process is simply an illustration of two of the conflicting pressures which underlie Land law: a desire to keep land in the family and the desire for land to be freely alienable.

THE CO-EXISTENCE OF ESTATES

It is fundamental to the understanding of the doctrine of estates, to appreciate that they can co-exist with regard to the same piece of land. The largest estate is the fee simple and it is out of this estate that the other, lesser, estates are carved. Some examples can be given.

1. X has a fee simple and grants a life estate in it to his son, S. This settlement does not exhaust X's fee simple. The position is that X has a fee simple in reversion: his right to possess the land reverts to him, or his heirs upon the death of S.
2. X has a fee simple and, by will, he leaves the land to his widow, W, for life, thereafter to his son, S, in fee simple. Upon X's death, W has a life estate and S a fee simple in remainder. The term remainder is used as it refers to what remains out of the original estate held by X.
3. X has a fee simple and creates a settlement under which he grants the land to his wife, W, for life, thereafter to his son, S, in fee tail. In this case, W has a life estate, S has a fee tail in remainder and X has a fee simple in reversion.

In all these examples, there exist future interests. In each case the estates are vested in the various parties. The element of futurity relates to the ability to take possession of the land. As existing estates they can be transferred to other people, although, it may be apparent that, precisely because they are future interests, it may be difficult to find a purchaser willing to pay money for them.

A second point that can be made is that where there exists a succession of interests, the finishing point is always a fee simple, because this is the largest estate. It follows that, as in example 3, X retains the fee simple simply because, under the settlement that he has created, he has failed to dispose of it. In example 2, where he has disposed of the fee simple, then no further

[8] See Megarry, *op. cit.*, pp. 40-46.

settlement is possible by X, because he has exhausted all of his rights in the land.

LEASEHOLD ESTATES

The other estate known to law is the lease. This form of landholding, whereby a tenant occupies land, normally for the payment of rent, originally developed outside of the feudal system and, technically was not recognised as belonging to the Law of Real Property. This is still true, but does not reflect the reality of the situation: the lease being an important form of land holding. To reflect this, leases are now referred to as chattels real and are invariably regarded as being within the ambit of a work on real property. Leases will be considered in a later Chapter.

CONCLUSION

The doctrine of estates is, therefore, a flexible means of allowing different rights with respect to land to be shared between different people. The doctrine remains at the centre of the theoretical basis of modern Land Law.

CHAPTER THREE

Law and Equity

A fundamental aspect of Land Law is the distinction between Law and Equity. This Chapter is concerned with this matter.

The Historical Basis of Equity

At the outset, the legal system was based upon local courts and the Royal Courts, the Courts of Common Law. The system that was in place was, however, bedevilled by an excess of formalism. Each action had to be started by the utilisation of a writ, issued by the Lord Chancellor. Unlike the position which pertains today, this was, in medieval times, an extremely technical procedure. Depending upon the relief that was being sought, a different writ would have to be used. This caused difficulty in that, if the wrong writ was used, the action would be discontinued and would subsequently have to be recommenced. Further problems arose, if there was not in existence an appropriate writ with which to commence the action. Even if the Lord Chancellor could be persuaded to issue a new writ, it did not follow that the courts would accept its validity.

A further problem facing litigants, particularly in the local courts, was that the opponent in the litigation may have been a powerful individual, able to exert considerable influence. The upshot might be that, although the one party might have the Law on his side, his right might not be vindicated in the local court.

Petitions to the King

As a result of dissatisfaction with the system then in place, disappointed litigants began the practice of petitioning the King directly, the King being regarded as the fountain of justice. At the outset, these petitions were directed to the King's Council, of which the Chancellor was a member. In time, they were directed directly to the Chancellor alone, who would determine the case.

The office of Chancellor was frequently held by an ecclesiastic and his decisions were frequently based upon an appeal to matters of conscience. Such an approach is, of course, inherently unpredictable: different people have different views as to the direction in which the dictates of conscience lead. Over time, the more individualistic approach to this jurisdiction declined and, instead, the basis of the jurisdiction to intervene became principled and systematised. The body of law that developed became recognised as that species of the law known as Equity.

In addition to the systematisation of the principles to be applied in cases where petitions were made, there was also seen an organisation of the court structure that administered the equitable jurisdiction. Various judges were appointed and, in time, a separate division of the High Court, the Court of Chancery, was established.

EQUITY ACTS IN PERSONAM

In order to grasp the nature of equitable intervention, it is important to appreciate the technique employed first by the Chancellor and, later, by the Court of Chancery. What did not occur was that the Chancellor disregarded the common law. Instead, having regard to the merits of the case would make an order directing one of the parties, personally, either to do something, or to refrain from doing something. *Penn v. Lord Baltimore*[1] concerned a dispute as to the boundary between Maryland and Pennsylvania and an agreement was made between the plaintiff and the defendant. When the plaintiff sought to enforce the agreement, it was argued that the court lacked jurisdiction to determine the boundary. This was not seen as a major problem. The Lord Chancellor said "The conscience of the party is bound by this agreement and being within the jurisdiction of this court . . . which acts *in personam*, the court may properly decree it as an agreement. . . ."[2] In other words, because the defendant's conscience was affected by the agreement, he could be ordered to implement it. The agreement was specifically enforced.

Equitable remedies.   A central feature of equitable intervention is the nature of the remedies afforded. Equity acts on the person

[1] (1750) 1 Ves. Sen. 444.
[2] *ibid*. at pp. 447-448.

by issuing a direction to do, or refrain from doing, something. The former usually is encompassed within the remedy of specific performance and the latter involves an injunction.[3] The penalty for non-compliance with such an order is that the defaulting party is in contempt of court and, therefore, subject to sanctions.

The principal equitable remedies of specific performance and the injunction are integral parts of the equitable process. The availability of either remedy depends upon the common law remedy being inadequate to compensate fully the aggrieved party. If, for example, A contracts with a car dealer to buy a mass produced car and B, in breach of contract, fails to deliver it, A is adequately compensated by an award of damages: he can easily buy another car of the same type. If, however, A has contracted to buy a rare item, such as an original Van Gogh, from B, then the award of damages, alone, is not an adequate remedy. What A wants is that particular picture. In recognition of this fact, Equity would normally award specific performance: B would be ordered to transfer the painting to A in return for the agreed purchase price.

A second factor which must be appreciated when considering the subject of equitable remedies is that, unlike the position at common law, the decision as to whether to grant such a remedy is a matter of discretion. This discretion is, of course, exercised judicially, so that the decision to grant or withhold the remedy is not a matter for the whim of an individual judge. If, for example, in the case of the contract for the sale of the Van Gogh, B had already contracted to sell it to another person prior to contracting to sell it to A, then equity would not order specific performance of contract between A and B as, to do so, would compel B to breach his earlier contract with X. In this circumstance, A would be left to his common law remedy of damages.

The availability of equitable remedies is an important matter in Land Law. As will be seen, their potential availability can be an important matter in determining whether a particular transaction gives rise to merely personal rights between the parties or whether a property right has been created.

TRUSTS

Equity, as it originally developed, operated to work on the conscience of an individual and to redress defects in the common law. What also developed in equity was a concept of major theoretical and practical importance: the trust.

[3] This is an overgeneralisation. For example, a mandatory injunction involves a party being ordered to do specified acts.

From early days a practice developed of land being conveyed to a person T for the use of another B. At law, the position was quite straightforward. T was the legal owner and the obligation undertaken in respect of B was disregarded. Equity, however, took the view that it would be unconscionable for T to disregard this undertaking and compelled T to comply with the use. In this way the actual benefit of the land was enjoyed by B.

Before considering how the early use developed into the modern trust, it is as well to consider why people adopted this course of action. If it was intended that B should benefit from the land, surely it would be simpler for the land to be conveyed to T directly. There were a number of reasons why the utilisation of the use was advantageous. Some of these reasons had a slightly romantic air; other were more prosaic.

Reasons for the use.   One reason for putting land into use occurred when the owner of the land was about to go abroad to fight in the crusades. In such circumstances land would be transferred to a nominee for the use of the departing knight, while he was away. A second reason advanced was that it was advantageous for certain religious orders who had taken vows of poverty. Because of these vows the monks could not own land. To avoid this, land was conveyed to nominees to be held to the use of the monks. Technically, therefore, because they did not have the legal ownership of the land, they had not broken their vows, while at the same time, being able to enjoy the benefit of the land. The third main reason involved tax.

Feudal dues.   An inherent part of the feudal system was that, when land passed to an heir by inheritance, various feudal dues became payable to the superior lord. The feudal dues, which may be likened to an early form of inheritance tax could be quite swingeing in nature. The device of the use was a valuable means of seeking to avoid such payments. What was sought to be achieved was to prevent the land from passing by inheritance.

The scheme adopted was for land to be transferred to a number of people, say T1, T2, T3 and T4 to be held to the use of B and his heirs. The effect of this was that the legal title was vested in the first four people, who would be subject to an obligation, enforceable in equity, to honour the use. When B died, to be succeded by his eldest son, S, the obligation imposed by the use was now owned by him. The important point to note was that, at law, there had been no change in the ownership of the property, which was still owned by T1, T2, T3 and T4. Consequently, the feudal dues which became payable when land passed by inheritance need not be paid. Of course T1, T2, T3 and T4 were not immortal. It was unlikely, however, that they would die simultaneously. So, when T1 died, T5 would be appointed as an additional legal owner. This ensured that, barring catastrophe, the legal title to the land would never pass by inheritance, the effect of this being that the payment of feudal dues was avoided.

The Statute of Uses 1535. For the leading barons the device of the use was extremely useful, in that it enabled them to avoid the payment of certain feudal dues to the King. It is true that their own tenants could also employ the use for the same purpose, with the result that dues were not paid to them. Nevertheless for these people the use was popular. For the King, however, the device was pernicious. As he was the ultimate lord and tenant of no-one, the effect of the use was to deprive him of valuable resources. To emasculate the use, Henry VIII forced through Parliament the Statute of Uses 1535.

The effect of the statute was to "execute" the use. If land was conveyed to T1, T2, T3 and T4 for the use of B and his heirs, the effect of the statute was to execute the use and cause the legal estate to vest in B. On the death of B, then feudal dues would become payable.

The use upon a use. Faced with this potentially lethal attack on the use, lawyers exerted a degree of ingenuity in seeking to side-step the statute. The method adopted was to employ two uses: the use upon a use. This device entailed that land would be conveyed to A and his heirs, to the use of B and his heirs, to the use of C and his heirs. Eventually, it was held that the effect of this contrivance was that the statute executed the first use but not the second, with the result that the legal title passed to B who held it to the use of C and his heirs.

The reasoning employed to achieve this result scarcely looks convincing but was evidence of the strong desire of the judges to resuscitate a popular legal device which might, otherwise, have become extinct. Over a period of time, the practice grew of describing the second use as a trust. Land was then conveyed unto the use of B and his heirs upon trust for C. The Statute of Uses was repealed in 1925[4] and the method now employed to create a trust such as that described above is for the land to be conveyed to B in fee simple upon trust for C. B is termed the trustee and C the beneficiary.

EQUITY FOLLOWS THE LAW

It is important to appreciate that at no stage did equity deny that the legal owner of the land was B. Equity took the view,

[4] L.P.A. 1925, Sched. 7.

however, that the trustee must use the land for the benefit of the trustee. From there, it was but a short step to say that, although B was the legal owner of the property, because the real enjoyment of the property belonged to C, he was regarded as the equitable, or beneficial, owner of the property.

Having accepted the notion of equitable ownership of land, the next question to determine was the nature of that ownership. The legal owner does not own the land itself; rather he owns an estate in the land. Equity adopted the same theoretical framework. Thus, as the common law permitted land to be held for A for life, to B in fee tail remainder to C in fee simple, equity enabled these estates to be held on trust in the same way. In addition to these legal estates, their equitable counterparts were also recognised. There could exist equitable life estates, equitable fees tail and equitable fees simple. This mirroring of the common law estates is an example of an important principle, applicable, as will be seen, to many areas of Land Law: Equity follows the Law.

The trust is a legal device which is widely used and embraces all sorts of property and not just land. It, nevertheless, occupies a pivotal role in Land Law. Although it is often the case that the legal owner of land is also the equitable owner of it, there are many situations where that is not so. In addition, some areas of law, such as co-ownership,[5] necessitate treating legal and equitable ownership separately. It is essential to an understanding of Land Law to grasp the dichotomy between the legal and equitable ownership of land. When the two coincide, then the person is described as the legal and beneficial owner of the land. In other cases, the legal owner of the land will hold the land on trust for another person who will be described as the beneficial owner or co-owner.

Other Equitable Interests

The extent of equitable intervention was not limited to the development of the trust. True to its origins as a court of conscience equity intervened to modify, substantially, other areas of law, the best example being the law of mortgages.[6] In addition to this, equity recognised the existence of other rights in land.

A feature of the creation of legal rights in land is that strict formal requirements are insisted upon. This usually involves the execution of a deed. In the absence of a deed, it is often the case

[5] See *post*, Chap. 7.
[6] See *post*, Chap. 12.

that the purported transaction is ineffective to create a particular legal interest. Equity, however, has taken a more relaxed view of the need for formalities. So, if a particular transaction is ineffective to create a legal interest, it may well be effective to create the equitable counterpart. For example the purported creation of a right of way (an easement) may be ineffective at law, due to the absence of a deed, but effective in equity to create an equitable right of way. Again, equity follows the law, so that if a particular right is capable of existing as a legal right in land, there is an equitable equivalent. Rights such as leases, mortgages and easements are recognised at law; they can also be created in equity.

The creation of equitable interests. There are various circumstances when an equitable interest can be created. These can be enumerated here and elaborated at various stages hereafter.

1. *Lack of formality.* As has just been mentioned an equitable interest can be created if the formalities necessary to create a legal interest have not been complied with.

2. *Possession of an equitable interest.* If a person only holds an equitable estate inland, he can only create equitable rights over it.

3. *Time.* As will be seen in the next Chapter, to exist as a legal right, the right in question must exist for the equivalent of either a fee simple absolute in possession or for a term of years. If the right does not satisfy these requirements then it can only exist in equity. For example, if A purports to grant B a right of way over his land for life, then this right of way, or easement, can, since 1925, only exist in equity.

4. *Right only recognised by equity.* There are certain rights in land that have only ever been recognised in equity. An example of such a right is a restrictive covenant: for instance when A covenants with his neighbour that he will only use the property as a private residence. Such an obligation is capable of existing as a property right but has only ever been so recognised by equity.

THE ENFORCEABILITY OF LEGAL AND EQUITABLE RIGHTS

Of paramount importance in Land Law is the question of the enforceability of rights against subsequent owners of the land.

When considering this issue, it is vital to distinguish between legal and equitable rights.

Legal Rights

If a legal right affects land, then anybody who subsequently acquires that land takes subject to that right. It is immaterial if the person knew of the right, or even whether it was possible for him to have discovered it. A legal right binds the world. A good example is provided by *Wyld v. Sylver*.[7] A property developer bought land, his intention being to build houses upon it. It later transpired that, by a private Act of Parliament of 1799, villagers had been granted the right to hold an annual fair on the land, although no such fair had taken place for 80 years. An injunction was granted to restrain the planned building, which would have prevented the villagers from exercising their legal right to hold a fair. In other words, the purchaser was bound by a legal right of which he had no prior notice.

Equitable Rights

Unlike legal rights, equitable rights are not enforceable against the world. The original basis of equitable intervention was that the conscience of a land owner was affected by some obligation that he had undertaken towards another. The question which then fell to be considered was in what circumstances a successor in title would also be affected by that obligation. The rule that developed was that the conscience of every subsequent owner of the land would be affected except for the bona fide purchaser of a legal estate for value without notice of the equitable right.[8]

The doctrine of the bona fide purchaser (as this is typically abbreviated) must now be considered.

THE BONA FIDE PURCHASER

Bona fide.   Although good faith is said to be an independent part of the definition,[9] no examples exist where this notion has played a separate part in the decision. Its use serves essentially to emphasise the importance of lack of notice.

Purchaser for value.   The technical meaning of "purchaser" is someone who acquires property by the act of the parties and not

---

[7] [1963] Ch. 243.
[8] See *Pilcher v. Rawlins* (1872) 7 Ch. App. 259.
[9] *Midland Bank Trust Co. Ltd v. Green* [1981] A.C. 513 at 528, *per* Lord Wilberforce.

by operation of law. Thus, someone who acquires property under a will is technically a purchaser, whereas someone who acquires property under an intestacy is not. In neither case has value been given. A purchaser who has not given value is bound by equitable interests affecting the land.

Value includes more than money. It includes anything that the common law would regard as consideration. In addition, it also includes marriage consideration. This is an ante-nuptial promise to settle property. Within the marriage consideration are the spouse and any issue of the marriage.

To take free from equitable interests, the purchase must be of a legal estate. This obviously includes a purchaser of a freehold estate but also includes a purchaser of a leasehold estate and a mortgagee. If the purchaser acquires only an equitable estate, the general rule is that he will be bound by prior equitable interests on the basis that the first in time prevails.

There are exceptions to this rule.

(a) Better right to legal estate. If the purchaser of an equitable estate has, in consequence of his purchase, a better right to the legal estate than the holder of a prior equitable interest, he will take free from it. An example of this is when the legal title is transferred to a trustee for the purchaser.[10]

(b) Later acquisition of the legal estate. A purchaser of an equitable estate without notice will take free from a prior equitable interest if he subsequently acquires the legal estate, even if he, then, has notice of the equitable interest.[11] This is so, unless he knowingly acquires the legal interest in breach of trust, in which case, he will take subject to the interests under that trust.[12]

(c) Mere equities. A purchaser of an equitable interest will take free of "mere equities" of which he has no notice. Mere equities are equitable rights which fall short of a full equitable interest in land and are ancillary to the land itself. They are, in essence, claims to equitable relief, such as a right to have an instrument rectified on the ground of mistake. While such a right is capable of binding a purchaser, a purchaser of an equitable interest without notice will take free from it.[13]

Without notice. The final element of the concept of the bona fide purchaser is the one which has generated most debate: that

---

[10] *Assaf v. Fuwa* [1955] A.C. 215.
[11] *Bailey v. Barnes* [1894] 1 Ch. 25.
[12] *McCarthy & Stone Ltd v. Julian S. Hodge & Co. Ltd* [1971] 1 W.L.R. 1547.
[13] See, generally, *Latec Investments Ltd v. Hotel Terrigal Pty. Ltd* (1965) 113 C.L.R. 265.

of notice. There are three types of notice: actual, constructive and imputed. These will be considered in turn.

(a) Actual notice.   Because of the system of registration of land charges, to be discussed in the next Chapter, this form of notice has increased in importance. Traditionally, it was less important than other sources of notice. A purchaser is regarded as having actual notice of an equitable interest if information about it has come to his attention from a reputable source and not, simply, from casual conversations.[14]

(b) Constructive notice.   If it were the case that a purchaser would only be bound by equitable interests of which he actually knew, prior to the purchase, then those interests would be extremely vulnerable. It would be in the purchaser's interest to know as little as possible about such interests when buying the land. To avoid this from happening, equity developed the doctrine of constructive notice: matters which a purchaser should have discovered. The test to determine what a purchaser should have discovered is what would have been discovered if he had made such inquiries and inspections as ought reasonably to have been made by him.[15] This then prompts the question as to what inquiries and inspections ought reasonably to be made. The answers to this are investigation of title and inspection of the land.

(1) Investigation of Title

It should be said, at the outset, that, owing to the extension of registration of both land charges and title, this source of constructive notice is of much less importance than was previously the case. What is entailed is the discovery of equitable interests in the course of investigating the vendor's right to sell the land.

As has already been seen, a large number of different rights can exist, simultaneously, with regard to the same piece of land and the fact that the person purporting to sell it is in physical possession of the property is not, on its own, sufficient evidence that he owns the land in fee simple: he could be a tenant, a life tenant, or even a squatter. To establish his ownership of the fee simple, the vendor must show documentary evidence of how the land came to be vested in him.

The process of proving his right to sell the property, referred to as deducing title, involves the vendor showing how he came

[14] *Lloyd v. Banks* (1868) L.R. 3 Ch. App. 488.
[15] L.P.A. 1925, s.199(1)(ii)(a).

by the property. The starting point would be to show the conveyance of the land to him. Having seen the conveyance to the vendor, the purchaser may then wish to know whether the person who conveyed the land to the vendor was, himself, entitled to do so. This then involves showing the conveyance by which that person acquired the property. This process could then be further repeated again and again, requiring the vendor to show the devolution of the property from the date when time began.

For obvious reasons, such a procedure would not be practical and a time limit was imposed on the length of time that a purchaser was expected to go back in order to investigate the vendor's title. The original period established at common law was 60 years but this was reduced to 40 years in 1874, to 30 years in 1925 and to 15 years in 1969.[16] Because it is unlikely that there will be a conveyance exactly 15 years old, the period specified is a minimum. So, if there are conveyances 12 years old and 20 years old, the purchaser should go back to the older conveyance. It is the first conveyance that is at least 15 years old.[17] This conveyance is termed the root of title.

The relevance of this for the purpose of constructive notice is that the purchaser will be considered to have constructive notice of all equitable interests that he would have discovered if he had inspected all the deeds, going back to a root of title of the appropriate age.[18]

(2) INSPECTION OF THE LAND

A second source of constructive notice is that generated by occupiers of the land. In *Hunt* v. *Luck*,[19] Vaughan Williams L.J. said:

"... if a purchaser ... has notice that the vendor ... is not in possession of the property, he must make inquiries of the person in possession – of the tenant who is in possession – and find out from him what his rights are, and, if he does not choose to do that, then whatever title he acquires as purchaser ... will be subject to the title or right of the person in possession."

The rule in *Hunt v. Luck*, whereby a purchaser was fixed with notice of the rights of persons in actual possession of the land,

---

[16] Vendor and Purchaser Act 1874, s.1; L.P.A. 1925, s.44(1); L.P.A. 1969, s.23.
[17] See *Re Cox and Neve's Contract* [1891] 2 Ch. 109, 118 *per* North J.
[18] See *Re Nisbett and Pott's Contract* [1906] 1 Ch. 386.
[19] [1902] 1 Ch. 428, 433.

seems eminently sensible when the vendor is not, himself, in possession of the land. If a person was purporting to sell a house in which he did not live himself but was occupied by another person, then, even a purchaser unversed in Land Law might be at the least curious as to who the occupier was and what he was doing in the house. His occupation is visibly inconsistent with a claim by the vendor to be losely entitled to the land. Rather greater difficulty has arisen where the vendor shares occupation with the vendor.

Shared occupation.   In *Caunce v. Caunce*,[20] a matrimonial home was, legally, in the sole name of the Mr Caunce but his wife was a beneficial co-owner of it, she having contributed to its purchase.[21] Without telling her, he mortgaged the house to a bank who made no inquiries of her before granting the mortgage. The main issue in the case was whether the bank had constructive notice of her equitable right and was, therefore, bound by it.

Stamp J. held in favour of the bank. Mindful of a recent dictum that "It has been the policy of the law for over a hundred years to simplify and facilitate transactions in real property",[22] he considered that it would be unreasonable to expect banks to make inquiries of the spouse of a legal owner of property. Instead he held that if a vendor, or mortgagor, is in possession of property then the purchaser or mortgagee is not affected with constructive notice of the rights of any other person who is also resident in the property and whose presence is not inconsistent with the title offered.[23]

The approach taken in *Caunce* articulated clearly one of the competing pressures involved in disputes concerning land: the desirability of simplifying the conveyancing process. The fewer inquiries that a purchaser or mortgagee is required to make, the easier his task will be. On the other hand, the price to be paid for favouring this interest is the rights of people, like Mrs Caunce, who live in a house are given less emphasis.

Caunce v. Caunce was criticised, *obiter*, in a later case,[24] and came under more direct re-consideration in the leading case of *Williams & Glyn's Bank Ltd v. Boland*.[25] Save that the case involved registered land, the facts of *Boland* were substantially the same as those in *Caunce*. Again, a husband was the sole legal

[20] [1969] 1 W.L.R. 286.
[21] See *post*, pp. 93–99.
[22] *National Provincial Bank Ltd v. Ainsworth* [1965] A.C. 1175, 1233 *per* Lord Upjohn.
[23] [1969] 1 W.L.R. 286, 293.
[24] *Hodgson v. Marks* [1971] Ch. 892, 934–935 *per* Russell L.J.
[25] [1981] A.C. 487.

owner of the matrimonial home but his wife was a co-owner in equity. Without consulting his wife, he mortgaged the house to the bank who made no inquiries of Mrs Boland prior to granting him the mortgage. The action in this case arose when the bank sought possession as a result of Mr Boland defaulting on the mortgage and this action was resisted by Mrs Boland who claimed that her interest was binding on the bank.

Because title to the land was registered, the legal issue in *Boland* was slightly different from that in *Caunce*. In *Caunce*, the main issue was whether the ambit of reasonable inquiries extended to making inquiries of an occupier who shared accommodation with the legal owner of the house. In *Boland*, it was whether Mrs Boland was in actual occupation of the house within the meaning of section 70(1)(g) of the Land Registration Act 1925.[26] The policy issue was, however, the same. Does one decide for the bank and give priority to the conveyancing dimension, or does one decide for Mrs Boland and favour the protection of people who hold informal interests in a house?

The House of Lords decided in favour of Mrs Boland. In reaching this decision, it was clear that the Law Lords were mindful of the social importance of the case.[27] In a modern society, it is quite common for wives and partners to go out to work and contribute to the acquisition of the family home, thereby acquiring an interest in it. To decide for the bank, in cases such as this would mean that her interest in the home would be put at risk by activities of her partner about which she had no knowledge. To decide in favour of Mrs Boland would, as the House of Lords were fully aware,[28] make life more difficult for conveyancers but this was considered to be an acceptable price to pay.

Although *Caunce v. Caunce* was not formally overruled, it was evident that it could not stand in the light of the decision in *Boland*. Subsequently, it came as no surprise when it was held that a purchaser would have constructive notice of the rights of people in occupation of property, even if the legal owner was also in occupation.[29] The conflict between the rights of occupiers and the rights of mortgagees has given rise to some complexity and will be returned to in a later Chapter.

(c) Imputed notice. A purchaser will have imputed notice of anything of which his agent has notice, provided that the agent

---

[26] *Post*, pp. 52–57.
[27] See, in particular, the speech of Lord Scarman.
[28] [1981] A.C. 487 at 508 *per* Lord Wilberforce.
[29] *Kingsnorth Finance Co. Ltd v. Tizard* [1986] 1 W.L.R. 783. See M.P. Thompson [1986] Conv. 283.

acquires notice in the course of the transaction with which the purchaser is involved and not from a previous transaction.[30]

Successors in Title

If the land is acquired by the bona fide purchaser, then he will take free from equitable interests which previously affected the land. They are said to have been overridden. They are not revived, if the land is subsequently conveyed to a purchaser who does have notice of the interest,[31] unless the person who acquired the land was originally bound by the interest.[32]

[30] L.P.A. 1925, s.199.
[31] *Wilkes v. Spooner* [1911] 2 K.B. 473.
[32] *Gordon v. Holland* (1913) 82 L.J.P.C. 81.

CHAPTER FOUR

The 1925 Legislation

A feature of the doctrine of estates is that it allowed for the fragmentation of rights among many people. In addition to the existence of legal estates, there was also in being equitable counterparts of those estates. As well as it being quite possible for a number of different estates to exist simultaneously with regard to the same plot of land, there could also be a number of third party rights, such as easements or restrictive covenants, enjoyed over it.

One of the consequences of this was that transactions involving the land became very difficult. A purchaser will normally want to purchase the maximum number of rights in a piece of land: a fee simple. In addition, he will not wish to make onerous inquiries as to the existence of equitable rights prior to the purchase. He will wish the position to be easily ascertainable. One of the principal aims of the 1925 legislation was to simplify the law in order to make it easier to buy and sell land. To achieve this objective, various means were adopted.

LAND LAW AFTER 1925

In implementing the general policy of simplifying the Law, a number of features of the legislation emerge.

1. Reduction in legal estates and interests.   As the common law developed, various different legal estates could exist at law. The 1925 legislation reduced the number of legal estates which could exist to two: the fee simple absolute in possession and the term of years absolute. All other estates must now be equitable. In addition to this, the number of third party rights, which would bind a purchaser regardless of notice, was reduced.

2. Registration of land charges. The reduction in the number of legal estates and interests led to a corresponding increase in the number of equitable interests. Prior to 1925, the purchaser was faced with an onerous task of inquiry to ensure that he would not be regarded as having notice of such rights. To facilitate the task of the purchaser, and also to secure the protection of the holder of an equitable interest, provision was made for the registration of many such rights. This process made the enforceability of such rights dependent upon their having been registered. The task of the purchaser, in theory at least, was made simpler as he could discover the existence of such rights by the simple expedient of making an appropriate search.

3. Registration of title. The traditional method of proving one's ownership of land was to examine the title deeds. These would display the devolution of the land through various transactions to establish the vendor's entitlement to deal with it. This is a time consuming business and one where mistakes can be made. Registration of title is a process designed to make such a practice obsolete. Once title to the land is registered, the general idea is that a purchaser can discover who is the owner of the land and what rights affect it by searching the register.[1] In this way, the conveyancing process is made more straightforward.

4. Extension of overreaching. The existence of a number of freehold estates affecting the same property was normally indicative of there having been created a family settlement. A settlement to A for life, remainder to B in fee tail, remainder to C in fee simple would normally occur within a family. That being the case, it was unlikely that A, B or C had actually bought their interests in the land. The effect of the settlement, however, was to make it extremely difficult for the land to be sold, because none of the people involved had an estate which was intrinsically attractive to a purchaser. The doctrine of overreaching is designed to overcome this problem.

In a situation such as that above, a mechanism is imposed to allow A to dispose of a legal fee simple. To safeguard the interests of B and C the purchase money is paid to two trustees. The interests of A, B and C are then transferred from the land to the money and the purchaser takes the land free from the interests under the settlement. Those interests are then said to have been overreached.

---

[1] This is an overgeneralisation, in that it does not deal with overriding interests. See *post* pp. 52–57.

5. Reform of co-ownership. It is common for land to be co-owned, the most common situation probably being when a matrimonial home is in the joint names of husband and wife. The structure of co-ownership in existence before 1925 led in many cases to the fragmentation of ownership of the legal title. By means of reform introduced in 1925, this possibility was eradicated.

REDUCTION IN LEGAL ESTATES

Section 1 of the Law of Property Act 1925 provides that: The only estates in land which are capable of subsisting or of being conveyed or created at law are-

(a) An estate in fee simple absolute in possession;
(b) A term of years absolute.

Section 1(2) also reduces the number of legal interests in land capable of subsisting or being conveyed or created at law. Of these interests, the most important are:

(a) An easement, right or privilege in or over land for an interest equivalent to an estate in fee simple absolute in possession or a term of years absolute;
(b) A rentcharge in possession issuing out of or charged on land being either perpetual or for a term of years absolute;
(c) A charge by way of legal mortgage; and
(d) Rights of entry exercisable over or in respect of a term of years absolute or annexed, for any purpose, to a legal rentcharge.

It is provided by section 1(3) of the Act that all other estates, interests, and charges in or over land take effect as equitable interests.

A number of points should be noted.

1. Capable of existing as legal estates. Section 1 of the Act lays down which estates and interests are capable of being legal estates and interests. It should not be thought that if a particular interest comes within the definition that it is necessarily legal. In general, to create a legal estate or interest, it is necessary to use a deed. If this is not done, then the interest will generally not be legal but may well take effect as an equitable interest. A term of years absolute may, therefore, be either legal or equitable.

2. Estates and interests. Section 1 refers separately to estates and interests in land. This is a helpful division, in that the idea

of an estate connotes ownership rights in land, whereas an interest in land generally means rights enjoyed over another person's land.

3. Legal estates.

(a) Fee simple.   The two estates capable of existing at law are the fee simple absolute in possession and the term of years absolute. The notion of the fee simple absolute in possession has already been considered. Outside the definition would be estates such as a determinable fee or a base fee. Certain problems arose in connection with defeasible fees simple, particularly with regard to rights of re-entry in connection with rentcharges, but these problems have now been resolved.[2] Possession is used to mean a present estate as opposed to an estate in remainder or in reversion. If land is subject to a lease, the fee simple remains in possession, as possession includes the right to receive rents and profits.[3]

(b) Term of years absolute.   This, somewhat unhelpful, definition refers to leasehold property. Term of years includes periods of less than a year, as well as a period of a year or years.[4] What it entails is that there is a term that is certain, or is capable of being made certain upon service of a notice to quit.[5]

The word "absolute" seems to have little meaning in that a lease which is determinable or liable to forfeiture is, nevertheless, a term of years absolute.

4. Legal interests.   Various interests are capable of subsisting as legal interests. The most important of these rights are as follows.

(a) Easements, rights and privileges.   An easement is a right over another person's land, a classic example being a right of way. Included, also, within the definition is a right known as a *profit à prendre*. This is the right to go onto another person's land and take something from it, for example, wood. In either case, to be legal, the rights must be equivalent to the two legal estates. An easement for life is, therefore, necessarily equitable.

(b) Rentcharges.   A rentcharge is a right for the owner of it to receive a periodical payment from the owner of the burdened

---

[2] See Megarry, Manual of the Law of Real Property (7th ed.), p. 73.
[3] L.P.A. 1925, s.205(1) (xix).
[4] *ibid.* s.205 (xxvii).
[5] *Prudential Assurance Co. Ltd v. London Residuary Body* [1992] 2 A.C. 386. *Post,* p. 116.

land. This right is independent of any other interest in the land. To be legal, the rentcharge must be either perpetual or for a term of years absolute and take effect in possession.[6] Except for certain limited purposes, no new rentcharges may be created after 1977 and those in existence will expire, at the latest, by 2033.[7]

(c) A charge by way of legal mortgage. A mortgage of land is one of the most important rights which can exist over another person's land and will be considered in a later Chapter.

(d) Rights of re-entry. A right to re-enter the land is the normal sanction imposed upon either a tenant who fails to comply with the covenants in the lease or with terms imposed by a rentcharge.

EQUITABLE RIGHTS

Unless a right is within one of the definitions given above, it must necessarily be equitable. These equitable interests differ, however, in nature. Although there is no formal statutory division of equitable interests, they do divide into one of two groups: family interests and commercial interests.

1. Family interests. If one considers a settlement, to A for life, remainder to B in fee tail, remainder to C in fee simple, it should be apparent that, after 1925, neither A, B or C have legal estates in land. A and B do not have a fee simple. C does have a fee simple but it is in remainder and not, therefore, in possession. The effect of section 1 of the Law of Property Act 1925 is to convert their legal estates into equitable estates.

To enable the land to be sold, the Settled Land Act 1925 provides for a legal fee simple to be vested in A. A takes on a dual role. He owns the life estate beneficially but is a trustee of the legal estate, which he is empowered to sell. To prevent him from selling the property and misappropriating the proceeds, two trustees are appointed. The purchase money is paid to them and a conveyance of the legal estate is made by A. The purchase money is then invested and distributed among the beneficiaries in accordance with their beneficial interests. The shifting of their interests from the land to the proceeds of sale is not unfair, in that, this being a family settlement, it is highly unlikely that either A, B or C will have paid for their interests in the property.

---

[6] Possession, here, has an extended meaning. See Megarry, *op. cit.*, p. 75.
[7] Rentcharges Act 1977, ss.2, 3.

2. Commercial interests. A person may own land and covenant with his neighbour only to use the property as a private
residence. This obligation, termed a restrictive covenant, is
capable of binding successive owners of the land affected. It
should be apparent that this type of right is unlikely to have
been granted for nothing. It will have been paid for. Moreover,
it is the type of right which cannot sensibly be transferred to
money. It is meaningless to talk of a restrictive covenant
affecting money. For the right to have any utility, it must remain
attached to the land through successive periods of ownership.
This equitable, commercial interest cannot be overreached and
its enforceability is made dependent upon registration.

A basic strategy of the 1925 legislation was to categorise
equitable interests into family interests, which, by implementing
the correct procedure, can be overreached and commercial
interests which would depend for their continued enforceability
upon registration. As will be seen, however, this dichotomy is
not all embracing. There exists a third category of equitable
right which is neither overreachable nor registrable, the enforceability of which depends upon the traditional doctrine of
notice.

THE REGISTRATION OF LAND CHARGES

An aim of the legislation was to make the enforceability of
various equitable rights dependent upon registration. To this
end, the Land Charges Act 1925, which has since been superseded by the Land Charges Act 1972, was enacted. This Act
introduced five separate registers, of which the most important,
and the only one which will be discussed, is that dealing with
land charges.

Before considering the structure of the Act, a number of
introductory points can be made. First it is important not to
confuse the system of land charges with either local land
charges or with registered land. The former relates to various
charges in favour of local authorities under the Local Land
Charges Act 1975. Registered land is a system of land ownership
whereby the actual title to the land is registered, the register
giving an authoritive version of the ownership of the land itself
and, subject to overriding interests, revealing the obligations to
which the land is subject.[8] It is important to be clear that
unregistered land and registered land are separate systems and
that land charges are relevant only when title is unregistered.

It may also be helpful, at the outset, to state the two basic
principles which apply to the registration of land charges:—

[8] See *post*, pp. 52–58.

(1) the registration of a land charge constitutes actual notice of the interest registered[9]; and

(2) non-registration of an interest as a land charge will make it void against certain classes of purchaser.[10]

Registrable Interests.

Land charges are divided into various classes, defined by section 2 of the Land Charges Act 1972. Some of the classes are, themselves, subdivided. Only the most important will be considered here.[11]

1. Class C. This class is sub-divided into four cateogries

C(i): A puisne mortgage. A puisne (pronounced puny) mortgage is a mortgage that is not protected by deposit of title deeds. Although it is a legal interest in land, it is required to be registered, the reason being an entirely practical one. In the case of a mortgage protected by the deposit of title deeds, that fact alone will tell any further potential lenders of the existence of the mortgage. Were it not for the registration provison, however, one could not know how many other legal mortgages had been created and one could not, therefore, safely lend money on the security of the land. To avoid this problem this type of mortgage is made registrable, despite it being a legal interest in land.

C(ii): A limited owner's charge. This is relatively unimportant.

C(iii): A general equitable charge. This is a residuary class. It is defined in an essentially negative manner and is an equitable interest which—

(a) is not included in any other class of land charge;

(b) is not protected by a deposit of documents relating to the legal estate affected; and

(c) does not arise, or affect any interest arising, under a trust for sale or settlement (and so be overreachable). An example of an equitable right within this definition is an unpaid vendor's lien on land.[12]

C(iv): An estate contract. This is an important class of land charge. It is a contract to convey or create a legal estate, made

---

[9] L.P.A. 1925, s.198.
[10] L.C.A. 1972, s.4.
[11] For a full list, see Megarry, *op. cit.*, pp. 78–84.
[12] *Uziell–Hamilton v. Keen* (1971) 22 P. & C.R. 655.

by a person who either owns a legal estate, or is entitled at the date of the contract to have a legal estate vested in him. While this definition obviously embraces contracts to purchase the fee simple, it is wider that that. It includes also options to purchase, rights of pre-emption and like rights. Included as well, are contracts to create a lease,[13] an option to renew a lease and an obligation to offer to surrender a lease to the landlord before seeking to assign it.

D(ii) Restrictive covenants.   Covenants that restrict the use of a person's land are registrable provided that:

   (a) they were created after 1925; and
   (b) they are not entered into between landlord and tenant.

For covenants created before 1925, the old rules as to notice to apply. This is also the case for covenants between landlord and tenant, unless the rules relating to the transmission of covenants affecting leasehold estates are applicable.[14]

D(iii) Equitable easements.   This class of land charge relates to easements created after 1925 which are merely equitable. This will include easements that are not equivalent to an estate in fee simple or to a term of years absolute. An easement for life will, therefore, be registrable under this class. A specifically enforceable contract to create an easement is also registrable.[15]

The definition of this class of land charge includes the words "right or privilege over or affecting land." This is wide enough to include an equitable *profit à prendre*, but does not include a number of informal rights, most notably rights arising under the doctrine of estoppel[16] which, again, are enforceable under the old doctrine of notice.

F: A spouse's statutory right of occupation.   This class of land charge was first introduced by legislation in 1967.

The backdrop to this statutory right was the abolition by the House of Lords of a rule which had been developed in a series of cases in the 1950's known as "the deserted wife's equity".[17] The gist of this rule was that, if a wife had been deserted by her husband, she had an equitable right to remain in the matrimonial home. This right was enforceable not only against her

---

[13] See *post*, pp. 121–123.
[14] *Post*, pp. 130–132.
[15] *E.R. Ives Investment Ltd v. High* [1967] 2 Q.B. 379. Arguably, it is also registrable as an estate contract.
[16] See *E.R. Ives Investment Ltd v. High, supra. Post*, pp. 175–181.
[17] See, *e.g.*, *Street v. Denham* [1954] 1 W.L.R. 624.

husband but was binding as well upon all but the bona fide purchaser. Consequently, if the husband mortgaged the house, the mortgagee would have constructive notice of the rights of the deserted spouse and would be unable to get possession as against her. This rule was highly controversial and in *National Provincial Bank Ltd v. Ainsworth*,[18] the House of Lords held there to be no such interest known to the law as the deserted wife's equity and that she did not, therefore have any right capable of binding the mortgagee.

This decision was, itself, controversial in that it was considered to leave a spouse in an unacceptably vulnerable position. To remedy this perceived failing in the law, the Matrimonial Homes Act 1967 gave a statutory right of occupation of the matrimonial home to both husband and wife.

The relevant provision, which is now contained in the Matrimonial Homes Act 1983, gives a spouse, who is not the legal owner of the home, a right not to be excluded from the home and, if not in possession of it, the right, with leave of the court, to enter it. This right is, if registered as Class F land charge binding upon a purchaser, including the trustee in bankruptcy.

It is true that, by registering the Class F a wife can prevent a disposition of the matrimonial home to which she does not consent.[19] The problem, however, is that, unless a wife is in receipt of legal advice, she is unlikely to know anything about the Class F and may not register it in time to prevent her husband from entering into a disposition, such as a mortgage, without informing her.

The history of the Class F reveals an underlying tension between protecting the rights of occupiers and promoting the sanctity of conveyancing transactions. Had the House of Lords approved the doctrine of the deserted wife's equity then they would have upheld the existence of a an informal right in land which was potentially binding upon a purchaser but was not capable of registration. The effect of this would have been that a purchaser could no longer rely on discovering the existence of all equitable rights by the simple expedient of searching in the land charges registry. In addition, further inquiries would need to be made, thereby complicating the conveyancing process. It is evident that this consideration weighed heavily in the House, Lord Upjohn pointing out that it has been the policy of the law for over a hundred years to simplify and facilitate the conveyancing process.[20]

---

[18] [1965] A.C. 1175.
[19] For a graphic illustration, see *Wroth v. Tyler* [1974] Ch. 30.
[20] *National Provincial Bank Ltd v. Ainsworth* [1965] A.C. 1175, 1233.

The legislative response was consistent with this policy. A wife (and so too, of course, a husband) is given a statutory right to occupy but its enforceability against purchasers is made dependent upon registration. The effect of this is that, in general, the conveyancing process will continue to operate smoothly and the reliability of the register of land charges enhanced. The cost of this is that people, who are not familiar with the Law of Real Property may lose their homes through ignorance of the need to register rights. As will be seen, this tension between competing interests re-emerged over the years but that rather different responses to it were to occur.

THE REGISTRATION OF LAND CHARGES

Having considered the scope of the most important classes of land charge, it is now necessary to consider the system in operation.

1. The effect of registration.   Under section 198 of the Law of Property Act 1925, the effect of registration of any matter as a land charge is deemed to constitute actual notice of the fact of registration to all persons and for all purposes connected with the land affected.

The ambit of this important section must be noted. If an interest is registered as a land charge then, subject to limited exceptions, a purchaser cannot claim not to have notice of it. Registration constitutes notice. The purpose of the Act is to do away with the old doctrine of notice in respect of matters which are registrable. What it does is to supply a replacement source of notice. If, however, something is registered as a land charge that is not, in itself, a valid interest in land then registration does not confer validity upon it.[21]

2. Registration against the estate owner.   The most serious flaw affecting the Land Charges legislation is the method of registering land charges. Section 3(1) of the Land Charges Act 1972 provides that:

A land charge shall be registered in the name of the estate owner whose land is intended to be affected.

The requirement that registration be effected against the estate owner rather than against the land itself has caused a number of avoidable difficulties.

(a) What name?   It has been decided that the correct name to register a land charge against is the name which appears in the

---

[21] *Cf. Cato v. Newman* [1940] 1 K.B. 415. (Registration of a positive covenant on the register of title).

title deeds and not any different version of the name, for example the name which appears on a birth or marriage certificate.[22] Achieving this may not be as easy as it might seem. In *Diligent Finance Co. Ltd v. Alleyne*,[23] a wife sought to register her statutory right of occupation against her husband. She did so in the name by which he was to known to her: Erskine Alleyne. Unfortunately, unknown to her, he had a middle name, Owen. The company searched against his full name, Erskine Owen Alleyne, and recieved a clear certificate of search. It was held that the purported registration was ineffectual against the company.

A mistake such as this is easy to make. A question which has also arisen is what the result should be when both the purported registration and the intended search use the wrong name. This comedy of errors occurred in *Oak Co-operative B.S. v. Blackburn*.[24] Mr Blackburn's actual name was Francis David Blackburn. Registration of a land charge was against the name under which he traded, Frank David Blackburn. A search was made against the name, Francis Davis Blackburn. In other words, both the registration and the search were against incorrect versions of his name. The Court of Appeal held the registration to have been effective. It was held that registration in what is a fair approximation of the correct name is effective against a purchaser who either does not search at all or who searches in the wrong name.

At first sight, this seems illogical in that, if the registration is in the wrong name, then it cannot be discovered by a purchaser save for the unlikely situation where the purchaser makes precisely the same error as the person seeking to register the land charge. Nevertheless, on pragmatic grounds, there is something to be said for the decision. When a person seeks to register a land charge, this may be a hostile act and the owner of the legal estate may not co-operate. In this event the person seeking to register will not have access to the title deeds and will have to make an educated guess as to how the estate owner's name appears in the deeds. When a person is making a search, however, this will normally be because he is engaged in a transaction with estate owner, in which case he will obtain access to the deeds. Hence, there is no excuse for an incorrect search, while an incorrect registration is more understandable. Such a problem would not have arisen had registration been against the land, rather than the estate owner.

[22] *Standard Property Investment Plc v. British Plastics Federation* (1985) 53 P. &. C.R. 25.
[23] (1972) 53 P. &. C.R. 346.
[24] [1968] Ch. 730.

(b) Who is the estate owner? In addition to the difficulty in ensuring that the registration is against the correct name of the estate owner, a more fundamental problem that can arise is to identify who the estate owner actually is. *In Barrett v. Hilton Developments Ltd*,[25] a person, B, had contracted to buy land from A and, before that contract had been completed, contracted to sell the same land to C. C registered the estate contract against B but this was held to be an ineffective registration because the estate owner was A and not B, although C could not have known this.

A similar problem can arise if an estate owner dies. In such a case, registration should be against the personal representatives of the deceased, if he died testate, and against the President of the Family Division if he died intestate. Registration against the name of the deceased was ineffective although the position has since been changed.[26]

(c) Undiscoverable land charges. Perhaps the most serious flaw in the system of registration against names is that certain land charges may not be readily discoverable by an intending purchaser, despite the fact that have been properly registered. This problem is best illustrated by an example.

1925. A conveys to B.
1935. B conveys to C.
1945. C conveys to D.
1955. D conveys to E.
1965. E conveys to F.
1982. F conveys to V.
1995. V contracts to sell the land to P.

This example lists the actual changes in ownership of the land from 1925 until the present day. It is possible that a land charge may have been registered against any of the different land owners since that date. The difficulty that P faces is that, in investigating title, he need only go back to a transaction at least 15 years old. The first transaction of that vintage, the root of title,[27] is the conveyance in 1965. P is able, therefore to requisition searches against the names V, F and E. If, however, a land charge, for example a restrictive covenant, was registered against C, P will, because of section 198 of the Law of Property Act 1925, be deemed to have notice of it, although he cannot discover it.

---

[25] [1975] Ch. 237.
[26] Law of Property (Miscellaneous Provisions) Act 1994, s.15.
[27] See *ante*, p. 11.

The existence of this problem has been recognised for a long time.[28] Because it was not considered to be feasible to dismantle the system that had been implemented and replace it with a more sensible one, where registration was against the land rather than the owner of it, the only remedy to this problem was to provide for the payment of compensation. The general rule, introduced by section 25 of the Law of Property Act 1969, is that a purchaser is entitled to compensation in respect of land charges which are behind the root of title.

3. Non-registration of land charges. Just as the effect of registration is clear cut, so too is the consequence of non-registration. Although certain differences exist in respect of the different classes of land charge, the sanction for non-registration is the same: the interest is void for non-registration against a purchaser for value.[29]

The leading case is *Midland Bank Trust Co. Ltd v. Green*.[30] A father, Walter, granted his son, Geoffrey, an option to purchase a farm, of which he was the tenant, at a price in the region of £22,000, the option to be exercisable for a ten year period. Some six years later, by which time the value of the farm had nearly doubled in value, Walter discovered that the option had not been registered as a land charge. To take advantage of this, Walter conveyed the farm to his wife, Evelyn, for £500. The principal issue in the litigation, by which time the farm was worth in the region of £454,000, was whether the option was binding upon her, it being common ground that she actually knew about the existence of the option.

Reversing the majority decision in the Court of Appeal, the House of Lords unanimously held that the option was not binding upon Evelyn. The Land Charges legislation was not to be watered down by the introduction of the concept of good faith. When the Act laid down that an estate contract was void for non-registration against a purchaser for money or money's worth, it meant precisely that. Although £500 was clearly an undervalue, it was unquestionably money and the case was regarded as a clear one.

Not surprisingly, this decision attracted criticism, the question being asked "would it really cause the collapse of civilised conveyancing if the . . . statutes were altered to make actual notice of an unprotected interest binding upon a purchaser?"[31]

---

[28] Report of Committee of Land Charges 1956 (Cmnd. 9825).
[29] L.C.A. 1972, s.4. See also L.P.A. 1925, s.198. For the differences between the different classes of land charge, see Megarry, *op. cit.* pp. 87, 88.
[30] [1981] A.C. 513.
[31] Stuart Anderson (1977) 40 M.L.R. 600 at 606. See, also, Brian Green (1981) 97 L.Q.R. 518 at 520.

While such views are readily understandable, in that the mother's case seemed short of merit, there is also much to be said in favour of the decision.

First, the decision engenders certainty into this branch of the law. Although the facts of *Green*, itself, were such that one can instinctively sympathise with the son, Geoffrey, other cases where issues of good faith may arise are quite likely to be less clear cut, involving less dramatic undervalues. In such circumstances, the motivation to water down the clear legislative provisions may be less strong.

A second point is that the transaction involved in the *Green* case is precisely the type of transaction where one would expect legal advice to be taken. To insist that rights should be protected by registration should not cause undue hardship, in that one would expect a competent solicitor to effect the necessary registration and a failure to do so will lead to an action in negligence.[32] Again, an alternative cause of action for breach of contract would be sustainable against his father for breach of contract although, given the likely level of damages, this may be of very limited utility. Further, it was assumed in subsequent litigation that the father and mother would be liable, in tort, to their son for conspiracy.[33] This assumption has, however, been criticised, partly on the basis that Property Law and the Law of Tort should not produce opposite results on the same set of facts.[34]

A final point to make about the *Green* litigation is that Geoffrey was in actual occupation of the farm at all material times. Had title been registered, this, as will be seen, would have had a significant effect on the outcome of the case. In general, where title is registered, an equitable interest is enforceable against a purchaser if, either, the holder of it has protected it by registration, or he is in actual occupation of the land.[35] That this is not so when title is not registered is a result of a legislative accident[36] and is an unfortunate anomaly.

4. The system in operation. Having described the effect of registration and non-registration of land charges, attention must now be given to how the system operates. The intending purchaser should requisition an official certificate of search. The effect of this is that the search is conclusive according to its

---

[32] *Midland Bank Co. Ltd v. Hett, Stubbs & Kemp* [1979] Ch. 384. But contrast *Bell v. Peter Browne & Co.* [1990] 2 Q.B. 495.

[33] *Midland Bank Trust Co. Ltd v. Green (No. 3)* [1982] Ch. 529.

[34] M.P. Thompson [1985] C.L.J. 280 at 293–295.

[35] *Post*, pp. 52–57.

[36] See H.W.R. Wade [1956] C.L.J. 216 at 228.

tenor.[37] If the certificate wrongly states that there are no subsisting entries, the purchaser can rely on this. This means that, if he completes the transaction within the specified period, he will not be bound by the land charge which was correctly registered. The remedy for the person who has suffered the loss of his interest in land is to sue the registry in negligence.[38]

A purchaser, obviously, cannot rely on a search certificate indefinitely. Under section 12 of the Act, the purchaser is protected in respect of land charges registered after the search was made, provided that the transaction is completed within 15 working days of the date of the certificate.

(i) Priority notices. It is normal for a purchase of land to be financed by way of a mortgage. This could present difficulties for a person seeking to register a land charge, such as a restrictive covenant, against the purchaser. The problem is that the land charge may be void for non-registration against the mortgagee, the mortgage being created simultaneously with the conveyance. To meet this difficulty a procedure was put in place to allow for the registration of a priority notice. In essence, the procedure involves the incumbrancer applying for registration of the land charge before the conveyance to the purchaser and then completing the registration subsequently.[39]

5. Unregistrable interests. As has been seen, the basic division of equitable interests is between the family type of interests, which are overreachable, and the commercial type of interests which are registrable. There is also in existence a third category of equitable interest which is neither registrable nor overreachable. The issue of whether it is binding upon a purchaser is then dependent upon the traditional doctrine of notice.

It has long been accepted that certain types of equitable right do not fall into any class of land charge and were, also, not overreachable. Some of these rights are relatively arcane, such as a tenant's right to remove fixtures,[40] or an equitable right of re-entry.[41] Of much greater general significance are informal rights of co-ownership, involving the law of trusts, or rights arising from estoppel.

(a) Informal rights. A phenomenon which has, in modern times, exercised the courts is where a house is conveyed into one

---

[37] L.C.A. 1972, s.9.
[38] *Ministry of Housing and Local Government v. Sharp* [1970] 2 Q.B. 223. See, also, *Murphy v. Brentwood D.C.* [1991] 1 A.C. 398 at 486.
[39] See Megarry, *op. cit.* pp. 89, 90.
[40] *Poster v. Slough Estates Ltd* [1969] 1 W.L.R. 1807.
[41] *Shiloh Spinners Ltd v. Harding* [1973] A.C. 691.

person's name and another person has an equitable interest in the property. This most frequently occurs in situations where the parties are married or are living together in a stable, but non-marital relationship. The normal scenario is that the legal title is in the man's name and his partner is an equitable co-owner. Problems arise if he then mortgages the house, without consulting his partner, and then defaults on the mortgage. The mortgagee's claim for possession is then met by a defence by the woman, who claims that her equitable interest in the house is binding upon the mortgagee.

A main problem here is that the framework for co-ownership of land is based upon the idea that there should be two owners of the legal estate. If that is the case, then, as will be seen, the interests of all the beneficial co-owners will be overreached by a conveyance made by the two legal owners.[42] As there is only one legal owner, the conveyance by him will not have that effect. Neither is there any land charge which would include within its definition the type of interest in question. Accordingly, the issue of the enforceability of the equitable interest is dependent upon the traditional doctrine of notice.

Where there is beneficial co-ownership, in circumstances such as that referred to above, the woman has acquired her interest under a trust. To qualify for such an interest, it is normally necessary for her to have made some financial contribution to the purchase of the house. For example, she may be in paid employment and her salary is used, at least in part, to pay the mortgage instalments. It is also possible for her to acquire an equitable interest in the house through the still more informal medium of proprietary estoppel.

Proprietary estoppel, to be examined in rather greater depth in a later Chapter, is a flexible, equitable doctrine, whereby a person may acquire an interest in another's land. Its essence involves a situation where one person, A, encourages another person, B, to believe that they either have, or will acquire, an interest in A's land. B then relies on that belief in circumstance where it would be unfair, or unconscionable, for A to deny B some right in the land. An equity arises and it is in the court's discretion as to how this equity should be satisfied. The main point, for present purposes, is that this equity is capable of binding purchasers but is neither overreachable or registrable.

When faced with the question of the enforceability of such informally created rights, the original attitude of the courts, as has been seen, was to give the doctrine of notice a narrow ambit and to hold that, in cases where the holder of the equitable

---

[42] *City of London B.S. v. Flegg* [1988] A.C. 54. See *post*, pp. 89–90.

interest shared the property with the owner of the legal title, then a purchaser would not have constructive notice of the equitable interest.[43] Latterly, the courts have taken a different line and held that reasonable inquiries includes making inquiries of people sharing a home with the legal owner of the house.

This trend to protect people in actual occupation of the home could be reversed by legislation. The rights could be made registrable by the creation of new land charges, the result of which would be that the rights would be lost as against a purchaser unless registered. The result of this would be to give priority to the conveyancing dimension. On the other hand, people who acquire rights in land through informal transactions are unlikely to know of the registration requirement. It is improbable, unlike the position in *Green*, that these people will be in receipt of legal advice. For this reason, it can be argued that it is desirable to allow informally created rights, which will frequently subsist in relation to a person's home, to be enforced on the basis of notice and insist that rights of a more commercial nature be dependent upon registration.

REGISTRATION OF TITLE

The traditional method of proving ownership of land was by reference to the title deeds. These are all the documents relevant to the ownership of the land, such as conveyances. When it was proposed to sell the land, the vendor would allow the purchaser access to those deeds and it would be for the purchaser to satisfy himself that all was well. He would also seek to discover from the deeds the existence of various third party rights affecting the property. Moreover, he would also need to requisition the appropriate searches in the Land Charges Registry. This is a repetitive process. It is also not foolproof. The process of registration of title is designed to obviate this process and to enhance the security of conveyancing transactions. To replace the title deeds, the central idea is that a person is registered as owner of the land. In addition, the third party rights affecting the land are entered on the register. The main aim is for an intending purchaser to find out all that he needs to know about the land that he is buying by the simple process of searching the register. As will be seen, however, matters are not so simple in practice.

1. The Principles of Land Registration.

Theodore Ruoff, a former Chief Land Registrar, and renowned writer on the subject, once identified three basic principles which underlie the system of land registration. These are:

[43] *Ante*, p. 26.

1. The mirror principle;
2. The curtain principle; and
3. The insurance principle.[44]

What is meant by these statements is, first, that the register accurately reflects the state of a person's title. Secondly, any equitable interests that will be overreached by a transaction affecting the property will be kept, or curtained, off the title. Thirdly, the state guarantees the accuracy of the register and will compensate any person suffering loss by reason of a mistake in the register. While Ruoff, himself, recognised that these principles were not inviolate, it is useful to bear them in mind when considering the subject of land registration.

(a) The register of title. Under section 1(1) of the Land Registration Act 1925, the Chief Land Registrar is required to keep the register of title to freehold and leasehold land. The term "register", in this context means the sum total of titles registered at the Land Registry. The Land Registry, itself, is made up of various District Land Registries where the individual titles are maintained.

Implicit in what has been said is that the term "register of title" means also the individual titles to land in England and Wales. Indeed, this is the normal use of the term.

(b) Divisions of the register. Each register of title is divided into three sections: The Property Register, the Proprietorship Register and The Charges Register.

(i) The property register. This section of the register contains a verbal description of the land and estate comprised in the registered title together with an individual filed plan.[45] It will contain, also, notes relating to the ownership of the mines and minerals.

(ii) The proprietorship register. This section of the register states the name and address of the proprietor and the nature of the title. In the case of freehold property, the title is usually an absolute title, although it is possible for there to be either a possessory title or a qualified title. There is the same gradation in respect of leasehold titles. This part of the register also contains any restrictions or inhibitions affecting the proprietor's right to deal with the property.

---

[44] Ruoff, *An Englishman Looks at the Torrens System,* p. 8.
[45] This plan will only identify general boundaries: L.R. Rules 1925, r. 278.

(iii) The charges register. This part of the register relates to matters adversely affecting the property, such as covenants, easements and mortgages. Matters which are registrable as land charges, where title is unregistered, should appear in this section of the register. One effect of this is that when title is registered, it is unnecessary to have regard to the Land Charges Register. The relevant information should appear in this section of the register of title. Hence the systems of registration of land charges and registration of title are mutually discreet.

2. Interests Capable of Registration

After 1925, the only two estates which are capable of substantive registration are the fee simple absolute in possession and the term of years absolute for a period of not less than 21 years. Substantive registration means that a separate individual title may be created in respect of these interests. In the case of any other legal estate which, by virtue of section 3 (xi) of the Act, is quite widely defined, they cannot be separately registered. Rather registration is effected against the estate to be affected. Thus, in the case of a mortgage, registration is effected by the Registrar entering the name of the mortgagee and the details of the mortgage in the Charges Register of the relevant title.

3. The Need to Register

The process of registering title to all the land in England and Wales has been a gradual one. It was never intended that all estate owners should go out and register title to their land. Such a plan would not have been feasible. Instead, the policy was followed of promoting a type of rolling registration; the need to register being governed by the occurrence of two triggering events.

The first triggering event that caused registration of title to be compulsory was that the area in which the land was situate was designated an area of compulsory registration. The process of extending the areas of compulsory registration of title was a gradual one, with the final piece of the jigsaw being put into place in 1990,[46] whereafter the whole of England and Wales is now an area of compulsory registration of title.

The fact that a particular area has become an area of compulsory registration does not mean that all land must then be registered. It is only upon certain transactions that registration of title becomes compulsory. These are a conveyance on sale of a

[46] S.I. 1989 No. 1347.

fee simple, or the grant or assignment of a lease of more than 21 years. On the occurrence of either event after an area has become one of compulsory registration, the sanction for non-registration is provided by section 123 of the Act. The effect of this section is that, unless an application for registration is made within two months, the conveyance shall become void as regards the grant or conveyance of the legal estate.[47] The legal title then re-vests in the vendor or grantor, who will hold it on a bare trust for the purchaser or the grantee.

It should be appreciated that, because the spread of compulsory registration of title has been gradual, it will be quite some time before title to all land in England and Wales will be registered. Even when an area has been designated as an area of compulsory registration for a long period, it may be quite some time before all land within that area is registered. Quite simply, it may remain unsold for a prolonged period. For this reason, it remains necessary to be familiar with both systems of land ownership.

A second, not unrelated point, should also be made at this stage. This is that, once title is registered, all future dealings with the land must be completed by registration.

FIRST REGISTRATION OF TITLE

When a conveyance on sale has occurred in an area of compulsory registration of title, the purchaser then applies to be registered as proprietor. The Chief Land Registrar will then investigate the purchaser's title and, when satisfied, register the purchaser with an absolute title[48] and the purchaser is furnished with a land certificate, which is a copy of the register at the time of registration. The effect of this is then governed by the statute.

Section 5 of the Land Registration Act 1925 provides that:

> Where the registered land is a freehold estate, the registration of any person as first proprietor with an absolute title shall vest in the person so registered the estate in fee simple in possession of the land, together with all rights, privileges and appurtenances belonging or appurtenant thereto, subject to the following rights and interests, that it is to say,—
>
> (a) Subject to the other incumbrances, and other entries, if any, appearing on the register; and
> (b) Unless the contrary is expressed on the register, subject to such overriding interests, if any, as affect the registered land . . .

---

[47] This sanction does not apply to cases where the property is misdescribed in the application for registration: *Proctor v. Kidman* (1985) 51 P. & C.R. 67.
[48] The other, less satisfactory titles will not be considered.

but free from all other estates and interests whatsoever, including estates and interests of [Her]
Majesty.

This a key provision to the working of the Act. The first part
of the section may be regarded as the credit part and the latter
parts the debit side. They will be considered in turn.

1. The statutory magic. As section 5 makes clear, a proprietor
registered with an absolute title has vested in him a fee simple
in possession. This is so, regardless of whether or not the person
who conveyed the property to him was entitled so to do. Such a
situation occurred in *Re 139 High Street, Deptford.*[49] A vendor
conveyed to a purchaser a freehold shop together with an annex
and the purchaser was registered as proprietor with an absolute
title. In fact, the annex had not belonged to the vendor but had
been owned by another party. The litigation concerned an action
by that party to have the register rectified to restore the annex to
its rightful owner. The point, for present purposes, is that it was
quite clear that the effect of section 5 had been to transfer to the
purchaser an estate that the vendor had no power to convey.
Had the case involved unregistered land, the conveyance would
have been entirely ineffective to transfer the legal estate which
the vendor did not own. The magic of section 5 was to perform
this very feat.

As was just pointed out, the actual litigation in this case
centred on a claim to have the register rectified[50]; to undo what
section 5 had done. This action succeeded and the proprietor
was deprived of the annex. He was, however, entitled to an
indemnity to compensate for his loss. Here is a manifestation of
important features of the system of registration of title. Unless
rectified in subsequent proceedings, the fact of registration is
conclusive as to questions of ownership of of the legal estate.
Secondly, the state provides a guarantee to a person who suffers
loss as a result of a mistake in registration. This is an illustration
of the insurance principle referred to above.[51]

2. Third party rights. As has been seen, section 5 vests the
legal estate in the registered proprietor. It also makes clear what
burdens he must take subject to. These are defined as
incumbrances and other entries appearing on the register, on the
one hand, and overriding interests on the other. These matters
will be looked at in turn.

[49] [1951] Ch. 884.
[50] See, *post*, pp. 58–60.
[51] See, *ante*, p. 46.

When title is unregistered, interests in property can be categorised into a six-fold category. These are:

1. Legal estates;
2. Legal charges;
3. Legal interests;
4. Equitable interests.

The fourth group is sub-divided into three sub-categories:

(a) Registrable interests;
(b) Overreachable interests; and
(c) Interests neither registrable nor overreachable.

In the case of registered land, a similar classification may be made, save that there are fewer groups. These are:

1. Registrable interests;
2. Registrable charges;
3. Minor interests;
4. Overriding interests.

Category 3 can be sub-divided into:

(a) Overreachable interests; and
(b) Non-overreachable interests.

This section deals with the latter two categories.

MINOR INTERESTS

Minor interests are defined in section 3(xv) of the Act and broadly correspond with equitable rights in unregistered land. To bind a purchaser then, subject to what is said later, they must be protected by being entered on the register. The manner of their registration will generally indicate whether they are family interests, which can be overreached, or commercial interests, which cannot. There are four methods by which an interest may be protected on the register, although only three of these methods will be discussed here.

1. Restrictions. A restriction, as the name suggests, is a limitation on the power of the registered proprietor to deal with the property. The terms of the restriction must be complied with before any dealing with the property can be registered.[52]

A restriction is used when land is subject to family interests which, if the appropriate machinery is employed, can be over-

[52] L.R.A. 1925, s.58.

reached. If, for example, land is settled upon A for life, remainder to B then, as has been seen, the strategy of the 1925 legislation is to allow these equitable interests to be overreached. The legal estate is vested in A but, to safeguard B's position, the purchase money must be paid to two trustees. Where title is registered, A is registered as proprietor and a restriction is entered to the effect that no dealing with the property by A will be registered unless the capital money is paid to two trustees. It should be noticed that the nature of the equitable interests are not revealed on the register of title. This is an application of the curtain principle.

2. Notices. The effect of the registration of a notice is that the proprietor is bound by the matter that is protected and, in any subsequent dealing, the next proprietor will take subject to the particular incumbrance.[53] This is subject to the qualification that the incumbrance that is sought to be protected is inherently valid.[54]

The types of interest that can be protected by the entry of a notice are various and would include a lease of less than 21 years, which is not, itself, capable of substantive registration. It includes, also, matters which were registrable under the Land Charges Act 1972. Thus, those matters which were registered as land charges prior to first registration of title will, thereafter, be protected by the entry of a notice on the register.

3. Cautions. The registration of a notice is usually done with the co-operation of the registered proprietor. Where such co-operation cannot be obtained, the alternative course of action is to lodge a caution. There are two types of caution, a caution against first registration and a caution against dealings. The second type of caution is more common. In each case, however, the essential nature of the caution is the same.

Under section 54 of the Act, any person interested in any land or charge registered may lodge a caution to the effect that no dealing with the land or charge on the part of the proprietor is to be registered until notice has been served upon the cautioner. Upon the giving of such notice, the cautioner has 14 days in which to object to the registration. If he fails to respond within this period, the registration takes effect as if no caution had been lodged. It is said to have been "warned off".[55] If, on the other hand, he does object, then the Registrar will determine the

---

[53] L.R.A. 1925, s.52.
[54] See *Kitney v. M.E.P.C Ltd* [1977] 1 W.L.R. 981.
[55] L.R.A. 1925, s.55; L.R. Rules 1925, r. 218.

matter and decide whether the caution should be removed or, alternatively, that the register be modified to give effect to the cautioner's interest.[56]

OVERRIDING INTERESTS

The registered proprietor takes subject to overriding interests. These interests are, by definition,[57] interests which are not entered on the register and, as such, provide a major exception to the "mirror principle", whereby the register is supposed to reflect accurately the state of the proprietor's title. The closest analogy to them in unregistered land is with legal interests which are binding upon a purchaser regardless of notice. The analogy should not be pushed too far, however, because, as will be seen, a number of equitable interests are capable of existing as overriding interests.

Section 70(1) defines what constitutes overriding interests. Only the more important matters will be considered here.

1. Easements. Under paragraph (a), a quite diverse collection of rights are listed as being overriding interests. Of these the most important are easements and *profits à prendre*. The definiton clearly included legal easements and profits but it was not clear whether equitable easements were also overriding interests. The elliptical wording of the paragraph refers to "other easements not being equitable easements required to be protected by notice on the register." The problem is that there is nothing in the Act that requires equitable easements to be so registered.

This matter was considered in *Celsteel Ltd v. Alton House Holdings Ltd*,[58] where Scott J. held that equitable easements which were openly exercised for the enjoyment of adjoining land were overriding interests. This will, in practice, include most equitable easements.

2. Adverse possession. Under paragraph (f), rights acquired, or being acquired, under the Limitation Act 1980 are overriding interests. This is concerned with adverse possession, a topic which will be discussed in a later Chapter.

3. Actual occupation. Paragraph (g) is the most important of the section. It provides that "The rights of every person in actual

---

[56] L.R. Rules 1925, rr. 219, 220.
[57] L.R.A. 1925, s.3(xvi).
[58] [1985] 1 W.L.R. 204 (reversed, in part, on a different point: [1986] 1 W.L.R. 512). See M.P. Thompson [1986] Conv. 31; (1987) Law Com. No. 185, paras. 2.25–2.35 recommending a reversal of this decision.

occupation of the land or in receipt of the rents and profits thereof, save where inquiry has is made of such person and the rights are not disclosed" are overriding interests. In construing this section, it is helpful to treat separately the question of what is meant by rights and what is meant by actual occupation.

(a) Rights. It is a common misconception to assume that if a person, other than the registered proprietor, is in actual occupation of land then, this alone, means that the occupier has an overriding interest. This is not so. The person must first establish that he has a right in that land.

The basic pre-requisite is that the person claiming to have an overriding interest has some recognisable property right in that land. Thus, in *National Provincial Bank Ltd* v. *Ainsworth*,[59] the House of Lords held that there was no such right known to Property Law as "the deserted wife's equity". Consequently, because this was the only right in the property that she had, she could not have an overriding interest, despite being in actual occupation of the property. Similarly, in *City of London B.S.* v. *Flegg*,[60] rights which had been overreached could not take effect as overriding interests.

Bearing this in mind, a large collection of rights have been held to be overriding interests within this paragraph and have included an option to purchase the reversion of a lease[61] and an interest under a bare trust.[62] It is not intended to catalogue which rights have been held to be within this section. Some comment should be made, however, on the relationship between minor interests and overriding interests.

(i) Upgrading of Minor Interests

An important issue is whether a right, which is within the statutory definition of a minor interest, will take effect as an overriding interest, if the owner of that right is also in actual occupation of the land. This was one of the issues which arose in the leading case of *Williams & Glyn's Bank Ltd* v. *Boland*.[63] Mr Boland was the sole registered proprietor of a matrimonial home and it was conceded that Mrs Boland was an equitable co-owner of it. The effect of this was that the house was subject to an implied trust for sale.[64] He, without consulting his wife,

---

[59] [1965] A.C. 1175.
[60] [1988] A.C. 54.
[61] *Webb v. Pollmount Ltd* [1966] Ch. 584.
[62] *Hodgson v. Marks* [1971] Ch. 892.
[63] [1981] A.C. 487.
[64] See *post*, pp. 105–106.

mortgaged the house to the bank, who did not address any inquiries to Mrs Boland prior to granting the mortgage. She argued that she had an overriding interest which was binding upon the bank.

One of the arguments advanced on behalf of the bank was that, because the interest that Mrs Boland had in the property was included within the statutory definition of a minor interest, it followed that it could not be an overriding interest. The two categories of interest were, it was contended, mutually exclusive. Depite finding this argument "formidable",[65] Lord Wilberforce rejected it. He took the view that there was no reason, in principle, why a minor interest could not, in effect, be upgraded to an overriding interest, if the person was in actual occupation of the land.

The effect of *Boland* on this point is to establish, as a general rule, that a minor interest coupled with actual occupation equals an overriding interest. This is so, unless the statute specifically provides that a particular right can only take effect as an overriding interest, the most important examples of this being the rights of a beneficiary under a strict settlement and a spouse's statutory right of occupation of the matrimonial home.[66]

The effect of this decision is that the rights of a person in actual occupation of land are binding upon a subsequent purchaser despite that person not having protected that right by registering it. This is in marked contrast to the position in unregistered land where, as has been seen,[67] non-registration of a land charge means that the interest will be void against a subsequent purchaser notwithstanding that the owner of the right is in actual occupation. The position in registered land is, it is suggested, preferable, in that, if a person is in actual occupation of land, he may well feel that his interest in it is safe, without perceiving the need to consult a solicitor to gain advice about the need to register it. The effect of this paragraph is, in the words of Lord Denning, to "protect a person in actual occupation from having his rights lost in the welter of registration."[68]

(b) Actual occupation. In addition to having a proprietary right in land, the person must, in order to establish an overriding interest, also be in actual occupation of the land. There are two

[65] [1981] A.C. 487 at 508.
[66] L.R.A 1925, s.86(2); Matrimonial Homes Act 1983, s.2(8)(b).
[67] *Ante*, pp. 13–14.
[68] *Strand Securities Ltd v. Caswell* [1965] Ch. 958 at 979.

questions involved in this; determining what is meant by actual occupation and deciding what is the crucial time when the person must be in actual occupation.

(i) MEANING

In considering the meaning of the phrase actual occupation, the courts have had to address the key question of whether, if the registered proprietor is in actual occupation of the land, other people may also be. It was argued, at one time, that, by analogy with the position concerning constructive notice in unregistered land, this would not be the case. This argument had some initial success, so that it was held, at first instance, in *Hodgson* v. *Marks*[69] that actual occupation should be construed to mean "actual *and apparent* occupation." On appeal, however, this view was rejected and it was held that the meaning of "actual occupation" was a matter of fact.[70] This was confirmed by the House of Lords in *Williams & Glyn's Bank Ltd v. Boland*, where the argument that a wife could not be considered to be in actual occupation of a home in which her husband lived, on the basis that her occupation should be regarded as but a shadow of his, was condemned as "heavily obsolete".[71]

It was reiterated in *Boland* that the question of whether a person is in actual occupation of land was one of fact. Cases can, therefore, only be illustrative. Some points do, however, emerge. To count as actual occupation, the presence in the property must be more than merely fleeting; hence, access to the property for the purpose of measuring up for curtains will not constitute actual occupation[72] and neither will the intermittent parking of a car.[73] On the other hand, temporary absence from the home because, for example, of a stay in hospital, will not cause the person to cease being in actual occupation.[74] In cases where a person is absent from the property for any appreciable length of time, it may be the case that the courts will take the view that some visible indication of an intention to return will be necessary for the person still to be regarded as being in actual occupation, although the point is yet to be decided.[75]

The fact that "actual occupation" is given a literal interpretation has various consequences. First, it means that a prudent

---

[69] [1971] Ch. 892, 916, *per* Ungoed–Thomas J.
[70] *ibid.* at pp. 931, 932 *per* Russell L.J.
[71] [1981] A.C. 487, 505, *per* Lord Wiberforce.
[72] *Abbey National B.S. v. Cann* [1991] 1 A.C. 56.
[73] *Epps v. Esso Petroleum Ltd* [1973] 1 W.L.R. 1071. Contrast *Kling v. Keston Properties Ltd* (1985) 49 P. & C.R. 212.
[74] See *Chhokar v. Chhokar* (1983) 5 F.L.R. 313.
[75] See Peter Sparkes [1989] Conv. 342.

purchaser must, in general, make inquiries of all occupants of the property. It is not sufficient simply to address inquiries to the proprietor of the land.[76] This task may be onerous and complicates the conveyancing process; again, evidence of the tension between the desire to protect the rights of occupiers, on the one hand, and the wish to facilitate conveyancing on the other. This tension is most acute in the context of mortgages and the matter will be reconsidered in a later Chapter.

A second point to make is that, because the question of whether a person is in actual occupation of land is one of fact, results may differ depending upon whether or not title is registered. If title is unregistered then, to decide whether a purchaser will be bound by an equitable interest, one must consider whether it should have been discovered by making reasonable inquiries. In registered land, the issue is whether the person was in actual occupation of the land. One can envisage circumstances when a person is held to be in actual occupation, although this was not discoverable by making reasonable inquiries.

(ii) RENTS AND PROFITS

A person who is not in actual occupation of land will nevertheless have an overriding interest if he is in receipt of the rents and profits from the land. If a person with a registrable interest allows a friend or relation to occupy a house in return for £1 per week, then he, as someone in receipt of rents and profits will have an overriding interest.[77] It is not obvious why such a person should enjoy the protection given to occupiers of the land and the Law Commission have recommended the removal of such protection.[78]

(iii) TIME OF OCCUPATION

On the transfer of registered land, the purchaser acquires the legal title when he is registered as proprietor. This, inevitably, is some time after the actual transfer document is executed. An important question is whether the relevant time for determining if a person is in actual occupation is the date of transfer or the date of registration. In the interest of convenience, it was held in *Abbey National B.S. v. Cann*,[79] to be the earlier date. Provided that the person was in actual occupation of the land at that time, it does not matter if he subsequently vacates the property.[80]

---

[76] *Hodgson v. Marks* [1971] Ch. 892, 932, per Russell L.J.
[77] *Cf. Strand Securities Ltd v. Caswell* [1965] Ch. 958.
[78] (1987) Law Com. No. 158, para. 2.70.
[79] [1991] 1 A.C. 56.
[80] *London & Cheshire Insurance Co, Ltd. v. Laplagrene Property Co. Ltd.* [1971] Ch. 499.

4. Local land charges. These are charges in favour of local authorities and are within paragraph (i) of the section.

5. Leases. A legal lease of less than 21 years is not capable of substantive registration with its own title and takes effect, under paragraph (k) as an overriding interest. In practice, leases which are not overriding interests under paragraph (k) are likely to have such status under paragraph (g) in that the tenant will usually be in actual occupation of the land.

DEALINGS WITH REGISTERED LAND

Once title to the land has been registered, then any future dealing with that land is effected by the new owner of the estate being registered as the proprietor. The nature of his title is then governed by section 20 of the Act, which is to the effect that in the case of a freehold estate[81] registered with an absolute title, a disposition of registered land for valuable consideration shall, when registered, confer on the transferee an estate in fee simple or the term of years absolute, together with all appurtenant rights, subject to: (a) interests noted on the register; and (b) overriding interests but free from all other estates and interests, including those of Her Majesty.

The section, which is cast in similar terms to section 5, seems clearly to preclude any role for the application of the doctrine of notice, or of good faith. Nevertheless, in *Peffer v. Rigg*,[82] such concepts were employed. As part of a divorce settlement, a house was transferred from D1 to D2 for £1 and D2 was registered with an absolute title. D1 had held the house on an express trust for P and D2 was aware of this. It was argued that the effect of section 20 was that D2 took free from the trust which had not been protected by entry on the register. Graham J. held that D2 was bound by P's beneficial interest.

There were three reasons given for this surprising decision. One of these involved a highly convoluted reading of various sections of the Act to justify the conclusion that the Act required a purchaser to act in good faith. This reading of the Act is, however, unsustainable and the decision, which in any event can be regarded as being made *per incuriam*,[83] is widely considered to be wrong. Notice of an unprotected interest should not, of itself, mean that a purchaser cannot rely on clear statutory

---

[81] This, somewhat confusingly, includes leaseholds.

[82] [1977] 1 W.L.R. 285. For criticism, see, *e.g.*, D.J. Hayton (1977) 36 C.L.J. 341; M.P. Thompson (1985) 44 C.L.J. 280, 285–289.

[83] A case which rejected the applicability of the doctrine of notice which was not cited was *De Lusignan v. Johnson* (1974) 230 E.G. 499.

provisions.[84] If, on the other hand, a purchaser expressly agrees to take subject to an unprotected interest then, it seems, it is fraudulent for him to go back on his agreement and a constructive trust is imposed to give effect to the unprotected interest.[85]

RECTIFICATION AND INDEMNITY

As has been seen, it is possible for a person to be mistakenly be registered as proprietor of land. Other errors in the registration process can occur. It is, therefore, necessary that provision exists whereby such errors can be rectified. Accordingly, jurisdiction is conferred by section 82 of the Act to allow the register to be rectified. Where this jurisdiction is exercised, a person who suffers loss as a consequence of rectification is generally entitled to an indemnity from state funds. This is the manifestation of the insurance principle referred to above.

RECTIFICATION

There are eight statutory grounds upon which the register may be rectified. These grounds are not mutually exclusive and it is possible that a case for rectification can be made out under a number of different heads. What should, however, be stressed is that it is not sufficient to make out a case for rectification under one of the statutory heads. One is not entitled to have the register rectified; it is always a matter of discretion for the court. So if, for example, the effect of rectification would be more serious to the proprietor than would the refusal of rectification to the person seeking rectification, then the order will be refused.[86]

1. Jurisdiction to rectify.   There are eight grounds for rectification set out in the statute. Of these, the first two grounds give the court exclusive jurisdiction to order rectification and, in the case of the remaining six, either the court or the registrar may make the order. Of the grounds themselves, with the exception of ground (c), they can roughly be divided into cases of either entitlement to an interest in the property, or to cases of mistakes occurring in the registry.[87] The grounds for rectification can now be, briefly, described.

---

[84] See, in the context of the Land Charges Act 1972, *Midland Bank Trust Co. Ltd v. Green* [1981] A.C. 513.

[85] *Lyus v. Prowsa Developments Ltd* [1982] 1 W.L.R. 1004; *Ashburn Anstalt v. Arnold* [1988] 2 All E.R. 147. For criticism, see M.P. Thompson [1988] Conv. 201, 205–206.

[86] See *Epps v. Esso Petroleum Co. Ltd* [1973] 1 W.L.R. 1071.

[87] *Norwich & Peterborough B.S. v. Steed* [1992] Ch. 116, 134 *per* Scott L.J.

(a) *Entitlement.* A court may order rectifcation when it has decided that a person is entitled to to an estate, right or interest in the land. A notice, caution or restriction may be entered under this head.

(b) *Aggrieved by entry.* This seems to overlap to a considerable extent with the above ground and allows a court to order rectification where any person is aggrieved by the making or omission of an entry on the register.

(c) *Consent.* The register may be rectified with the consent of all interested parties.

(d) *Fraud.* If registration has been secured by fraud, then the court or registrar may rectify the register. The fraud in question refers to fraud practised on the registry. This was established in the leading case of *Norwich & Peterborough B.S. v. Steed.*[88] A son, who was the registered proprietor of a house had given his mother power of attorney over it. By means of fraud, she was prevailed upon to transfer the house to her daughter and son-in-law, who in turn mortgaged the house to the building society, whose charge was duly registered. The son then sought rectification of the register, as against the building society. The Court of Appeal held that there was no jurisdiction to do so. The mortgage which had been lodged with the registry was not fraudulent. If the transfer, itself, was a forgery and a mortgage had subsequently been executed, it was envisaged that rectification could be expected.[89]

(e) *Two people registered as proprietor.*

(f) *Mortgages.* If a mortgagee is registered as proprietor of the land, the register may be rectified. This is unlikely to happen. The possibilty arises because conveying the land to the mortgagee was the method of mortgaging land before 1925.

(g) *Wrong person registered.* Where a person who is registered as proprietor would not have been the owner of the land had title been unregistered, then rectification may be ordered. If land is wrongly included in a conveyance, as occurred in *Re 139 High Street, Deptford,* the register may be rectified under this head.

(h) *Just to rectify.* Although this appears to give the court and the registrar an untrammelled discretion to rectify the register

---

[88] [1993] Ch. 116,
[89] *ibid.* at p. 132 *per* Scott L.J.

when it is considered appropriate to do so, this is not the case. It was held in *Norwich & Peterborough B.S. v. Steed*, that it is only applicable in cases where a mistake has been made in the registry. The paragraph was seen as a form of safety net, to allow rectification in the case of a mistake that had not been identified in any of the preceding paragraphs.

2. Restrictions on right to rectify.   The grounds on which the register may be rectified when the registered proprietor is in possession of the land are more restricted, this reflecting a policy of the Act in affording greater protection to people who occupy land than to those who do not. It is provided by section 82(3) of the Act, as amended, that the register shall not be rectified so as to affect the title of of the proprietor in possession unless one of four exceptions are satisfied. These are:

(a) Overriding interests.   The register may be rectified to give effect to an overriding interest. As the proprietor takes subject to such interests in any event, this simply enables the register to be rectified to give effect to the true position.

(b) Court order: the register may be rectified to give effect to a court order.

(c) Lack of proper care.   If the registered proprietor has contributed to the error in registration by a lack of proper care, then the register may be rectified. As originally drafted, this exception allowed rectification if the proprietor had simply contributed to the error. This included the lodging of a inaccurate conveyance.[90] This construction deprived the proprietor in possession of much of the protection it was intended that he should have and an innocent error will no longer have this effect.

(d) Unjust not to rectify.   If the person seeking rectification can persuade a court or the registrar that it would be unjust not to rectify. The onus is on the person seeking rectification and this onus will not be easy to satisfy.

INDEMNITY

A remedy, which is complementary to that of rectification, is the payment of an indemnity. Because the jurisdiction to rectify the register is a discretionary one, there is provison to indemnify not only a person who suffers loss by reason of rectification but also a person who suffers loss by reason of non-rectification.

---

[90] See S. Cretney and G. Dworkin (1968) 84 L.Q.R. 528.

(a) Rectification. A person who suffers loss by reason of rectification of the register is, in general, entitled to be paid an
indemnity,[91] such indemnity being payable out of public funds.
Thus, if, in error, a person is wrongly registered as proprietor of
land to which he is not entitled, the indemnity will amount to
the value of that land which, by process of rectification is
returned to the true owner of it. The indemnity is, however,
payable only in respect of loss caused by rectification. If
rectification is ordered to give effect to an overriding interest,
then rectification has not caused loss; the proprietor was, in any
event bound by this interest. In this circumstance, no indemnity
is payable.[92] This is subject to the qualification that the applicant
or his predecessor in title has not contributed to the error by a
lack of proper care, provided that the applicant has not acquired
title under a disposition for valuable consideration.[93] It is
expressly provided by section 83(4) of the Act, that a proprietor
claiming in good faith under a forged disposition shall, where
the register is rectified, be deemed to have suffered loss and be
entitled to an indemnity.

(b) Non-rectification. If, in the exercise of discretion, it is
decided not to rectify the register, then the person who suffers
loss as a result is entitled to an indemnity. Unfortunately, the
amount of this indemnity is calculated by reference to the time
when the error in registration occurred,[94] which may be some
considerable time before rectification proceedings are brought.

---

[91] L.R.A 1925, s.83(1).
[92] See *Re Chowood's Registered Land* [1933] Ch. 574.
[93] L.R.A. 1925, s.83(5).
[94] L.R.A. 1925, s. 83(6); see, also, *Epps v. Esso Petroleum Co. Ltd* [1973] 1 W.L.R.
1071, 1081.

CHAPTER FIVE

The Transfer of Freehold Estates

The two main ways in which freehold estates are transferred are by sale and upon death. This Chapter is concerned with these two issues.

SALE

When land is sold, it is normal for there to be two stages involved: contract and conveyance. It is also usual for there to be a gap of up to four weeks between the two stages of the transaction. There are a number of reasons for this. One reason is that it is common for transactions to be linked. A person buying a house will often be selling one as well. It is important that the two transactions are synchronised to avoid the prospect of being saddled with two houses and, as a result, two mortgages, with potentially catastrophic financial consequences, or being left with no house at all. Secondly, as will be seen, there are a number of tasks to be performed between contract and conveyance, it not being usual to perform these tasks prior to the existence of a binding contract.

A practice has, also, developed of forming a contract by the exchange of identical documents signed, respectively, by each party to the contract. As a matter of terminology, the two stages in the transaction are frequently referred to as exchange of contracts and completion; the latter term being synonymous with the conveyance stage, where the legal title is actually transferred.

Contract

Unlike contracts for the sale of most other commodities, contracts for the sale of land have, for over three hundred years, been subject to statutory requirements regarding formalities. So, whereas a contract for the sale of a car can be made orally and will be fully enforceable, this is not so in the case of land. The matter of formalities must now be considered.

1. Contracts made before September 27, 1989. Until the coming into force of the Law of Property (Miscellaneous Provisions) Act 1989, it was perfectly possible to make an oral contract for the sale of land. Such a contract was, however, unenforceable by action. First by section 4 of the Statute of Frauds 1677, which was superseded by section 40(1) of the Law of Property Act 1925, it was provided that:-

> No action may be brought upon any contract for the sale or other disposition of land or any interest in land, unless the agreement upon which action is brought, or some memorandum or note thereof, is in writing, and signed by the person to be charged or by some other person thereunto by him lawfully authorised.

Although this section has now been repealed, a number of points can usefully be made about it. First, although repealed, the section continues to apply to contracts made before September 27, 1989, when the new Act came into force. While it is highly unlikely that many contracts for the sale of land will be affected by section 40,[1] other transactions may continue to be affected for some time to come, notably contracts for leases and options to purchase. The other points about the section one needs to make are necessary to enable the changes introduced by the new legislation to be properly understood.

1. Contract unenforceable. The effect of section 40 was to make contracts for the sale of land unenforceable unless there was sufficient written evidence of it. In the absence of such evidence, neither party could sue upon the contract but there was nothing to prevent it being used as a defence to an action, for example, a vendor could retain a deposit paid by the purchase under an oral contract of sale if the purchaser declined to complete the transaction.[2]

A second point is that the evidence required by section 40 insisted only that the party to be charged, or defendant, sign the note or memorandum. This meant that if only one party had signed the documentation then he could be sued upon the contract but the other party to it could not.

---

[1] Although see *Morritt v. Wonham* [1993] N.P.C. 2; M.P. Thompson [1994] Conv. 233.
[2] *Monnickendam v. Leanse* (1923) 39 T.L.R. 445.

2. Part performance.   As has been seen, a contract which did not comply with the formal requirements of section 40 was not void. It was a perfectly valid contract but could not be enforced by action upon it. The parties, themselves, may not have been aware of this and proceeded on the basis that the contract between them was fully binding. If one of the parties realised at a later stage that the contract was not enforceable, he may seek to refuse to complete. If the other party has relied on the contract being enforceable, to allow the other side to refuse to continue with the implementation of the contract may result in injustice.

To meet this difficulty, equity developed the doctrine of part performance, a doctrine given statutory recognition by section 40(2) of the Act. Under this doctrine, about which a fair amount of case law developed, if one party had performed a sufficient act of part performance of an oral contract then an equity arose in his favour. To satisfy this equity, the court had a choice "between undoing what has been done (which is not always possible, or, if possible, just) and completing what has been left undone."[3]

The basis of this equitable doctrine was the prevention of fraud; it being regarded as fraudulent for one party to a contract to allow the other to act on the basis that the contract was enforceable and then, subsequently, turn round and plead that the lack of a written memorandum resulted in the contract being unenforceable. To this, essentially equitable basis was added an evidentiary role, that the act, or acts, relied upon pointed to the existence of a contract between the two.[4]

A classic example of part performance, by both parties to the contract, was if the purchaser was allowed to take possession of the vendor's land. In such circumstances, the contract would be enforceable by both vendor and purchaser. Indeed, despite the element of choice in satisfying the equity, referred to above, the effect of a successful act of part performance was to operate as an alternative to a written memorandum. The oral contract between the parties was enforced.

2. Contracts made after September 26, 1989.   Section 40 of the Law of Property Act 1925 was considered by the Law Commission, who considered that reform was appropriate,[5] the principal considerations being that the idea that a contract enforceable against only the person who signed a memorandum was unfair

---

[3] *Maddison v. Alderson* (1883) 8 App. Cas. 467 at 476, *per* Earl of Selborne L.C.
[4] See *Steadman v. Steadman* [1976] A.C. 536.
[5] (1987) Law Com. No. 164.

and that the notion of a valid, but enforceable contract was confusing. This Report was implemented by section 2 of the Law Reform (Miscellaneous Provisions) Act 1989. Section 2(1) provides that:–

A contract for the sale or other disposition of an interest in land can only be made in writing and only by incorporating all the terms that the parties have expressly agreed in one document or, where contracts are exchanged, in each.

On the question of the signatures of the parties, section 2(3) provides that the document incorporating the terms or, where contracts are exchanged, one of the documents incorporating them (but not necessarily the same one) must be signed by or on behalf of each party to the contract.

This section applies to all contracts for the sale or disposition of an interest in land except for a contract for a lease of less than three years, a contract made in the course of a public auction or to a contract regulated by the Financial Services Act 1986.

1. Made in writing. The crucial difference between section 2 and its predecessor is that an agreement that does not satisfy section 2 is not a contract at all. There is now no such thing as an oral contract for the sale of land. Various consequences flow from this.

A first point to make is that, like section 40, which it superseded, section 2 applies not just to contracts for the sale of land but to every type of disposition of interests in land. This will include, unless within one of the exceptions listed by the Act, interests such as leases, mortgages and easements. One difficulty that the new Act has created relates to the informal creation of such interests. As will be seen, it is a long established principle of Land Law that an attempt to create such an interest without using a deed, as is generally required, is not entirely ineffective. It will normally be construed as a contract to create the particular interest in land. This, in turn, may result in the transaction being effective to create an equitable version of the interest in question.[6] It now seems to be the case that an informal transaction which does not comply with the new statutory regime cannot take effect as a contract to create the particular interest in question and may lead to a particular transaction being entirely ineffective.[7]

A related problem concerns options to purchase land. An option gives the grantee the right to enter into a contract for the

---

[6] See *post*, pp. 121–122.
[7] See *United Bank of Kuwait v. Sahib* [1994] *The Times*, July 7. See M.P. Thompson [1994] Conv. 465.

sale of the grantor's land. This is dependent upon the grantee electing to exercise the option. One perceived difficulty was whether the document purporting to exercise the option must comply with section 2. If so, a problem may well arise in that the document exercising the option may well not be signed by the grantor. This issue was addressed in *Spiro v. Glencross Properties Ltd.*[8] In that case, it was held to be sufficient if the option itself satisfied the section. For this purpose, the option was treated as a conditional contract. The effect of this decison is that an option granted prior to the coming into force of section 2 but exercised after that date will continue to be governed by the old law.

2. *Abolition of part performance.*   A second consequence of the Act insisting that contracts for the sale of land actually are in writing is that the doctrine of part performance is abolished in respect of agreements to which the Act applies. The effect, in the past, of a successful act of part performance was that the previously unenforceable contract for the sale of land became enforceable. Because there is now no such thing as an oral contract for the sale of land there can be no possibility of there being part performance of it.

The Law Commission was quite well aware that the effect of the proposed reform would be to abolish part performance. The view was expressed that, what were part performance cases in the past, would now be determined upon the principles of equitable estoppel.[9] The difficulty with this, however, is that it is a feature of the doctrine of estoppel that the court has considerable discretion as to how any equity that has arisen should be satisfied.[10] In cases of part performance, the normal reaction of the court was to enforce the agreement that the parties had actually made. While it is possible that the courts will adopt this course of action in estoppel cases that arise as a result of section 2, there is no guarantee that this will be the case. Instead, a court may adopt a more discretionary approach.[11] The result may be to increase the element of uncertainty in cases of this nature, which is unfortunate, particularly given that one of the aims of the legislation was to simplify the law.

3. *All terms.*   The section makes clear that all the terms that have been expressly agreed between the parties must be in writing. Under the old law, to be adequate as a memorandum,

---

[8] [1991] Ch. 537.
[9] (1997) Law Com. No. 164, paras. 5.4, 5.5. See, also, L. Bentley and P. Coughlin (1990) 10 L.S. 325.
[10] See *post*, pp. 178–180.
[11] See *Morritt v. Wonham* [1993] N.P.C. 2.

the written evidence had, also, as a general rule, to make reference to all the terms agreed beween the parties. In considering whether the memorandum was adequate in this regard, the courts adopted a fairly liberal view as to what constituted an acceptable reference to a particular term and, if an otherwise vague reference could be clarified, the courts were generally willing to allow such clarification to be made, in order to avoid the contract being held to be unenforceable.[12] A similar approach is likely to be continued in construing the new section. Where there will be a difference between the old law and the new is the consequence of the writing omitting a term that has been expressly agreed between the parties.

Under the old law, if a memorandum omitted a term of the contract which was solely for the benefit of one of the parties to it, he could opt to waive the term and enforce the contract upon the terms evidenced in writing.[13] In the converse situation, the other party could submit to perform the omitted term.[14] Under the new law, neither approach is possible because all the terms of the contract that have been expressly agreed must be in writing. There are two possible solutions to this problem. The first is to treat the omitted term as an independent collateral contract, to which the Act does not apply.[15] The second, and more generally applicable solution is to seek to have the written contract rectified to reflect the actual agreement.[16] If this course is adopted, then, section 2(4) of the Act provides that the date of the contract is deemed to be the date of the rectification rather than the date that the original document was signed.

3. Exchange of Contracts. The method of entering into a contract for the sale of land which is most commonly employed is to adopt a process known as exchange of contracts. This practice, which is expressly recognised by the 1989 Act, involves each party signing an identical document. When both parties are ready to commit themselves to being legally bound to proceed with the sale, these documents are then exchanged and it is at that moment that the contract comes into being. Where the process of exchange is envisaged, no contract comes into being until exchange is actually effected[17] and either party is free to withdraw from the contemplated transaction.

[12] See, *e.g., Harewood v. Retese* [1990] 1 W.L.R. 333; Megarry, *Manual of the Law of Real Property* (27th ed.), pp. 119, 120.
[13] See, *e.g., North v. Loomes* [1919] 1 Ch. 378.
[14] See *Scott v. Bradley* [1971] Ch. 850.
[15] *Record v. Bell* [1991] 1 W.L.R. 853.
[16] See *Wright v. Leonard* [1994] N.P.C. 49.
[17] *Eccles v. Bryant* [1948] Ch. 93.

1. Synchronising transactions.   The principal reason for the adoption of this practice is the need to synchronise various transactions. It is quite common for a house purchase to form part of a chain of linked transactions. A, a first time buyer, is buying a house from B. B, in turn, is buying a house from C, who is buying a house from D. It is important for each of these people that the contracts are synchronised. B will not wish to commit himself to the sale of his house to A until he has secured the existence of the contract to buy C's house. The process of exchanging contracts facilitates this synchronisation by seeking to ensure that all exchange simultaneously. Indeed, to further enhance this process, the practice has developed of constructive exchange of contracts by telephone, practitioners phoning their counterpart and each agreeing to hold their client's contract on behalf of the other side.[18]

2. Gazumping.   A principal reason for conveyancing transactions to be protracted is the need for everyone involved in the chain to be ready to exchange contracts at the same time. While the parties are waiting for this to happen, they are in something of a state of limbo, having agreed in principle upon the purchase of a particular property but being unable to commit themselves to the transaction. At this stage, the parties have only agreed "subject to contract". Either side is free to withdraw from the transaction for any reason. A practice which attracted notoriety in the 1970s and has surfaced from time to time, thereafter, is that of gazumping. This practice, which can only occur when house prices are volatile, is for the vendor having agreed to sell the property for a certain price, that agreement being subject to contract, then informing the purchaser that he will withdraw from the transaction unless he agrees to an increase in the purchase price. If the purchaser cannot or will not agree to this, he loses the transaction and will also have incurred a degree of wasted expenditure. He is said to have been gazumped. This practice, which has attracted considerable opprobrium, has proved very difficult to eradicate[19] and, to some extent, is an economic rather than a legal problem. It stems, however, from the delay involved in the parties being able to proceed to an exchange of contracts. It should, however, be stressed that gazumping can only occur prior to exchange of contracts. Once contracts have been exchanged, neither side is free, unilaterally, to withdraw from the contract.

---

[18] See *Domb v. Isoz* [1980] Ch. 548.
[19] For a recent attempt involving a "lock-out" agreement, see *Pitt v. PHH Asset Management Ltd* [1993] 40 E.G. 149.

3. Forms of contract. A contract for the sale of a house which had as its agreed terms only the contracting parties and the price to be paid would be perfectly valid but not workable. Certain other terms, such as the date for completion would need to be implied by law. A contract which contains only the bare essential described above is termed an open contract and is unusual in practice. Normal practice is to use a standard form, printed contract, the one currently in use being the second edition of the Standard Conditions of Sale. As the name suggests, these forms contain a host of conditions regulating the sale, such as the payment of a deposit. There a number of general conditions which are, in principle, applicable to all sales but there is also a need to introduce special conditions to deal with the particular details of the individual contract.

4. The effect of the contract. Once contracts have been exchanged, the legal Rubicon has been crossed and both parties are thenceforth committed to the transaction. As is the case with all contracts, if either party defaults on the contract, the other party can sue for damages. In the case of land contracts, however, the remedy of specific performance is routinely available, so that if, say, the vendor declines to proceed with the sale, the purchaser can secure a court order compelling him to do so. The availability of the equitable remedy of specific performance has certain important consequences.

Until the contract is actually completed, the vendor remains the legal owner of the property. In the eye of equity, however, the person who should be the owner of the land is the purchaser. This is because of the existence of the specifically enforceable contract of sale. It is a maxim of equity, that equity looks upon that as done which ought to be done. In other words, because equity takes the view that the purchaser should have the land conveyed to him, he should be regarded from the date of the contract as being the owner of the property. The effect of this approach is that the vendor is regarded as trustee of the property in favour of the purchaser.

1. Vendor as trustee. The imposition of the trust means that the vendor is subjected to various duties with regard to the property to be sold, pending the completion of the property. Of these duties, the most important is to take reasonable care of it. This duty extends not only to acts committed by himself, or his agents, but also to seek to prevent acts of damage by third parties or the effects of the weather.[20]

---

[20] See *Clarke v. Ramuz* [1891] 2 Q.B. 456 (damage done by trespassers); *Lucie-Smith v. Gorman* [1981] C.L.Y. 2866 (burst pipes in winter).

2. Purchaser as beneficiary.   The purchaser, as beneficial owner of the property, is entitled to the benefit of any increase in the value of the land pending completion. Much more importantly, however, he must, as beneficial owner of the land, bear the risk of damage to the property during this period. If, without default on the part of the vendor, the property is damaged, or even destroyed, the conventional wisdom is that the purchaser must nevertheless pay the agreed purchase price in full.[21] The result of this is that the purchaser needs to insure the property from the date of the contract, it not being safe, for various reasons, to rely upon the vendor's insurance policy.[22]

The rule that the risk of damage to the property between contract and completion passes to the purchaser has undesirable consequences. First a purchaser may be unaware of the rule and, secondly, when he is aware of the rule, guarding against it may lead to a duplication of insurance, with both vendor and purchaser simultaneously insuring the same property. The Law Commission was impressed by these criticisms and provisionally recommended that the rule be reversed by legislation.[23] Since then, Condition 5 of the Standard Conditions of Sale, in effect, provides that the risk of damage to the property between contract and completion remains with the vendor and no legislation has ensued.

2. CONVEYANCING

In the period between contract and conveyance a number of tasks need to be performed before the transaction is completed and the purchaser acquires the legal title to the land. The procedure varies, depending upon whether or not title to the land is registered.

1. Unregistered Land.   The essential task to be performed, at this stage of the transaction, is for the purchaser to check that the title that the vendor can establish to the land is in accordance with that which has been promised by the contract. This process is known as the investigation and proof of title and when, as is usually the case, the contract is governed by the Standard Conditions of Sale, a time scale for these procedures is stipulated in the contract.

1. Delivery of abstract or epitome of title.   The vendor must prove his title to the land in accordance with the contract of sale. To do

---

[21] See *Lysaght v. Edwards* (1876) 2 Ch.D. 499 at 507 *per* Sir George Jessel M.R. For an attack on this "conventional wisdom", see M.P. Thompson [1984] Conv. 43.
[22] See *Rayner v. Preston* (1881) 18 Ch.D. 1; *Castellain* v. *Preston* (1883) 11 Q.B.D. 380.
[23] (1988) Law Com. W.P. 109.

this, he traces the devolution of title from the root of title to the present day. An abstract of title is a condensed summary of all the documents comprised in that title, together with a recital of relevant events, such as births, deaths and marriages. The production of an abstract of title is a skilled, and dying, art. Nowadays, it is more common for the deeds to be photocopied and sent to the purchaser, together with what is, effectively, an index. This index is termed an epitome of title.

2. *Consideration of abstract.* Upon receipt of the abstract, the purchaser considers the abstract or epitome and considers whether the title to the land is good. The abstract, or photocopies, must then be compared with the actual deeds.

3. *Requisitions.* Having received the abstract, the purchaser frequently requires further information concerning some matter revealed in the title, such as the date of a death, or an assurance that an existing mortgage will be discharged upon completion. These inquiries are termed requisitions on title. The vendor then replies to these requisitions and, if the answers are not satisfactory, the purchaser may then make further requisitions.

4. *Draft conveyance.* The purchaser drafts the conveyance to be used on the completion of the transaction. This is then sent to the vendor for his approval and emendation until, finally, an agreed document is completed which awaits execution.

5. *Searches.* At this stage, the purchaser searches in the land charges register. It is important that the subsequent completion takes place within the priority period.

6. *Conveyance.* The time has then arrived for the transaction to be completed. The vendor will receive the purchase money and the purchaser will obtain the legal title. For this latter event to occur, the vendor must execute a deed.[24] Traditionally, to be a deed, a document had to be signed, sealed and delivered. This is no longer the case. Under section 1 of the Law of Property (Miscellaneous Provisions) Act 1989, to be a deed, an instrument must make clear on its face that it is intended to be a deed by the person making it and it is validly executed. The deed will be validly executed if it is signed in the presence of a witness who attests the signature, or is signed at his direction and in his presence and in the presence of two witnesses who each attest the signature, and is then delivered as a deed.

---

[24] L.P.A. 1925, s.52.

7. First registration.   Because all of England and Wales is now subject to compulsory registration of title, the purchaser will, within two months of the execution of the conveyance, need to lodge the title deeds, together with the conveyance, with the land registry and apply for first registration of title.

2. Registered land.   The purchaser's task, when title is registered, is essentially the same as when title is unregistered. The procedure is, however, rather different.

1. Inspection of register.   The register has, since the bringing into force of section 1 of the Land Registration Act 1988 in 1990, been open to inspection. The vendor will, on the first instance supply office copies of any documents entered on the register and the purchaser will requisition an official search of the register. He should, also, seek to discover the existence of any overriding interests.

2. Requisitions on title.   Although, subject to overriding interests, the register gives an authoritative account of the vendor's title, there is still a role for requisitions on title. The contract may not have disclosed some interest noted on the register, or given only an inadequate account of it.[25] In such cases, the same procedure regarding requisitions as pertains in the case of unregistered land will take place.

3. Draft transfer.   As is the case with unregistered land, the transfer document is prepared by the purchaser and sent to the vendor for approval.

4. Transfer and registration.   The transfer document is similar to the conveyance where title is registered. The main difference is that it does not, of itself, operate to transfer the legal title. Once the transfer has been executed, the purchaser should apply to be registered as proprietor of the land. Although the legal title does not pass until the purchaser is registered as the new proprietor, for the purposes of section 70(1)(g) of the Land Registration Act, the relevant time to establish if a person has an overriding interest is the date of the transfer and not the later date when the application for registration is made.[26]

DEVOLUTION ON DEATH

The second method by which freehold interests in land are commonly transferred is upon death. This section outlines the

---

[25] See *Faruqi v. English Real Estates Ltd* [1979] 1 W.L.R. 963.
[26] *Abbey National B.S. v. Cann* [1991] 1 A.C. 56; *ante*, p. 56.

procedure by which this occurs, dealing with both testate and intestate succession and also the statutory jurisdiction by which the courts may make orders in favour of certain dependants of the deceased.

1. Freedom of testation. The general position under English Law was that a testator had total freedom to dispose of his property as he saw fit. This freedom was modified in 1939 and the current legislative provision is the Inheritance (Provision for Family and Dependants) Act 1975. As the title of the Act suggests, its purpose is to allow a court to make orders in favour of various dependants of the deceased, for whom proper provision was not made by the deceased. The Act applies in cases of both testacy and intestacy and does not operate to prevent the normal rules of succession from operating. Instead, it allows certain people to make applications which, if successful will operate to vary the effect of those rules.

1. Who can apply? There are four categories of people who can make applications under the Act. These are:-

    (a) the wife or husband of the deceased;
    (b) the former wife or husband who has not remarried;
    (c) a child of the deceased. This includes a child not yet born at the time of death, an illegitimate child, an adopted child and one treated as a child of the deceased's family;
    (d) any other person who immediately before the death of the deceased was maintained, either wholly or partly, by the deceased.

2. Applications under the Act. Applications under the Act must be made within six months of the grant of probate or letters of administration. The basis of the application is that the deceased has failed to make reasonable financial provision for the applicant. The meaning of this term varies depending upon the status of the applicant.

    (i) In the case of a spouse, unless judicially separated, it means such financial provision as it would be reasonable in all the circumstances for a husband or wife to receive, whether or not it is required for the purpose of maintenance. The court must have regard to such provision as a court would make had the marriage terminated by divorce rather than death.
    (ii) For others, it means such financial provision as it would be reasonable in all the circumstances for the applicant to receive for his or her maintenance.

3. Orders.   Once an application has been made, the court may make an order affecting any property which the deceased had power to dispose of by will. The court possesses a wide discretion in making orders under the Act and regard is had to the financial needs of the applicant. The test as to whether reasonable provision has been made for the applicant is an objective one.[27]

2. Testate Succession.   For a will to be valid, it must, in general, comply with certain formal requirements. These requirements do not apply to a class of people who are entitled to make what are termed privileged wills. The privileged group consists of soldiers on actual military service, which has been held to include soldiers on duty in Northern Ireland,[28] a mariner or sailor at sea and a member of the Naval or Marine Forces so circumstanced that, had he been a soldier, he would have been in actual military service.[29] Such people can make valid, informal wills.

1. Formalities.   To be valid, a will must comply with the formal requirements prescribed by section 9 of the Wills Act 1837, as amended by section 17 of the Administration of Justice Act 1982. The will must be in writing and be signed by the testator, or by someone else in his presence and acting under his direction. Prior to the amendment introduced by the Administration of Justice Act 1982, the signature had to appear at the end of the will. In the case of those dying after 1983, it is sufficient if the signature appears on any part of the will, provided that it appears that the testator intended by his signature to give effect to the will.

The testator must either sign the will or acknowledge his signature in the simultaneous presence of two witnesses. The witnesses must then both sign the will. It is important that a witness to the will does not receive any benefit under it. If this is the case, then, subject to certain exceptions, section 15 of the Wills Act 1837 operates to invalidate that part of the will. If a person who is to benefit from the will is allowed to witness the will and is, therefore, deprived of the intended gift, he may have a cause of action in tort against a solicitor employed to draft the will.[30]

2. Passing of Title.   On the death of the testator, his property vests in his personal representatives, who apply for a grant of

---

[27] *Re Coventry* [1980] Ch. 461.
[28] *Re Jones* [1981] P. 7.
[29] Wills (Soldiers and Sailors) Act 1918, ss.1, 2.
[30] *Ross v. Caunters* [1980] Ch. 297; *White v. Jones* [1995] 1 All E.R. 691.

probate of the will. After probate has been granted their task is to pass the deceased's estate to the people entitled under the will. In the case of land, the method employed to do this is to execute a document which is termed an assent. The documents of title are then the grant of probate and the assent. A subsequent purchaser is not entitled to see the actual will.[31] In the case of registered land, a similar procedure operates and the person entitled under the will will be registered as the new proprietor.[32]

3. Intestacy

When a person dies intestate, a stautory scheme operates to determine who is entitled to the deceased's estate, the details of which are beyond the scope of this book.[33] On the death of the intestate, his property vests in the President of the Family Division of the High Court.[34] Application is then made for the grant of letters of adminstration. The persons appointed will then dispose of the property in accordance with the rules governing intestacy.

---

[31] See Administration of Estates Act 1925, s.36(4), (7).
[32] See Ruoff and Roper *Registered Conveyancing* paras. 27.03, 27.04.
[33] See Megarry, *op. cit.*, pp. 157–163.
[34] A.E.A. 1925, s.9.

CHAPTER SIX

Settlements of Land

When looking at the doctrine of estates, it was seen that a
number of estates could exist simultaneously with respect to the
same piece of land. Land could be settled upon A for life,
remainder to B in fee tail, remainder to C in fee simple. As a
result of the reforms implemented by the 1925 legislation, none
of these estates are now capable of existing as legal estates. So,
in order for this land to be marketable, a mechanism was
necessary to enable a legal fee simple to exist and to be sellable.
In fact, there are two such mechanisms available to deal with
this type of situation: the strict settlement and the trust for sale.
This Chapter is concerned with these two legal devices.

SETTLED LAND

Section 1 of the Settled Land Act defines a settlement for the
purpose of the Act. The essential definition refers to any deed,
will, agreement for a settlement or other agreement, Act of
Parliament, or other instrument by which land stands for the
time being limited in trust for any persons by way of succession.
The Act then proceeds to give what are essentially examples of
such situations but, also, includes within the definition of settled
land the situation where a fee simple or a term of years is
conveyed to a minor. Section 1(7) of the Act expressly provides
that the definition of a settlement does not apply to land held
upon trust for sale.

The example given at the start of this Chapter will involve a
settlement within the meaning of the Act. Because neither A, B
or C have a fee simple absolute in possession, their estates are
necessarily equitable and, therefore, limited in trust. Although

all three have estates in the land, the right to possession of B and C will occur some time in the future and there is, therefore, the necessary element of succession.

1. Object of the Act. The principal object of the Act was to make land, which was subject to a succession of interests, marketable. To this end, the essential strategy was to vest a legal estate in the hands of one person, the tenant for life, and give to that person extensive powers to dispose of that estate. To safeguard the position of all the people with interests in the land, trustees are appointed; these trustees acting, effectively, as watchdogs to ensure that the tenant for life does not abuse his powers. When the tenant for life exercises his powers, the effect, in favour of the purchaser, is that the beneficial interests existing under the settlement are overreached and take effect against the money that has been generated. How these objectives are implemented can now be elaborated.

2. The tenant for life. A central character in the settled land system is the tenant for life. Section 4(2) of the Act requires that the land shall be conveyed, by a vesting deed, to the tenant for life, or, if more than one person, to them as joint tenants. Where the legal estate is already vested in the tenant for life, which will be the case when the legal owner of land creates a settlement whereby he retains a life interest in the property, then it is sufficient if the vesting deed declares that the land is vested in him for that estate.

Various issues arise. First, it must be determined who the tenant for life is and consideration given to the position where there is no such person. Secondly, attention must be given to the role and powers of the tenant for life. Thirdly, the role of the vesting deed must be examined.

1. Who is the tenant for life? The tenant for life is defined by section 19 of the Act as the person of full age who is for the time being beneficially entitled under the settlement to possession of settled land for his life. If there are two or more such persons then, together, they constitute the tenant for life. So, for example if land is settled to A for life, to B in fee tail and to C in fee simple then A will be the tenant for life. When A dies, B, or his lineal heir, will become tenant for life. When B dies, without lineal heirs, the settlement will be at an end and the land will simply be conveyed to C.[1]

Two situations can arise when there is nobody who satisfies the definition of tenant for life. These situations are when there

---

[1] For the procedures on death, see *post*, p. 84.

is no person entitled to possession of the land for life,[2] or if the person so entitled is a minor. In both cases, the Act makes provision for a person to act as the statutory owner.

2. *The statutory owner.*   If the tenant for life is a minor, the legal estate is vested in the statutory owner. This is the personal representative of the testator who has established the settlement where no vesting instrument has been executed or, alternatively, the trustees of the settlement. Where there is, otherwise, no tenant for life, the statutory owner is either the person of full age upon whom the settlement expressly confers the powers of the tenant for life, or, if there is no such person, the trustees of the settlement.[3]

3. **The powers of the tenant for life.**   The vesting deed has the effect of vesting in the tenant for life a legal fee simple in the land. He does not, however, have unfettered powers to deal with that estate. First, it must be appreciated that, while he owns his own equitable estate in the property beneficially, he holds the legal estate as a trustee. Certain proposed transactions can be prevented by others interested in the land if those transactions are in some way improper. Secondly, although the Act does confer a legal fee simple on the tenant for life, his power to deal with that estate are expressly elaborated by the Act. As will be seen, difficulties can arise if the tenant for life seeks to make a disposition of property which is not authorised by the Act.

(1) Trusteeship.   Because the tenant for life holds the legal estate on trust, he is subject to the normal duties of trusteeship in respect of his dealings with it. So, for example, in *Re Earl Somers*,[4] the tenant for life, who was a confirmed teetotaller, sought to grant a lease of The White Hart Hotel, the lease to contain a covenant prohibiting the sale of alcohol. The trustees of the settlement obtained a declaration that she was not entitled to do this, because the transaction was not in the best financial interest of the beneficiaries.

(2) Statutory powers.   The powers of the tenant for life are conferred by Part II of the Act. These powers, which can be increased, but not curtailed,[5] by the settlement include[6] the

---

[2] See, *e.g.*, *Re Frewen* [1926] Ch. 580; *Re Galenga's W.T.* [1938] 1 All E.R. 106.

[3] S.L.A. 1925, ss.23, 26.

[4] (1893) 11 T.L.R. 567. See, also, *Middlemas v. Stevens* [1901] 1 Ch. 574.

[5] S.L.A. 1925, s.106. *Post*, p. 81.

[6] For a fuller discussion of the powers of the tenant for life, see Megarry, *Manual of the Law of Real Property* (27th ed.), pp. 241–247.

power of sale, the power to grant certain leases and the power to mortgage the property for certain specified purposes. Before exercising these powers, the tenant for life is required to serve a written notice, not less than one month before the transaction, on the trustees of the settlement that he intends to exercise his powers. This safeguard is not, however, as strong as it might appear because, except in the case of a mortgage, it is sufficient if the tenant for life simply serves a notice on trustees to the effect that "I intend from time to time to exercise my powers under the Settled Land Act 1925." In addition, a purchaser, if in good faith, is not concerned to see that this requirement has been satisfied.[7]

(3) Unauthorised dispositions. Difficulties can arise if the tenant for life purports to make some disposition of the land which is not authorised by the Act. In such cases, one must distinguish between situations where what has been done appear to be totally unauthorised by the Act and cases where the problem appears to be more of a technical nature.

(i) Void Transactions

Section 18 of the Act provides that:

"Where land is the subject of a vesting instrument, and the trustees of the settlement have not been discharged under this Act, then—
(a)   any disposition by the tenant for life . . . other than than a disposition authorised by this Act . . . shall be void, except for the purpose of conveying or creating such equitable interests as he has power, in right of his equitable interests and powers under the trust instrument, to convey or create."

In *Weston v. Henshaw*,[8] G sold land to his son, F, who later resold the property to his father. Sometime later, G settled the land on F for life, remainder to F's sons. F then mortgaged the property for his own benefit: a transaction which he was not empowered to do under the Act. In doing this, he showed to the innocent mortgagee only the conveyance from G to himself. He suppressed the later documents, the result being that the mortgagee neither knew, nor had any means of knowing, that he was dealing with a tenant for life. The issue subsequently arose as to whether the mortgage was valid. Danckwerts J. held that it was not.

---

[7] S.L.A. 1925, s.101.
[8] [1950] Ch. 510.

In reaching this conclusion, the judge simply applied section 18 of the Act. He also rejected, however an argument based upon section 110 of the Act. This section, which is designed to protect purchasers, provides that:

"On a sale, exchange, lease, mortgage, charge, or other disposition, a purchaser dealing in good faith with a tenant for life . . . shall, as against all parties entitled under the settlement, be conclusively taken to have given the best price . . . that could reasonably be obtained . . . and to have complied with all the requirements of this Act."

The judge held that this section afforded no protection to the mortgagee because it applied only to situtations where the purchaser knew that he was dealing with the tenant for life.

(II) IRREGULARITIES

The interpretation given to section 110 in *Weston v. Henshaw* was doubted in *Re Morgan's Lease*.[9] In this case, the principal objection to a lease granted by a tenant for life was that the best rent reasonably obtainable had not been obtained. The judge, however, held that the tenants had acted in good faith and were, therefore protected by section 110. His disapproval of *Weston v. Henshaw* was, therefore, *obiter*. It is also, it is suggested, misplaced.

There is a fundamental difference between the two cases. In *Weston v. Henshaw*, the tenant had not been empowered by the Act to enter the particular transaction. It could be described as being *ultra vires*. In *Re Morgan's* lease, however, the transaction was, itself, one which was permitted by the Act. The problem relating to it concerned the issue of the rent: a matter which is within section 110. The conclusion which should follow, and one which is consistent with the most recent authority,[10] is that if the transaction is beyond the powers of the tenant for life then it will be void in so far as the legal estate is concerned. If the problem relates to incidental matters affecting an inherently authorised transaction then, provided that the purchaser is acting in good faith, he will obtain a good title. Although this is hard on an innocent purchaser, the result seems to follow from the scheme of the Act. Instead of simply giving the tenant for life a legal fee simple, and the powers that that entails, it gives him the legal estate and then lists the powers that he has with respect to it. Unfortunately, this can leave an innocent purchaser in an exposed position if he is victim of fraud.

[9] [1972] Ch. 1.
[10] *Bevan v. Johnston* [1990] 2 E.G.L.R. 33.

(4) No restriction on tenant for life's powers. Because the principal aim of the Act is to enable settled land to be bought and sold, it is necessary to proscribe any attempt to prevent the tenant for life from exercising the powers conferred upon him by the statute. To this end, section 106 renders void any provision in the settlement which would tend to have the effect of discouraging the tenant for life from exercising those powers. If, for example, the settlement gives A a life interest, determinable if he ceases to occupy the property, the determining event will be void, if the reason why the tenant for life has ceased to be in occupation is that he has sold the property.[11] If, however, the tenant for life simply chooses not to live in the property, then the determining factor is perfectly valid. The reason for ceasing to be in occupation is unrelated to the exercise of the statutory powers.[12]

4. The structure of settlements. It is now necessary to consider the mechanics employed to set up a settlement, before going on to look at the system in practice. Fundamental to the system is the adoption of a two-deed structure, whereby the equitable interests are kept separate from the legal title. The two deeds are, respectively, the vesting deed and the trust instrument.[13]

(1) The vesting deed. When a settlement is created, it is necessary to vest the legal estate in the tenant for life or, if the legal estate is already vested in him, to indicate the change in capacity of the owner of that estate. This is the function of the vesting deed. The vesting deed contains the following information.

(i) It describes the settled land;
(ii) It declares that the settled land is vested in the person or persons to whom it was conveyed, or in whom it is declared to be vested, upon the trusts from time to time affecting the settled land;
(iii) It states the names of the trustees of the settlement;
(iv) It states the names of any persons empowered to appoint new trustees of the settlement; and
(v) It states any additional powers conferred by the trust instrument.[14]

The role of the trust instrument will be explained shortly. First the question of the consequence of their not being a vesting deed will be addressed.

---

[11] See *Re Paget's S.E.* (1885) 30 Ch.D. 161; *Re Ames* [1893] 2 Ch. 479.
[12] See *Re Haynes* (1887) 37 Ch.D. 306.
[13] S.L.A. 1925, s.4(1).
[14] S.L.A. 1925, s.5.

(A) Section 13

Under section 13 of the Act, where a person is entitled to have a vesting deed executed in his favour, and this has not occurred, then any purported disposition of the land will not take effect, except as a contract to carry out the purported disposition after the vesting deed has been executed. An exception is made in favour of a purchaser of a legal estate without notice of the tenant for life having become so entitled. This protection of the purchaser contrasts with the position under section 18 and can be illustrated by an example.

S, who holds the legal estate in land, settles the land upon himself for life, remainders over. He does not, as he should, execute a vesting deed. He then mortgages the property for his own benefit; an unauthorised transaction. The effect of section 13 is to ensure that the mortgagee, assuming him to be in good faith, will get a good title. If, however, S did execute a vesting deed but, when creating the mortgage suppressed this document, then the effect of section 18, as established in *Weston v. Henshaw* is to render the mortgage void. Yet the mortgagee is equally innocent as in the first situation. This seems unjustifiable, but follows from the different wording of the two sections.

(2) The trust instrument. In addition to the need for a vesting deed, when creating a settlement, there must also be a trust instrument. The trust instrument contains the following:

(i) It declares the trusts of the settlement;
(ii) It appoints the trustees of the settlement;
(iii) It contains the power, if any, to appoint new trustees;
(iv) It sets out any extended powers given to the tenant for life; and
(v) It bears any ad valorum stamp duty which may be payable.[15]

Where land is settled upon death, the personal representatives of the deceased settlor vest the legal title in the tenant for life by a vesting assent and the will acts as the trust instrument.

The main difference between the vesting deed and the trust instrument is that the latter document sets out the beneficial interests that exist under the settlement. No mention is made of the beneficial entitlements in the vesting deed. The reason for this strict demarcation is the curtain principle, which is central to the scheme of the Act, and the overreaching procedure.

---

[15] S.L.A. 1925, s.4(3).

4. The curtain principle and overreaching. In enabling settled land to be sold, the Settled Land Act enables the beneficial interests existing under the settlement to be overreached: to be converted into interests in money. Because the interests will be overreached, the purchaser does not need to know what they are. Section 110(2) of the Act then follows the logic of this by not only discouraging the curious purchaser from discovering what the beneficial interests under the settlement are but, save for four exceptions of varying importance,[16] specifically prohibits him from inspecting the trust deed, where this information is contained. The equitable interests are hidden behind the curtain of the vesting deed, the particulars set out in which the purchaser is statutorily obliged to accept as correct.[17] The curtain principle will, also, operate where title is registered. The tenant for life will be registered as the proprietor and a restriction entered that no disposition of the land is to be registered unless capital money is paid to the trustees of the settlement. There will be no mention on the register of what the beneficial interests are.

If the purchaser is to overreach the beneficial interests under the settlement, he must take care to operate the correct machinery. This entails him taking the conveyance from the tenant for life and paying the purchase money to, or at the direction, of the trustees of the settlement or into court.[18] The capital money is then invested in accordance with the directions of the tenant for life, the objects of such investments being enumerated in section 73 of the Act, and the interests of the beneficiaries under the settlement take effect in those invetments. So, if the settlement was to A for life, remainder to B in fee simple, and A sells the property, the purchase money will be invested. A will then receive the income that is generated, this representing his interest under the settlement, and, on A's death, B will be entitled to the capital sum to do with as he sees fit.

5. Problems with the Settled Land Act. It is generally accepted that few strict settlements are created, deliberately, in modern times. One reason for this is that the desire to create dynastic settlements of land is probably less strong today than it was in the past. Another reason is the cumbersome nature of the system established by the Act.

(a) Complexity. The two deed system is an essential part of the structure introduced by the Act. So, too, is the need for the legal

---

[16] For these exceptions, see Megarry, *op. cit.*, p. 231.
[17] S.L.A. 1925, s.110(2). For a discussion of the position if the particulars are incorrect, see Megarry, *op. cit.*, pp. 230, 231.
[18] S.L.A. 1925, s.75.

title to be vested in the tenant for life. A consequence of this is that when changes to the beneficial ownership occur behind the curtain, new documents will need to be executed to reflect those changes and ensure that the legal title is vested in the new tenant for life. A good illustration of this occurs on the death of a tenant for life, in circumstances when the settlement continues in being; an example of this being a settlement whereby land is settled upon A for life, to B in tail and to C in fee simple. A then dies.

In this situation the land must be dealt with differently from the rest of A's estate. The part of his estate which is not subject to the settlement will vest in his personal representatives in the normal way. The land, however, will vest in the trustees of the settlement as his special personal representatives.[19] They will then vest the settled land in B, by way of a vesting assent. The upshot of this is that different people will be involved in the administration of A's estate; a factor which increases cost and complexity.

(b) Accidental settlements.   A second problem which can arise with regard to the Settled Land Act is that of accidental settlements. This can arise as a result of a "home made" will, whereby a testator leaves a house to the surviving spouse for life, remainder to their children. In such cases the full structure of the Act comes into play; a consequence which may well have been entirely unforeseen. Secondly, and rather more problematically, the Act can also apply to informal family arrangements.

In the leading case of *Bannister v. Bannister,*[20] the defendant sold two cottages to her brother-in-law. It was orally agreed, at the time of the sale that she could remain in one of the cottages, rent free, for the rest of her life. The purchase price reflected this agreement. Some time later, the brother-in-law sought to evict her arguing, principally, that the oral agreement was ineffective because of a lack of writing.[21] Not surprisingly, this argument failed. The Court of Appeal held that he held the cottage on a constructive trust for his sister-in-law. Under that trust, she was held to be entitled to a life interest in the property. This in turn meant that the land became settled land and she was the tenant for life.

A similar problem occurred in *Binions v. Evans.*[22] Tredegar Estate owned land upon which was a cottage in which lived Mr

---

[19] S.L.A. 1925, s.7; Administration of Estates Act 1925, s.22.
[20] [1948] 2 All E.R. 133.
[21] L.P.A. 1925, s.53(1)(b); see *post*, p. 98.
[22] [1972] Ch. 359.

and Mrs Evans, he being a long term employee of the estate. It was agreed that, in return for the Evanses keeping the cottage and garden in good order, they could remain in it for the remainder of their lives. Later, after Mr Evans had died, the Estate sold the cottage to Mr and Mrs Binions, expressly subject to Mrs Evans' right to live in the house. Notwithstanding this agreement, and the fact that the price of the cottage had been discounted to reflect this agreement, Mr and Mrs Binions sought to evict her from the property. The majority of the Court of Appeal, Lord Denning dissenting on this point,[23] held that the agreement meant that Mrs Evans was the tenant for life within the meaning of the Act.

The result of this case meant that Mrs Evans was entitled to have a vesting deed executed in her favour. She would then acquire all the powers of the tenant for life, including the power to sell the land. It is this consideration that led to Lord Denning's dissent and to a good deal of academic disquiet.[24] It is felt to be inappropriate that a person in the position of Mrs Evans should be given such powers as a result of a mere act of generosity.

This concern has led the courts on a number of subsequent occasions to seek to craft solutions to, not dissimilar, situations where it is sought to protect a person's right of occupation of property while avoiding the complications of the Settled Land Act 1925.[25] In other cases, however, courts have felt constrained to adopt the line taken in *Bannister*.[26]

While one can readily understand the concern felt in some quarters about the application of the Settled Land Act to informal situations of this nature, these results occur as a result of a long standing policy which is to prevent land from being unsellable for a considerable period. If, in the above instances, the court had been able to fashion a solution which allowed the occupier to remain in indefinite occupation, but without acquiring the statutory powers of the tenant for life, then that policy would be undermined. This, in a modern age, might be no bad thing. In the absence of such a review, however, a finding that people in the position of Mrs Evans will be tenant for life, within the meaning of the Act, is quite defensible.

---

[23] He did not, however, dissent in the result, whereby Mrs Evans was allowed to remain in the property. *Post*, pp. 171–175.

[24] See, *e.g.*, J.A. Hornby (1977) 93 L.Q.R. 561.

[25] See *Dodsworth v. Dodsworth* [1973] E.G.D. 233; *Griffiths v. Williams* [1978] E.G.D. 919.

[26] *Ungarian v. Lessnoff* [1990] Ch. 206; *Costello v. Costello* [1994] N.P.C. 32.

TRUSTS FOR SALE

An alternative method to the employment of the Settled Land
Act as a means of creating settlements of land is the trust for
sale. When land is held upon trust for sale, then the Settled
Land Act is inapplicable. One must first consider the meaning of
the term, trust for sale, and then examine the respective roles of
the trustees and the beneficiaries and the operation of
overreaching.

1. The trust for sale. A trust for sale is defined by section
205(1)(xix) as being an immediate binding trust for sale with or
without a power at discretion to postpone the sale. The trustees
for sale are the persons holding the land upon trust for sale.
Various aspects of this, seemingly unhelpful, definition need
elaboration.

(1) Duty to sell. To come within the definition of a trust for sale,
the trust must impose a duty upon the trustees to sell the
property. If a settlement provides for land to be conveyed to
trustees on trust for various people in succession, with power to
sell the property, then this will create a strict settlement and not
a trust for sale. If, however, the trust gives the trustees power
"to retain or sell the land", this is construed as a trust to sell
with power to postpone.[27]

(2) Immediate. The trust for sale must be immediate. This does
not mean that the trustees must sell the property at once.
Rather, it means that the obligation to do so must arise immediately. So, for example, a trust to sell land when X reaches a
specified age will not be a trust for sale.[28] The land will be
subject to the Settled Land Act 1925.

It should be reiterated that the existence of a trust for sale
does not mean that the land must be sold forthwith. It is normal
for the trustees for sale to be given a power to postpone the
exercise of the sale. Indeed, unless the contrary intention is
expressed, such a power is implied by statute.[29] This, at first
seems, paradoxical; the trustees being under a duty to do one
thing but with power to do the opposite. This is, however, by no
means unique to this type of situation: for example, trustees
may be under a duty to distribute income but also possess a
power to accumulate.[30] This contradistinction between the duty

---

[27] L.P.A. 1925, s.25.
[28] See *Re Hanson* [1928] Ch. 96. *Cf. Re Herklot's W.T.* [1964] 1 W.L.R. 583.
[29] L.P.A. 1925, s.25.
[30] See *McPhail v. Doulton* [1971] A.C. 424.

and the power may, however, have important consequences when the trustees cannot agree as to whether the land should be sold or retained.[31]

(3) Binding. The meaning of this term, at one time, was the source of considerable difficulty and debate.[32] Much of the sting has now gone out of this dispute and it is now generally taken to mean a trust which is binding upon the whole legal estate.

2. The creation of trusts for sale. A trust for sale can be created either expressly or be imposed by statute.

(1) Express trusts. In the case of an express trust for sale, it was normal for two documents to be used. This was in order to keep the trusts, which will not affect a purchaser, off the title. Where a trust for sale is created expressly, it is also normal for the trustees to be given the power to postpone the sale. It can also be provided that the property is not to be sold without the consent of a particular person. If a person is selected who, for whatever reason, is unlikely to give such consent, then the effect will be to make it difficult for the property to be sold.[33] In such circumstances, it will be necessary to petition the court to get an order for sale.[34] The paradoxical result is that it is actually easier to prevent land from being sold by using a trust for sale than by using the Settled Land Act 1925. If the consent of more than two persons is required before the property can be sold, then it is provided by section 26(1) of the Act that, in favour of a purchaser, the consent of two persons will be sufficient.

(2) Implied trust for sale. A trust for sale is imposed by statute in a number of situations. The most important are:

(I) CO-OWNERSHIP

In virtually all cases of co-ownership the land is held upon an implied, statutory trust for sale. It is, of course, common for the matrimonial home to be in the joint names of husband and wife. The result will be that the house is held upon a statutory trust for sale. As will be seen, it is also the case that, if the legal title to the house is in the name of one person but, there is co-ownership in equity, there will also be an implied trust for sale.[35]

---

[31] See *post*, pp. 112–113.
[32] See Megarry, *op. cit.*, pp. 252, 253.
[33] See *Re Inns* [1947] 1 Ch. 576.
[34] See *Re Beale's S.T.* [1932] 2 Ch. 15.
[35] *Post*, pp. 105–106.

(ii). Intestacy. When a person dies intestate, section 33 of the Administration of Estates Act 1925 provides that all the property of the intestate is held upon trust for sale.

3. The trustees for sale. A key difference between the strict settlement and the trust for sale is the location of the legal estate. In the case of the strict settlement, the legal estate is held by the tenant for life or statutory owner. The trustees of the settlement act as watchdogs of the settlement. By way of contrast, in the case of the trust for sale, the legal estate is held by the trustees. The trustees are then given all the powers of both the tenant for life and the trustees of the settlement.[36] If the trustees refuse to exercise their powers, then any person interested may apply to the court, under section 30 of the Act, and the court may make any order that it sees fit.

When land is held upon trust for sale, power rests in the hands of the trustees for sale. The person who is entitled to the income from the land occupies a far less important position than does his counterpart where the land is subject to the regime of the Settled Land Act. He is not, however, without rights. First, certain powers of management may be delegated to him under section 29 of the Law of Property Act 1925. This does not, however, include the power of sale. Secondly, his consent may be a prerequisite to the exercise of the power of sale. Thirdly, the trustees may be under a duty to consult the beneficiary prior to the exercise of the power of sale. This will be the case if the trust for sale arises by statutory imposition. This is, however, a fairly innocuous provision, given that consultation is not equivalent to a power of veto and, in any event, a purchaser is not concerned to see that any such obligation has been complied with.[37] Finally, as noted previously, if the trustees do not exercise their powers, a beneficiary may petition the court for an order to implement some transaction.

4. The doctrine of conversion. Because the trust in question is a trust for sale, rather than simply a trust with a power of sale, the interests of the beneficiaries have traditionally been seen as being in the proceeds of sale of the land rather than in the land, itself. This approach, termed the doctrine of conversion,[38] results from the application of the maxim, that equity looks upon that as done which ought to be done. The trust is a trust for sale.

---

[36] L.P.A. 1925, s.28.
[37] L.P.A 1925, s.26(3).
[38] For an excellent historical account of this doctrine, see S. Anderson (1984) 100 L.Q.R. 86.

Consequently, the trustees are under a duty to sell. Assuming that to have been done, the interests of the beneficiaries are in the proceeds of sale and not in the land.

This doctrine is a technical one and although one does, from time to time, see it being judicially endorsed,[39] it is now applied in a generally pragmatic way and largely confined to issues of succession. If, for example, a testator leaves his personal property to A and his real property to B then the testator's interest under a trust for sale will pass to A.[40] In this context, the doctrine is useful because, otherwise, the destination of the testator's bequest would differ depending upon the, possibly, random chance of the trustees exercising the power of sale the day before his death or the day afterwards. In other contexts, however, such as a contract for the sale of the beneficiary's interest, the doctrine has less utility and it is expressly provided by section 2(6) of the Law of Property (Miscellaneous Provisions) Act 1989 that such contracts are within the ambit of the section. Again, when the land which is subject to a trust for sale is used as a home, Lord Wilberforce has described the view that the interests of the beneficiaries have only an interest in the proceeds of sale as "just a little unreal".[41]

5. Overreaching. As is the case where land is subject to a strict settlement, when land is subject to a trust for sale, machinery exists for the beneficial interests behind the trust to be overreached. Although it may be argued that overreaching, in the strict sense, does not occur in that the interests of the beneficiaries are, throughout, regarded as being in the proceeds of sale, this is to adopt too purist a view. It is certainly more realistic to view the process as being overreaching; this is particularly the case when the overreaching machinery is not complied with.

Section 27 of the Law of Property Act 1925 provides that, so long as the capital money is paid to, or at the direction of, no fewer than two trustees for sale, a purchaser of the legal estate from the trustees shall not be concerned with the trusts affecting the proceeds of sale. This means that a purchaser will overreach the beneficial interests existing behind the trust for sale, provided that he pays the purchase money to no fewer than two trustees for sale. The leading case is *City of London B.S. v. Flegg.*[42]

(1) Two trustees. In this case, a property, known as Bleak House, was transferred to Mr and Mrs Maxwell-Brown, who

---

[39] *City of London B.S. v. Flegg* [1988] A.C. 54 at 82, 83, *per* Lord Oliver.
[40] *Re Kempthorne* [1930] 1 Ch. 268.
[41] *Williams & Glyn's Bank Ltd v. Boland* [1981] A.C. 487 at 507.
[42] [1988] A.C. 54.

were registered as joint proprietors. The Fleggs, who were the parents of Mrs Maxwell-Brown, made a significant financial contribution to the purchase of the property and, consequently, became equitable co-owners of it. The position was that the Maxwell-Browns held the property on trust for sale, the beneficiaries under the trust being themselves and the Fleggs. Without informing the Fleggs, they then executed a number of mortgages over the property and then, finally, mortgaged the property to the City of London B.S., the amount borrowed being sufficient to pay off the previous mortgages. When the Maxwell-Browns defaulted on the mortgage, the building society sought possession and the Fleggs argued that, as beneficial co-owners of the house who were in actual occupation of it at all material times, they had an overriding interest binding upon the society.

The House of Lords held in favour of the building society. The fact that the Fleggs were in actual occupation of the land was irrelevant. This was because they did not have rights which were capable of taking effect as an overriding interest. Their rights were overreached by the mortgage and the interest of the mortgagee, therefore, took priority.

This important decision firmly establishes that, so far as a purchaser is concerned, provided that he pays the purchase money to two trustees, he can ignore, totally, the interests that exist behind the trust for sale. It would not matter if there were four equitable co-owners or 44. The result would have been the same. It is true that the Maxwell-Browns would have been liable to the Fleggs for breach of trust. That, however, is not a matter of any concern to the purchaser. This is, also, very much an example of the courts giving priority to the conveyancing dimension at the expense of the rights of occupiers. This issue will be considered again in a later Chapter.[43]

(2) One trustee.   A vital feature of the decision in *Flegg* was that there were two trustees for sale. In *Williams & Glyn's Bank Ltd v. Boland*,[44] the house was in the sole name of Mr Boland and his wife was an equitable co-owner of it. The effect of this was that there was an implied trust for sale but only one trustee for sale. He then mortgaged the property for his own purposes. In this case, Mrs Boland was held to have an overriding interest. The crucial distinction was that there was only one trustee for sale and he could not, therefore, overreach his wife's interest. The argument for the bank that her interest could not affect them because, owing to the doctrine of conversion, it was only in the

---

[43] *Post*, pp. 198–204.
[44] [1981] A.C. 487.

proceeds of sale was rejected. She was held to be a person interested in the land, which was sufficient for the purpose of section 70 (1)(g) of the Land Registration Act 1925. Similarly, when title is unregistered, an interest behind a trust for sale will bind a purchaser, with notice, unless overreached.[45]

It is apparent then, that compliance with the overreaching machinery is essential whenever land is subject to a trust for sale. If a purchaser deals with two trustees for sale, he can safely disregard the interests of any person with an interest under the trust. If he does not, he may find himself bound by such interests.

A NEED FOR TWO SYSTEMS?

The strict settlement and the trust for sale both provide mechanisms by which a settlor can create various settlements in land. The main difference between the two systems is that, in the case of the former, the legal estate and the statutory powers are vested in the tenant for life and, in the case of the latter, these functions are performed by the trustees for sale. A question which arises is whether it is necessary to retain two systems; an issue which raises, also, the question as to which of the two systems is preferable.

There is little doubt that, of the two systems, the trust for sale is by far the simpler. The principal reason for this is the different documentation necessary to set up either mechanism. In the case of the strict settlement, it is essential that the legal estate is vested in the tenant for life. This means that, with every change that occurs behind the curtain, the legal position must be altered so that the next person entitled is duly constituted as tenant for life. This can be a cumbersome and expensive business. In the case of a trust for sale, however, this is unnecessary. Provided that there are two trustees, what happens behind the curtain to the beneficial interests is a matter to which the purchaser has no concern. If a trustee dies, it is a simple matter to appoint another as a replacement. From a conveyancing point of view, the trust for sale is clearly preferable.

The trust for sale is also preferable if the real aim of a settlor is to retain the land in the family. This can be done by making the sale subject to various consents. The trust for sale is also the more flexible of the two devices. Largely for these reasons, the suggestion has been made that it would be preferable if all

---

[45] *Kingsnorth Finance Co. Ltd v. Tizard* [1986] 1 W.L.R. 783.

settlements were to take place behind a trust for sale, the strict settlement being abolished.[46] This view has, in essence, been accepted by the Law Commission who have proposed the creation of a new trust of land, where the trustees would have the power (but not a trust) to sell the land and would have all the powers of an absolute owner.[47] Implementation of this proposal would have a beneficially simplifying effect on the law.

[46] G.A. Grove (1961) 24 M.L.R. 123.
[47] Law Com. No. 181 (1989).

CHAPTER SEVEN

Co-ownership

This Chapter is concerned with co-ownership of land. Various matters arise for consideration. The first issue which will be considered is how co-ownership occurs or, put another way, how one acquires an interest in land. The matters which will then be addressed are the legal framework of co-ownership, the difference between the position at law and in equity and, finally, the position of the beneficiaries and, in particular, the problems caused when the co-owners cannot agree as to whether the property should be sold or retained.

THE ESTABLISHMENT OF CO-OWNERSHIP

The most obvious way to establish co-ownership of land is for the property to be conveyed into joint names and there to be a declaration as to what the beneficial entitlement is to be. When this course of action is adopted then, in the absence of any claim to rectification,[1] such a statement is conclusive.[2] Unfortunately, in a number of cases, this is not done. In this event, disputes will arise as to the ownership of the home. These disputes fall to be resolved by the application of law of trusts and the equitable doctrine of estoppel.

1. Trusts.   Disputes as to whether property is the subject of co-ownership and, if so, what the respective shares in the property are, tend to occur in the context of a family home. In modern

---

[1] *Thames Guarantee Ltd v. Campbell* [1985] Q.B. 210.
[2] *Goodman v. Gallant* [1986] Fam. 106; *Turton v. Turton* [1988] Ch. 542.

times, these disputes usually occur when a couple have been living together in a non-marital relationship. Where a couple are married, the ascertainment of the respective beneficial interest of husband and wife in the matrimonial home will, as between themselves,[3] often not be very important because the courts have a wide discretion, under the Matrimonial Causes Act 1973, to reallocate property on divorce. When a couple are not married, there is no such statutory jurisdiction and so, the issue as to who owns the house must be determined by the law of property. This will frequently involve the law of trusts. The typical scenario involves a situation where a house is in the sole name of the name partner and, at the end of a relationship, his female partner claims to have a beneficial interest in the house.

(1) Resulting trusts. The principle upon which the resulting trust is based is, essentially, a simple one. If two people contribute to the purchase of a car and that car is then transferred to one of them alone, there are various ways of looking at the transaction. These are that the contributor made a loan of the money, that he made a gift of the money or that he intended to acquire some interest in the car, proportionate to the size of the contribution. If the transaction is a loan then the lender will, in general, acquire no interest in the property which has been bought.[4] If it is not a loan, then one of the other two consequences will ensue. The law of resulting trusts is predicated upon the basis that, in the absence of a particular relationship between the parties, the presumption is that a person who contributes to the purchase of a particular item intends to acquire an interest in that property. This presumption, unless rebutted by evidence of a contrary intention, is then given effect to by the creation of a resulting trust.

The resulting trust has, for a long time, been recognised as having a significant role to play in determining disputes with regard to the ownership of a home. Considerable difficulty has been experienced, however, in applying the basic rationale of the resulting trust in this context. These difficulties stem from the related questions as to determining the intentions of the parties as to the ownership of the home and to assessing what counts as a contribution towards the purchase of a house.

(1) Intention. The importance of ascertaining the intention of the parties with regard to the beneficial ownership of the home was stressed by the House of Lords in a pair of cases, *Pettitt v.*

---

[3] It may well be very important when a third party is involved.
[4] See, *e.g., Re Sharpe* [1980] 1 W.L.R. 219.

Pettitt[5] and *Gissing v. Gissing*,[6] the latter being the more important of the two decisions. In *Gissing*, a house was in the sole name of Mr Gissing, who paid the mortgage instalments and had supplied the original down payment. Mrs Gissing claimed to have an interest in the house, the basis of that claim being that she had spent some £220 on furnishings and laying a lawn, buying clothes for herself and her son and had also bought some extras around the house.

This claim was unanimously rejected by the House of Lords. It was held, relying on the earlier analysis conducted in *Pettitt*, that, for her to succeed, a court must be able to infer an agreement that she should have a share in the property. It was not open to a court to impute to the parties intentions, with regard to this matter which, as reasonable people, they ought to have had.[7] For the court to be able to infer any such intention, the claimant has to show that she has made a financial contribution to the purchase of the house.

This supposed dichotomy between imputing intentions to the parties and inferring what actually was intended, while causing judicial disagreement as to which is preferable, has, in truth, never been a real one. In most disputes of this nature, it is only too apparent that a couple entered into a relationship and started living together without giving any thought, at all, as to how property would be divided up on the termination of the relationship. After the relationship has foundered, and the court is seeking to reach a conclusion as to the ownership of the home, what is really in issue is the type of contribution that the claimant has to have made in order to raise the presumption of a resulting trust. To address this matter it is necessary to distinguish between direct and indirect contributions.

(i) Direct contributions. The most straightforward type of case is where both parties make a direct cash contribution to the purchase of the house. In *Re Roger's Question*,[8] a house was bought for £1,000. She paid a cash sum of £100 and the balance was provided by a mortgage loan for which he was solely responsible. It was held that the property was shared in proportion to their contributions. She owned one-tenth of the property and he owned nine-tenths. Similarly, if both partners go out to work and each person's salary goes towards meeting

[5] [1970] A.C. 777.
[6] [1971] A.C. 886.
[7] *ibid.* at p. 904 *per* Lord Diplock, who expressly recognised that the contrary view that he had articulated in *Pettitt* could no longer be sustained. Lord Reid continued to assert this view.
[8] [1948] 1 All E.R. 328.

the mortgage instalments, then the task of the courts is simply to calculate the value of each of their contributions. In principle, the cases are seen in much the same way as if the dispute related to the joint purchase of a car.

(ii) Indirect contributions. Cases which occasion considerably more difficulty are those where there is no direct contribution, in the sense described above, to the purchase of the house. Any contribution made is of a more indirect nature.

This matter was addressed in *Gissing v. Gissing*. In that case, it was recognised that the household expenditure may be organised in such a way that one income is directed towards the payment of the mortgage while the other goes towards meeting the other household expenditure. This type of arrangement, it was said, would entitle each party to a beneficial interest in the house. Where contributions to the family budget are relied upon to acquire an interest in the house, however, it was made clear that the contributions had to be such that, without it, the other partner could not have financed the purchase of the house.[9]

This approach to the issue of indirect financial contributions to the purchase of the house took an avowedly financial approach. An important matter of controversy was whether a contribution to the household, for example in situations where the female partner stayed at home looking after the house, her partner and any children would enable her to acquire an interest under a trust.

In a number of cases in the 1970s a more flexible approach was taken to this matter, frequently by holding that what was described as a new model constructive trust should be imposed whenever justice and good conscience required it.[10] The dictates of justice and good conscience were not dependent upon a financial contribution having been made to the acquisition of the house.[11] Rather it depended upon "all the circumstances and how much she has contributed – not merely in money – but also in keeping up the house, and, if there are children, in looking after them."[12]

This approach was controversial. First, it was difficult to reconcile with authority. Secondly, objections were raised on the basis that property rights should not be altered on the basis of the perceived fairness of an individual case[13]: a matter of considerable significance to third parties not immediately con-

---

[9] *Gissing v. Gissing* [1971] A.C. 886, 909 *per* Lord Diplock.
[10] *Hussey v. Palmer* [1972] 1 W.L.R. 1286, 1289 *per* Lord Denning M.R.
[11] See *Hazell v. Hazell* [1972] 1 W.L.R. 310 at 302–304 *per* Lord Denning M.R.
[12] *Hall v. Hall* [1982] 3 F.L.R. 379, 381 *per* Lord Denning M.R.
[13] See, *e.g.*, A.J. Oakley (1973) 26 C.L.P. 17.

nected with the individual dispute. Nevertheless, from a different perspective, one can also applaud this less orthodox attitude which affords economic significance to what, for want of a better expression, may be termed domestic labour: an attitude which is now fairly well marked in other jurisdictions.[14] In England, however, the resulting trust has resorted to more traditional lines.

In *Burns v. Burns*,[15] an unmarried couple had cohabited for 17 years in a house which was in the man's name and for which he had provided the finance. For a considerable period of time, when she was not in paid employment, she stayed at home looking after the house and their children. After a number of years she did gain employment as a driving-instructor and her earnings were used to pay items such as the rates and the telephone bill and she also bought some household chattels. On the breakdown of their relationship, it was held that she had no interest in the house. According to Fox L.J.: " What is needed is evidence of a payment or payments by the plaintiff which it can be inferred was referable to the acquisition of an interest in the house."[16] She was unable to adduce such evidence and, therefore, had no interest in the house.

This strict line of insisting upon what is, essentially, purchasing behaviour in order to acquire a beneficial interest in a house was emphatically endorsed by the House of Lords in *Lloyd's Bank Plc v. Rosset*.[17] Lord Bridge said:

"In this situation direct contributions to the purchase price by the person who is not the legal owner, whether initially or by payment of mortgage instalments, will readily justify the inference necessary to the creation of a constructive trust, but, as I read the authorities, it is at least extremely doubtful whether anything else will do."[18]

Evidently, therefore, for a person to acquire an interest under a resulting trust a financial contribution to the acquisition of the home is necessary; contributions to the household will not be sufficient.

2. Constructive trusts. Although the utilisation of the constructive trust as a flexible remedial device, imposed to meet the

---

[14] See *Sorochan v. Sorochan* (1986) 29 D.L.R. (4th) 1.
[15] [1984] Ch. 317.
[16] *ibid.* at p. 328.
[17] [1991] A.C. 107.
[18] *ibid.* at p. 133. Constructive trust, in this passage, is probably a slip for resulting trust.

perceived justice of a particular case, was abandoned, there does remain an important, but different, role for this category of trust in the present context. Unlike the position when resulting trust principles are being applied, where the courts make presumptions as to the intentions of the parties derived from financial contributions to the purchase of the house, where constructive trusts become involved is where there is evidence of an actual agreement between the parties as to the beneficial ownership of the home. The role of the constructive trust, in this context, is to prevent a statute from being used as an instrument of fraud: the statutory provision in question being section 53(1)(b) of the Law of Property Act 1925.

(1) Fraud.   Section 53(1)(b) of the Law of Property Act 1925 requires a declaration of a trust concerning land to be evidenced in writing. The lack of such writing will make the declaration of trust unenforceable. So, if a man tells his partner that he regards the house as being as much her's as it is his — a statement which, if made with respect to personal property, would be sufficient to create a trust[19] — this statement will have no legal effect. If, however, she relies on what she has been told and makes a contribution to the purchase of the house, for him to rely upon the lack of writing to deny her a beneficial interest in that house, would then enable him to be unjustly enriched at her expense. To prevent this, a constructive trust, which is exempt from the statutory requirement of writing,[20] is imposed to enforce the agreement.

(2) Enforcing the agreement.   It is important to appreciate that, when a constructive trust is imposed, it is to implement the actual agreement of the parties. The size of the contribution is not the issue. An excellent illustration of this is provided by *Re Densham.*[21] A husband and wife had agreed that they would share the ownership of the house but, seemingly by mistake, it was conveyed into his name, alone. It was found as a fact that she had made a financial contribution to the acquisition of the house, the size of that contribution amounting to one-ninth of the purchase price. Had the dispute been between husband and wife, as to the ownership of the house, then she would have been entitled to a half share: the extent of the agreement between them being enforced under a constructive trust. Had

---

[19] *Paul v. Constance* [1977] 1 W.L.R. 527.
[20] L.P.A 1925, s.53(2); Law of Property (Miscellaneous Provisions) Act 1989, s.2(5).
[21] [1975] 1 W.L.R. 1519.

there been no such agreement then, under a resulting trust, she would have been entitled only to one-ninth of the house. It was important, in this case, to differentiate between the two because the difference between the one-half share under a constructive trust and the one-ninth share, which she had "bought" under a resulting trust was set aside, as against his trustee in bankruptcy, as being a voluntary settlement made by the bankrupt.[22]

There are a number of cases where this principle has been applied. Often the agreement to share the beneficial ownership in the house is found by the fact that some pretext is given to one party as to why the house is not being put into joint names. In *Grant v. Edwards*,[23] for example, the woman was persuaded by her new partner that the house which they were buying should be put in his name alone because, otherwise, the house might be available to her husband in ensuing divorce proceedings. The need to give some sort of pretext indicates a common intention to share the ownership of the house.[24] Were that not so, no such pretext would be necessary. In cases of this type it is usual, but not invariable,[25] for the share to be one-half.

(3) Contribution. It is not sufficient for there, simply, to be an oral agreement that the ownership in the house is to be shared. It must, also, be fraudulent for the legal owner to refuse to give effect to the agreement. The basis of that fraud is unjust enrichment; that he would otherwise benefit, at her expense, were the agreement not to be enforced.[26] Applying this principle, it should be necessary for the claimant to show that she has made some contribution to the purchase of the house.

In some cases, however, there have been indications that non-contributory reliance might suffice.[27] Any such trend has the effect of blurring the distinction between the constructive trust and estoppel; a temptation which should be resisted,[28] the two doctrines having different theoretical bases.

3. Estoppel. Equitable estoppel is an old doctrine, the essence of which is that one person, A, has encouraged another person,

---

[22] Bankruptcy Act 1914, s. 42. See now Insolvency Act 1986, s. 339.
[23] [1986] Ch. 638.
[24] See, also, *Eves v. Eves* [1975] 1 W.L.R. 1338.
[25] See the somewhat exotic case of *Ungarian v. Lessnoff* [1990] Ch. 206 (life interest). The award of a one-third interest in *Eves v. Eves, supra,* is the least satisfactory part of the case.
[26] This line of authority stems from *Rochefoucald* v. *Boustead* [1897] 1 Ch. 196. See M.P. Thompson (1985) 36 N.I.L.Q. 358 at 364–370.
[27] *Grant v. Edwards* [1986] Ch. 638 at 657 *per* Sir Nicolas Browne-Wilkinson V.-C.; *Hammond v. Mitchell* [1991] 1 W.L.R. 1127. See A. Lawson [1992] Conv. 218.
[28] Contrast D. Hayton [1990] Conv. 370 and P. Ferguson (1993) 109 L.Q.R. 114.

B, to believe that they have, or will acquire an interest in A's land. B then acts on that expectation in circumstances where it would be unconscionable for A to deny some interest to B.[29] An equity arises in B's favour and it is in the court's discretion as to how that equity should be satisfied.[30]

An example is provided by *Pascoe v. Turner*.[31] The plaintiff and the defendant cohabited in a house owned by the plaintiff. He then bought another house and they moved into that house. He told her that the house, and everything in it were her's. In reliance on this, she, to his knowledge, spent money on various improvements to the property; the expenditure amounting to about one-quarter of her life savings. He then formed a relationship with another woman and gave her two month's notice to quit the property. She counterclaimed for a declaration that he held the house upon trust for her. It was held by the Court of Appeal that she had rights arising out of estoppel and, to satisfy the equity that had arisen, he was ordered to convey the house to her.

A number of points can be made about this case. The most obvious is that she appears to have received a considerable windfall, acquiring the house for a comparatively small financial outlay. While this is true, it should not disguise the fact that the court does have a discretion as to remedy. In the case, itself, the court did consider awarding her a less extensive right to the property. In the circumstances of the case, however, having regard to his behaviour, and also his comparative wealth, an order enforcing the full extent of her expectation was considered to be appropriate. This will not be true in all cases.[32]

The second point to make concerns the nature of her reliance on what had been said to her. In the case, itself, her reliance was of a financial nature. She had spent money on the strength of what she had been told. Reliance can, however, be of a non financial kind and yet still be sufficient to raise an estoppel. In *Maharaj v. Chand*,[33] a woman, who was in a stable relationship with the plaintiff, owned a flat of her own. He then acquired a house and told her that, if she moved in with him he would provide her with a permanent home. She gave up her flat to move in with him and, some time later, he moved out and sought possession. The Privy Council held that, due to the operation of estoppel, she had the right to remain in the house indefinitely.

[29] See *Taylors Fashions Ltd v. Liverpool Victoria Trustees Ltd* [1982] Q.B. 133n.
[30] See *Crabb v. Arun D.C.* [1976] Ch. 179 at 198.
[31] [1979] 1 W.L.R. 431.
[32] See, *e.g.*, *Dodsworth v. Dodsworth* (1973) 228 E.G. 115.
[33] [1986] A.C. 898.

The conduct, in this case, while clearly amounting to reliance on what he had told her, equally clearly did not take the form of any financial contribution to the purchase of the house. No question of unjust enrichment, therefore, arose. The different nature of the reliance from that required for the imposition of a constructive trust is an important reason for keeping separate the two doctrines. Because it is not necessary for the reliance to be of a financial nature, it is possible that the courts may construe behaviour such as giving up career prospects in reliance on an expectation of security in the home as being sufficient to give her a right in that home.[34] Were the law to develop in this way, that is accepting that estoppel principles should be applied in a fairly flexible way, then rather greater protection can be given to female cohabitees who devote significant periods of their lives to looking after a home, a partner and children than is currently afforded to them by the law of trusts.

THE STRUCTURE OF CO-OWNERSHIP

Today, there are two forms of co-ownership which are relevant. These are the joint tenancy and the tenancy in common. The different nature of the two forms of landholding must now be considered.

1. Joint tenancies. The essence of a joint tenancy is that the joint tenants are, as a group, viewed as one legal entity. As individuals, they own no separate, or individual, share in the property. They are a collective. An important, and distinctive consequence of this is the *ius accrescendi*, or right of survivorship.

The right of survivorship is one of the most significant features of the joint tenancy. If A, B and C are joint tenants and A dies, the effect of the doctrine of survivorship is that the ownership of the land automatically devolves upon B and C. It is quite immaterial that A has purported to leave his share in the property to another person, D. A did not have a share in the property and so there was nothing upon which his will could operate. He simply drops out of the picture. Similarly, if B then dies, he, too, drops out of the picture and C becomes the sole owner of the property. For this reason, it has been said of each joint tenant, that they each hold nothing and yet holds the whole.[35]

---

[34] See *Jones (A.E.) v. Jones (F.W.)* [1977] 1 W.L.R. 438 but contrast the somewhat unfortunate decision in *Coombes v. Smith* [1986] 1 W.L.R. 1306.

[35] *Murray v. Hall* (1840) 7 C.B. 441 at 455.

1. The four unities. For a joint tenancy to exist, there must be present what are known as the four unities. The four unities are possession, interest, title and time.

(i) Possession

The unity of possession is common to both types of co-ownership. It means, simply, that all the co-owners are equally entitled to possess the property; one cannot exclude the other. If one co-owner does exclude the other, then he will be liable to pay an occupation rent to the person ousted.[36]

(ii) Interest

To be joint tenants, each must be entitled to the same interest in the property. If, for example, A has a life interest and B has an entailed interest then they cannot be joint tenants. If, however, land is conveyed to A and B for life, remainder to B in fee simple, A and B can be joint tenants of the life estate despite B's entitlement to the remainder interest.[37]

(iii) Title

As no joint tenant has an interest to call his own, it must follow that they all acquired their interest in the same way, either by conveyance, upon death or by a joint act of adverse possession.[38]

(iv) Time

Following logically from the previous requirement, all the joint tenants must acquire an interest in the property at the same time.

2. Tenancies in common. The tenancy in common differs crucially from a joint tenancy. When a tenancy in common exists, each joint tenant is entitled to a separate share in the property. That share is not physically demarcated. Hence a tenancy in common is frequently referred to as an undivided share in the property. It is quite common for those shares to be of different sizes. If A and B hold land as tenants in common, it is quite possible for A to own three quarters of the property and B to own one quarter.

(i) No survivorship. Because each tenant in common holds an individual, undivided, share in the property, there is no room

---

[36] See *Dennis v. McDonald* [1982] Fam. 63.
[37] *Wiscot's Case* (1599) 2 Co. Rep. 60b.
[38] *Ward v. Ward* (1871) 9 Ch. App. 789.

for the doctrine of survivorship. On the death of a tenant in common, his share will pass either by will or upon intestacy.

(ii) Unity of possession. Each tenant in common has an undivided share in the property. The only one of the unities that needs be present is the unity of possession. One tenant in common cannot exclude another from the property. None of the other unities need be present.

CO-OWNERSHIP AFTER 1925

From a conveyancing point of view, there is no doubt that the joint tenancy is far more convenient than the tenancy in common. The reason for this is that the existence of tenancies in common leads to a fragmentation of ownership and a proliferation of the number of people interested in the land. If, for example, A and B held the land as tenants in common and A died leaving his share to C and D and then C died leaving his share to E and F, then, to sell the land, B, D, E and F would all have to be party to the conveyance. Had A and B been joint tenants, then B would have been left as the sole owner of the property.

While there are distinct conveyancing advantages to the property being owned by joint tenants, from the point of view of the joint tenants, themselves, the doctrine of survivorship can produce results which are unfair or inappropriate. Who survives the longest is a matter of chance. If A and B are joint tenants, A may not want his "share" in the property to go to B upon his death. He may prefer to leave it to members of his own family. One is left with a position that convenience favours the joint tenancy and fairness favours the tenancy in common. The 1925 legislation sought to accommodate both demands and did so by making it absolutely essential to distinguish between the position at law and in equity.

1. Legal joint tenancy. It is now no longer possible for a tenancy in common to exist at law. Section 1(6) of the Law of Property Act 1925 provides that "A legal estate is not capable of subsisting or of being created at law. . . .". In addition to this reform, it is further provided that the maximum number of legal owners of the property is four.[39] If land is conveyed to more than four persons then, under section 34(2) of the Act, the conveyance operates to vest the land in the first four persons named.

[39] Trustee Act 1925, s.34.

2. Position in equity.   It is no longer possible for there to be a legal tenancy in common. Co-ownership at law must take the form of a joint tenancy. There is no such restriction in equity. It is expressly provided by section 36(2) of the Act that, while it is not possible to convert a legal joint tenancy into a tenancy in common, by the process known as severance,[40] it is entirely possible for this to occur in equity. Thus, to reiterate, while it is impossible for co-owners to be anything other than joint tenants at law, in equity they can be either joint tenants or tenants in common. How the position in equity is ascertained will be considered shortly. First attention will be given to the imposition of a trust in cases of co-ownership.

3. The imposition of a trust for sale.   Because there can exist different forms of co-ownership in law and equity, it is necessary that the existence of co-ownership gives rise to a trust. The scheme of the legislation is that the existence of co-ownership should lead to the imposition of a trust for sale. The essential idea underlying this is that a purchaser can deal with the legal owners of the property, of whom, as has been seen, there can be a maximum of four. Any number of people can, however, be co-owners in equity. While this is important to the trustees and the beneficiaries, it is of no consequence to a purchaser who can pay the purchase price to the trustees, safe in the knowledge that all the beneficial interest will be overreached by the conveyance.[41] This end is achieved in various ways.

(i) Conveyance to tenants in common.   If land is conveyed to tenants in common, the effect of this, according to section 34(2) of the Act, is that the legal estate is vested in them as joint tenants under the statutory trusts. The statutory trusts are defined by section 35 of the Act. Under the statutory trusts, the trustees hold the land upon a trust for sale to give effect to the rights of the persons interested in the land. In the case of a conveyance to A and B as tenants in common, therefore, the effect is that A and B hold as joint tenants at law upon trust for sale for themselves as tenants in common. This may be represented as follows.

Law	A,B.	Joint tenants
		Trust for Sale
Equity	A and B	Tenants in Common.

---

[40] *Post*, pp. 106–110.
[41] *City of London B.S. v. Flegg* [1988] A.C. 54. *Ante*, p. 90.

(ii) Devise to tenants in common. Where property is left by will to A and B as tenants in common, a trust for sale is, again, imposed but there is a difference in the identity of the trustees. In this case, the land vests in the testator's personal representatives, say X and Y, who assume the role of the trustees for sale.[42] The position is:

Law	X,Y,	Joint Tenants
		Trust for Sale
Equity	A and B	Tenants in Common.

(iii) Conveyance to Joint Tenants. If property is conveyed to A and B as joint tenants, again, a trust for sale is imposed, although the method of so doing is a little tortuous. By section 36(1) of the Act, the effect of the conveyance is to vest the legal estate in A and B as joint tenants to hold the land upon the trust for sale in like manner as if the persons beneficially entitled were tenants in common, but so as not sever the joint tenancy in equity. The outcome of this convoluted section is this:

Law	A,B.	Joint Tenants
		Trust for Sale
Equity	A,B	Joint Tenants.

This latter position looks, at first sight, a little strange. The position at law and in equity is identical. What then is the purpose of the trust for sale? The main answer to this is that the position may not remain identical. The equitable joint tenancy may, in the future become converted into a tenancy in common. A purchaser, however, does not know this and does not need to know it. He may remain unconcerned with the position in equity, provided that he deals with the legal owners. It is always necessary, however, to understand the overall position to deal separately with the positions in law and equity and this is done regardless of whether or not the positions are identical.

(iv) Sole ownership at law; co-ownership in equity. A position which can arise is when land is conveyed to one person at law but there is co-ownership in equity. This will usually occur when the person who is not the legal owner has acquired a beneficial interest in the property under a resulting or constructive trust. The legal effect of this situation[43] was not

---

expressly dealt with in the legislation and has had to be dealt with by the courts.

In *Bull v. Bull*,[44] a house was conveyed into the sole name of a son but his mother had contributed to the purchase price. This made them tenants in common in equity, the sizes of their respective shares in the property being in proportion to their respective financial contributions. The Court of Appeal relied upon section 36(4) of the Settled Land Act 1925, which provides that an undivided share in land shall not be created except under a trust instrument or under the L.P.A. 1925 and then shall only take effect behind a trust for sale. This, it was held, meant that the son held the land upon an implied trust for sale on behalf of himself and his mother as beneficial tenants in common.

Although this reasoning has been subject to academic criticism,[45] it has been expressly endorsed by the House of Lords.[46] It means that all cases of beneficial co-ownership, except where the settlement takes effect under the Settled Land Act 1925,[47] will result in the imposition of a trust for sale, although it must be stressed that, where there is only one trustee for sale, the beneficial interests behind the trust cannot be overreached by a conveyance executed by only the one trustee.

SEVERANCE

As has been seen, the framework of co-ownership is that the legal owners can only be joint tenants and they will hold the property upon a trust for sale, either express or under a trust imposed by statute. The reason for this is to facilitate conveyancing. In equity, however, they can be either joint tenants or tenants in common. The present section is concerned with the related issues of, first, how one determines whether there was, originally, an equitable tenancy or a tenancy in common and, secondly, how one can convert an equitable joint tenancy into a tenancy in common.

1. Words of severance. It is open to the parties to provide, expressly, as to how the property is to be held in equity. The best way of doing this is for the conveyance to state expressly that the co-owners are to be either joint tenants or tenants in common. In the case of the latter form of co-ownership, it is not

[44] [1955] 1 Q.B. 234.
[45] See Bernard Rudden (1963) Conv. (N.S.) 51.
[46] *Williams & Glyn's Bank Ltd v. Boland* [1981] A.C. 487.
[47] See Thompson, *op. cit.*, p. 16.

essential for this wording to be used. It is sufficient if there is any indiciation that it is intended that the co-owners are to have specified interests in the property. Expressions, termed words of severance, which have had the effect of creating a tenancy in common include, "share and share alike", "equally" and "to be divided between". There is no magic in any particular wording. All that is necessary is to show an intention to create shares.

2. Implied severance. As has been seen the essential nature of a joint tenancy is that the individual joint tenants have no individual interests in the property and on the death of one joint tenant the surviving joint tenants take by survivorship. This has considerable conveyancing advantages but can work unfairly. In certain situations, equity presumed that this right of survivorship could not have been intended and so would presume that there was a beneficial tenancy in common. There are three such situations.

(i) Partnerships. If two people buy land together as a commercial investment, it is highly unlikely that they intend the right of survivorship to operate between them. Accordingly, based upon the principle that a joint tenancy is inappropriate as between merchants, equity will assume that a tenancy in common has been created.[48]

(ii) Mortgages. For the same reason that partners are assumed to take as tenants in common, it is also assumed that lenders of money will also take their security as tenants in common.[49]

(iii) Unequal contributions. A person may obtain a beneficial interest in a house by making a financial contribution to its purchase. Where the contributions are unequal in size, it is assumed that the parties intend the size of each share to be determined by the size of the contribution. This means that there will be a tenancy in common in unequal shares.[50]

(iv) Presumptions. It must be stressed that, in the three situations referred to above, equity presumes there to be a tenancy in common. That presumption can be rebutted. This will occur if there is an express declaration of a joint tenancy, which will prevail over a presumption on favour of a tenancy in common.[51]

---

[48] See *Malayan Credit Ltd v. Jack Chia-Mph Ltd* [1986] A.C. 549.
[49] *Petty v. Styward* (1632) 1 Ch.Rep. 57.
[50] *Lake v. Gibson* (1729) 1 Eq.Cas.Ab. 391.
[51] *Barton v. Morris* [1985] 1 W.L.R. 1257 (business transaction); *Goodman v. Gallant* [1986] Fam. 106 (unequal contribution).

3. Acts of severance.   It is open to beneficial joint tenants to convert that joint tenancy into a tenancy in common by a process termed severance. This must be done during the lifetime of the joint tenants. It cannot be done by will.[52] Severance can be effected in a number of ways. These are common law severance and statutory severance.

Section 36 (2) of the Law of Property Act 1925 provides that where a legal estate is vested in joint tenants beneficially, and any tenant desires to sever the joint tenancy in equity, he shall give to the other joint tenants a notice in writing of such desire or do such other acts or things as would, in the case of personal estate, have been effectual to sever the joint tenancy in equity. The effect of the section is to preserve the pre-1925 method of severance, as developed at common law, and add a new statutory method of severance by the serving of a written notice. These methods will be considered in turn.

1. Statutory severance.   Under the Act a joint tenant may sever the beneficial joint tenancy by serving upon the other joint tenants a notice of an intention to sever. It would appear from the wording of this that the notice must be served upon all of the other joint tenants. The notice, itself need not take any particular form and so, for example, a divorce petition which includes a summons asking for the property to be sold and that the proceeds of sale be divided equally has been held to have effected a severance.[53] On the other hand, in *Harris v. Goddard*,[54] a married couple held the matrimonial home as beneficial joint tenants. Divorce proceedings were instituted and a divorce petition was submitted which sought relief in the terms of section 23 of the Matrimonial Cause Act 1973 asking that such order might be made by way of transfer of the property in respect of the former matrimonial home as might be just. Shortly before the date of the hearing, the husband became seriously ill and died shortly afterwards. It was held that the joint tenancy had not been severed and, consequently the wife, whom one might suppose, was the last person he wanted to inherit his property took by survivorship. The reason for this was that the statement in the divorce petition was too equivocal to constitute severance. To be sufficient, there must be a present claim to a share in the property. In this case the claim made reference to some share in the future. While correct on the facts, the case is illustrative of the fact that it may not always be desirable for the property to be conveyed to a couple as joint tenants.[55]

---

[52] See *Re Caines (dec'd)* [1978] 1 W.L.R. 540 at 555.
[53] *Re Draper's Conveyance* [1969] 1 Ch. 486.
[54] [1983] 1 W.L.R. 1203.
[55] See, further, M.P. Thompson [1987] Conv. 29 and 275 but contrast A.M. Prichard [1987] Conv. 273.

2. Severance at common law. The Act retains the common law method of severing a joint tenancy. The classic exposition of the common law method of severance was given by Sir William Page-Wood V.-C. in *Williams v. Hensman*.[56] He said:

"A joint tenancy can be severed in three ways: in the first place, an act of any of the persons interested operating on his own share may create a severance as to that share. . . . Secondly a joint tenancy may be severed by mutual agreement. And in the third place, there may be a severance by any course of dealing sufficient to intimate that the interest of all were mutually treated as constituting a tenancy in common. When the severance depends upon an inference of this kind without any express act of severance, it will not suffice to rely on an intention, with respect to the particular share, declared only behind the backs of the other persons interested."

These three methods, together with a fourth method, homicide, not mentioned in this case, will be looked at in turn.

(i) Alienation. If one joint tenant transfers his interest in the property, or contracts to do so, this will effect severance.[57] Such transactions are not common and severance under this head is more likely to occur on an involuntary basis. If a person is declared bankrupt then, under section 306 of the Insolvency Act 1986, his property will vest in his trustee in bankruptcy. The effect of this provision is that the equitable joint tenancy will be severed and the bankrupt's share will vest in the trustee.[58] In similar vein, if one co-owner forges the signature of his other co-owner, in order to borrow money by way of mortgage, this transaction will sever the equitable joint tenancy and operate as a mortgage against his share in the property.[59]

Some doubt has arisen as to whether severance is possible under this head if one joint tenant orally informs the other of a wish to sever. Although support exists for the view that severance is possible by this method,[60] the better view is that this is not so. It would make little sense to introduce the statutory method of severance by means of a written notice, if one could sever by an oral declaration.[61]

---

[56] (1861) 1 J. & H. 546 at 557–558.
[57] See *Goddard v. Lewis* (1909) 101 L.T. 528.
[58] See *Morgan v. Marquis* (1853) 9 Exch. 145.
[59] *First National Securities Ltd v. Hegarty* [1985] Q.B. 850.
[60] *Hawkesley v. May* [1956] 1 Q.B. 304 at 311.
[61] *Nielson-Jones v. Fedden* [1975] Ch. 222 at 236–237.

2. *Mutual agreement and course of dealing.* These two methods are closely related. The leading case is *Burgess* v. *Rawnsley*.[62] Beneficial joint tenants entered into an oral agreement whereby one agreed to buy the other's interest in the property. It was held that, despite the oral agreement being unenforceable,[63] the fact that agreement had been reached was sufficient to effect a severance. Whether negotiations falling short of such an agreement would have had a similar effect was left open. Logically, it would seem that it should. If one joint tenant offers the other £20,000 for her share in the property and she declines, saying that she would accept £25,000 this must carry an implicit recognition that she has a share to sell. Otherwise their conversation has no meaning. This, it is thought, ought to be sufficient to amount to a severance but such authority as there is is against this view.[64] In all cases where severance is alleged, the onus of proof is on the person seeking to establish that severance has occurred.[65]

3. *Homicide.*   A long established principle of English law is that a criminal should not profit from his crime. So if A murders B, he cannot inherit under B's will or take under his intestacy.[66] This principle, which has been modified in respect of killings which do not amount to murder,[67] operates, also, in the context of a joint tenancy to prevent one joint tenant, who has killed the other from benefitting from the doctrine of survivorship. The effect of the homicide is to cause severance of the joint tenancy.[68]

4. The effect of severance.   The effect of severance is to give each joint tenant an equal share in the property, regardless of the fact that the joint tenants may have contributed unequally to the purchase of the property.[69] Where severance is not total, a similar principle operates. So, if A, B, C and D are beneficial joint tenants and A severs his joint tenancy, this does not affect the position of B, C and D as between themselves. The position will be that A has a one-quarter share in the property and B, C and D will hold the remaining three-quarter share as joint tenants.[70]

---

[62] [1975] Ch. 429.
[63] L.P.A. 1925, s. 40.
[64] See *Gore v. Carpenter* (1990) 60 P. & C.R. 456.
[65] *Greenfield v. Greenfield* (1979) 38 P. & C.R. 570.
[66] See, *e.g.*, *Re Crippen* [1911] p. 108.
[67] Forfeiture Act 1982.
[68] *Re K. (dec'd)* [1986] Fam. 180.
[69] *Goodman v. Gallant* [1986] Fam. 106.
[70] *Williams v. Hensman* (1861) 1 J. & H. 546.

5. Procedure on death. The effect of the death of a co-owner of property will be that the number of legal owners will decrease, owing to the operation of the doctrine of survivorship. When there is only one legal owner left this can place a purchaser in an awkward position as he will not know if co-ownership is continuing in equity. The position differs according to whether or not title to the land is registered.

1. Unregistered land. Suppose H and W bought a house together in 1980 and it was conveyed to them as beneficial joint tenants. H dies in 1994 and W is now proposing to sell the house. It is clear that she is the sole legal owner by survivorship. What is not known is the position in equity. If severance had occurred during H's lifetime and H had left his share in the property to S, then co-ownership is continuing in equity and, to get a good title, a purchaser will need to insist upon the appointment of another trustee for sale in order to overreach S's interest. If, on the hand, severance had not occurred, W is solely entitled in law and equity and it is not necessary for another trustee to be appointed. The problem, so far as P was concerned, is that he could not know what the position was and so, to be on the safe side, would insist upon the appointment of a second trustee in all cases of this nature. This problem was eradicated, in the case of unregistered land, by the Law of Property (Joint Tenants) Act 1964, which operates retrospectively back to 1925.

Under section 1 of the Act, the survivor of two or more joint tenants shall, as against a purchaser, be deemed to be solely and beneficially interested in the property if he conveys as beneficial owner or the conveyance includes a statement that he is so interested. This is so, unless a memorandum of severance is endorsed upon the conveyance or a bankruptcy order has been registered under the Land Charges Act 1972 against one of the joint tenants.

So, in the example above, if W is selling the property, P will see the conveyance to H and W as joint tenants. He will also be shown H's death certificate. Unless a memorandum of severance is endorsed upon the conveyance to H and W, he is bound to assume that W is the sole beneficial owner provided that she conveys in that capacity. If this is not the case, then W will have to account to the other beneficiary for his share of the proceeds of sale but the purchaser will nevertheless get a good title.

2. Registered land. The 1964 Act does not apply to registered land. In this case, the fact that severance has occurred ought to be indicated by the entry of a restriction, to the effect that the surviving proprietor cannot give a good receipt in respect of capital money. This is sufficient to indicate the existence of a beneficial tenancy in common. If there is no such restriction, then a purchaser who takes a transfer of the land from the survivor of two registered proprietors will take free from the interest of a co-owner, unless that person is in actual occupation of the land and, thereby, has an overriding interest.

DISPUTES AS TO SALE

Property that is subject to co-ownership is held upon trust for sale. It is by no means unknown for there to be disagreements as to when that trust should be executed and the property actually sold. If there is only one legal owner, but co-ownership in equity, then the beneficial co-owner can get an injunction to prevent the legal owner from selling the property.[71] In any event, the purchaser would run a substantial risk of being bound by the interest of the co-owner. Where there is legal co-ownership, and agreement cannot be reached as to whether the property should be sold, the court will have to adjudicate. Different principles apply depending upon who is seeking the sale.

1. Disputes between co-owners.   When the co-owners cannot agree on whether the property is to be sold then, anyone interested may apply to the court under section 30 of the Law of Property Act 1925 for a vesting order or other order giving effect to the proposed transaction or for an order directing the trustees for sale to give effect thereto and the court may make such order as it sees fit.

At one time, the courts, when faced with a petition under section 30, were strongly influenced by the fact that the trust was a trust for sale. If the trustees were not unanimous in deciding to exercise the power to postpone the sale, then effect would be given to the mandatory nature of the trust and a sale would be ordered.[72] The modern tendency is to recognise that the trust for sale is a technical device and that the purpose of the trust for sale may be to provide a family home. In these cases the court may look to family law considerations and be less willing to make such an order.

If property is bought as a financial investment and the co-owners disagree as to whether the property should be sold then, in the absence of some prior agreement regulating this matter,[73]

---

[71] *Waller v. Waller* [1967] 1 W.L.R. 451.
[72] *Re Mayo* [1943] Ch. 302.
[73] See *Re Buchanan-Wollaston's Conveyance* [1939] Ch. 738.

there is no reason why the court should not order a sale. If a couple buy a house in which to live, then different considerations apply. If only the couple themselves are involved, and the relationship breaks down, a sale will normally be ordered, the effect of which will be to allow a clean break to be made between the two.[74] When children are involved, however, a sale may be less desirable.

When children are involved, the courts are anxious to see that they continue to have a secure home. In such cases, a court is likely to postpone a sale at least until the youngest child has reached the age of 18,[75] or, even indefinitely. The effect of such a postponement may be that one of the co-owners, usually the father, derives no benefit from the property and is precluded from realising the capital value of the house. To mitigate this the court may order that the mother pay an occupation rent.[76] In such cases, the courts use their jurisdiction under section 30 to achieve results, in cases on non-marital cohabitation, in line with those arrived at under the divorce jurisdiction when the couple are married.[77]

2. Bankruptcy. When one co-owner becomes bankrupt his beneficial share in the property vests in the trustee in bankruptcy, who will then seek an order that the property be sold. Although the court retains a discretion, the approach that has been consistently adopted is to give priority to the claims of the trustee, and through him, the creditors,[78] and order that the property be sold. Only in exceptional circumstances[79] will the court refuse, or postpone significantly, an order for sale and the fact that the bankrupt's family will lose their home is not regarded as an exceptional circumstance but, rather, a normal incident of bankruptcy.[80] Under section 336 of the Insolvency Act 1986, if the trustee in bankruptcy seeks a sale of a dwelling-house at least a year after the dwelling vested in him, then the court is required to assume (unless the circumstances are exceptional) that the interests of the creditors outweigh all other considerations.

---

[74] See *Jones v. Challenger* [1961] 1 Q.B. 176.
[75] *Re Evers' Trust* [1980] 1 W.L.R. 1327.
[76] *Dennis v. McDonald* [1982] Fam. 63.
[77] See M.P. Thompson [1984] Conv. 103.
[78] For the position when a creditor seeks a sale, see *Abbey National Plc v. Moss* (1994) 29 H.L.R. 249.
[79] See *Re Holliday* [1981] Ch. 405.
[80] See *Re Bailey* [1977] 1 W.L.R. 278; *Re Lowrie* [1981] 3 All E.R. 353; *Re Citro* [1991] Ch. 142.

CHAPTER EIGHT

Leasehold Estates

The lease originally developed outside the feudal structure of estates. This was because it was principally a commercial relationship rather than one based upon status. For that reason, leases were not originally regarded as real property at all. This is, of course, only of historical interest. Leasehold estates are now extremely important forms of land holding, both in the residential and the commercial context. This Chapter will seek to cover the general principles relating to leasehold property but will not become involved with the detail of the statutory systems which regulate leases, save to set the context in which leases and, in particular, residential leases, are set. Before doing that, it is useful to refer to the terminology that is customarily used.

1. Terminology. The term demise is sometimes used instead of the word lease. Similarly, term of years, tenancy and lease are frequently used interchangeably. The person who grants the lease is referred to as the landlord or the lessor and the grantee of the lease, the tenant or the lessee. The landlord, after granting the lease retains the freehold in the property. This is referred to as the reversion. This can be assigned to another person, that person being referred to as the assignee of the reversion. Similarly, the tenant can usually assign the lease; again the person to whom the lease is assigned being termed the assignee of the lease. Finally, instead of the tenant assigning the lease, he can carve out of his interest a lesser leasehold interest. If, for example, the tenant has a 99-year lease, he can create out of that period, termed the head lease, a lease of, say, 50 years. This is termed a sub-lease. The tenant will then occupy a dual position.

He is the tenant of the landlord under the head lease and is also the sub-landlord under the sub-lease.

THE CONTEXT OF LEASES

Leases occur in four main contexts. These are private sector residential properties, public sector residential properties, commercial leases and agricultural lettings. In each case, there exists a complex series of statutory regulations affecting either rent levels, security of tenure, or both. It is beyond the scope of this book to describe these various statutory regimes in any detail. A little must be said, however, about the private sector regime because the existence of the statutory background has had a significant effect on the development of certain fundamental principles affecting the creation of leases.

Since 1915, there has been in existence some form of statutory regulation of the landlord and tenant relationship. The various statutory provisions, known collectively as the Rent Acts, have provided various forms of protection for tenants. This protection has essentially been two-pronged. Limits have been set on the level of rents that can be charged and the tenant has been afforded security of tenure. This latter element has amounted to conferring on a residential tenant a status of irremoveability, the effect of which, on the landlord, is to make it virtually impossible, in many cases, to regain possession of the property from the tenant. Taken together, the effect of the Rent Acts on the landlord can be drastic. His inability to secure a commercial rent from the property, coupled with his inability to regain possession, has a depressing effect on the value of the reversion. Consequently many landlords have sought, at times by exercises reminiscent of the tax avoidance industry, to create relationships to which the Rent Acts do not apply.

The degree of protection afforded to tenants has varied over the years, reflecting the different political outlook of successive governments. Currently the level of protection under the Housing Act 1988 is considerably less than was previously the case. The effect of earlier Rent Acts, however, was to cause freeholders to go to some lengths to seek to create a transaction, whereby a financial return is secured from a property, without that transaction being within the terms of the relevant legislation. A principal device used to achieve this end is to create a licence to which the Acts do not, in general apply, rather than a lease. A consequence of this is that the task of distinguishing between a lease and a licence has frequently proved to be difficult. The cases that turn on this distinction can only be properly understood, however, if the motivation behind a particular transaction is appreciated.

THE ESSENTIALS OF A LEASE

The two main essentials of a lease is that there must be certainty of duration and the tenant must enjoy exclusive possession. These will be looked at in turn.

1. Certainty of duration.   A lease must have both an ascertainable starting date and finishing date. Thus, in *Lace v. Chantler*,[1] a lease expressed to last for the duration of the war was held to be void. This rule was recently confirmed by the House of Lords in *Prudential Assurance Co. Ltd v. London Residuary Body*.[2] The lease, in this case, which concerned a strip of land, had been granted in 1930 and was expressed to continue until the land was required by the council for the purpose of widening the highway. It was unanimously held that this was not valid. As one could not determine when this event would occur, the purported lease was void.

This requirement of certainty is subject to some modifications. For example, one type of lease is a periodic tenancy, one which continues from week to week or from month to month, until determined by the service of a notice to quit.[3] At the outset, one cannot tell how long such a lease will last. It is nevertheless valid because the length of each period is certain and it is in the power of both parties to the lease to bring it to an end, thereby making the term certain. In a case such as *Lace v. Chantler*, the determining factor is outside the control of either party to the lease. A second modification to the rule concerns tenancies for life. If this is granted for a rent then section 169(6) of the Law of Property Act 1925 converts the lease into a 99-year lease determinable on death. If it is not for a rent, then the matter is governed by the Settled Land Act 1925.

2. Exclusive Possession.   A tenant holds an estate in land. One of the incidents of that estate is his right to exclude all others, including the landlord, from the property. This right, the right to exclusive possession, is the hallmark of a lease. It is also a contentious issue. To avoid granting a tenancy, freeholders frequently assert that what has been created is a licence and not a lease. To that end, it is often denied that exclusive possession has been granted. The courts have often been faced with the task of identifying the true position when presented with documentation that seeks to disguise the reality of a transaction.

---

[1] [1944] K.B. 368.
[2] [1992] 2 A.C. 386.
[3] *Post*, p. 133.

1. *Single occupancy.* In determining whether exclusive possession has been given, it is helpful to treat, separately, situations where there is only one occupier of property and situations where a property is subject to multiple occupancy. In the case of single occupancy, the leading case is *Street v. Mountford*.[4] Mrs Mountford signed an agreement, termed a licence, which permitted her to occupy a room in return for a "licence fee" of £37 per week. The freeholder conceded that exclusive possession had been granted but denied that a lease had been created. The House of Lords held that there was in fact a lease.

Lord Templeman, who gave the only speech, held that if a person had been granted exclusive possession of property, for a term at a rent[5] then, regardless of what the parties may call the transaction, it is a lease. Were that not the case, it would be impossible to distinguish between a lease and a licence. The crucial component is exclusive possession. As to this, he said:

> "An occupier of residential accommodation at a rent for a term is either a lodger or a tenant. The occupier is a lodger if the landlord provides attendance or services which require the landlord or his servants to exercise unrestricted access to and use of the premises."[6]

The distinction between a lease and lodgings is crucial and had, to an extent, been obscured in earlier cases by the misuse of terminology and, in particular, the use of the term exclusive possession when what was meant was exclusive occupation.[7] The latter expression is merely a factual description. A student, who has a single room in a hall of residence is in exclusive occupation of it. It is not shared. Because of the high degree of access to the room required by the hall authorities, for purposes such as cleaning, the student does not have exclusive possession and, in Lord Templeman's terms is a lodger. Such will normally be the case in hotels, or an old people's home.[8]

As well as making the distinction between a lease and lodgings, Lord Templeman also referred to cases where a person was seemingly in exclusive possession but was held not to be a tenant. In such cases, what was involved was some act of generosity where there was no intention to enter into contrac-

---

[4] [1985] A.C. 809.
[5] Strictly speaking, the payment of rent is not essential: L.P.A. 1925, s.205(1)(xxvii).
[6] [1985] A.C. 809 at 817–818.
[7] See, in particular, *Marchant v. Charters* [1977] 1 W.L.R. 1181 at 1185, *per* Lord Denning M.R. For a helpful discussion, see M.C. Cullity (1965) 28 Conv.(N.S.) 336.
[8] *Abbeyfield (Harpenden) Society Ltd v. Woods* [1968] 1 W.L.R. 374.

tual relations.[9] Without a contract, there cannot be a lease. If the transaction is a commercial one, and exclusive possession is given, the relationship is normally one of landlord and tenant.[10] Attempts to disguise this by the inclusion of artificial terms requiring the tenant to vacate the room for a set period each day are likely to be regarded as bogus and be unsuccessful.[11]

2. *Multiple occupancy.* Where a property is occupied by more than one person, quite different problems can arise in determining whether exclusive possession has been granted. In this context a scheme developed of entering into separate agreements with each occupier of the property. The aim of this was to prevent the occupiers from being joint tenants. If successful, the result was that no individual had exclusive possession because each had to share with another; as a group they did not have exclusive possession because they were not joint tenants.

The case which brought this device to prominence was *Somma v. Hazelhurst*.[12] A cohabiting couple sought to rent a room. They signed separate "licence" agreements, which were in identical terms. Each agreement made each occupier liable for a fixed sum of money which amounted to half of the total payable for the flat. Each agreement required the occupier to share the property with another licensee and the licensor. The issue subsequently arose as to the status of the occupiers. The Court of Appeal held them to be licensees and not tenants.

The crucial aspects of the reasoning were the reservation of the right of the licensor to move into the room with the couple, this not being regarded as contrary to public policy, and the provisions regarding rent. Joint tenants are jointly and severally liable for the rent. This means either joint tenant can be pursued for the total rent payable. In this case, however, each occupant was only liable for one-half of the rent. As they were not jointly and severally liable, they were not joint tenants. Neither, as individuals did they enjoy exclusive possession and, so, they were licensees.

The effect of this decision was to afford landlords a facile method of avoiding the Rent Act in cases of multiple occupancy. Accordingly, there was some relief when *Somma* was overruled in *Street v. Mountford*. Unfortunately the reasoning employed in

---

[9] See *Booker v. Palmer* [1942] 2 All E.R. 674; *Marcroft Wagons Ltd v. Smith* [1951] 2 K.B. 496.

[10] *Facchini v. Bryson* [1952] 1 T.L.R. 1386.

[11] *Crancour Ltd v. Da Silvaesa* (1987) 18 H.L.R. 265; *Aslan v. Murphy (No. 1)* [1990 1 W.L.R. 766. Contrast *Westminster C.C. v. Clarke* [1992] 2 A.C. 288 (hostel for homeless men).

[12] [1978] 1 W.L.R. 1014.

Somma was not addressed. The case was overruled on the basis that the purported transaction was a sham. According to Lord Templeman, who regarded the couple as joint tenants,

> "the sham nature this obligation would have been only slightly more obvious if H. and S. had been married or if the room had been furnished with a double bed instead of two single beds."[13]

While this approach to *Somma* was quite understandable, given the highly artificial nature of the documents that the couple had signed, the reasoning did not, however, provide much guidance as to what the position would be in other cases of multiple occupancy, where the separate documentation might be rather more genuine than was the case in *Somma*. These difficulties came to light in a number of cases after *Street v. Mountford*[14] leaving the matter to be reviewed, again, by the House of Lords in the conjoined appeals in *A.G. Securities Ltd v. Vaughan* and *Antoniades v. Villiers*.[15]

The two cases involved very different facts. In *Vaughan*, the property in question was a furnished four-bedroomed flat. Individual agreements were entered into with each occupier. Under these agreements, the rent payable differed in respect of each occupier as, in some cases, did the length of the occupancy agreement. When one occupant left, he was replaced by another who entered into a new agreement with the freeholder. In *Villiers*, the facts were virtually identical to those of *Somma* and it was clear that the documents that had been signed by the couple had been modelled on those used in *Somma*. Each licence agreement gave the "licensor" the right to introduce a third occupant into the flat. The only distinction between this case and *Somma* was that this was a two-bedroomed so that the introduction of a third person was at least more feasible than was the case in *Somma*. The House of Lords, in both cases reversing decisions of the Court of Appeal, held that individual licences had been created in *Vaughan* but that in *Villiers* the two occupiers were joint tenants.

The distinction between the two cases was, in essence, that the documents in *Vaughan* represented the reality of the situation, whereas in *Villiers* they did not. In *Vaughan* what was envisaged was that the occupiers of the flat should be a fluctuating body of people with whom individual agreements made obvious sense.

---

[13] [1985] A.C. 809 at 825.
[14] See *Brooker Settled Estates Ltd v. Ayres* (1986) 19 H.L.R. 1375; *Hadjiloucas v. Crean* [1988] 1 W.L.R. 1006.
[15] [1990] 1 A.C. 417.

There was no unity of time, title or interest between the occupiers. The agreements were independent and it was impossible to see how they could, together, be regarded as joint tenants. In *Villiers*, on the other hand, the documents were interdependent. One would not have signed the document without the other. Accordingly, the documents should be read together with the effect that they were joint tenants. The reservation of the right to install a third licensee was regarded as a sham provision and one that was, in any event, contrary to the Rent Act.

These two cases have not resolved all the difficulties in determining disputes as to the status of occupiers who are required to sign separate occupancy agreeements. The difficulty is more one of applying the principle to a particular factual situation, to determine if the documents are independent or interdependent.[16] It may be difficult to determine, for example, if four students who rent a house together are joint tenants or licensees. It should be appreciated, however that the nature of the problem is not usually to distinguish between a lease and lodgings in the sense previously described.

THE CREATION OF LEASES

For a lease to be legal, it must satisfy the definition set out in section 1(1)(b) of the Law of Property Act 1925. It must be for a term of years absolute. Term of years is defined to include terms of less than a year, so there is nothing to prevent a six month tenancy from being a legal lease. As well as satisfying the definition of a legal lease, certain formalities must also be complied with. A failure to do so will, as will be seen, not mean that the proposed transaction is entirely ineffective.

1. Legal leases. Section 52 of the Law of Property Act 1925 establishes the basic rule which is that all conveyances of land or any interest therein are void for the purpose of conveying or creating a legal estate in land unless made by deed. An exception is then made by section 54(2) of the Act. This exemption extends to a lease taking effect in possession for a period not exceeding three years at the best rent reasonably obtainable without taking a fine. In other words, the general rule is that to create a legal lease a deed must be used. To leases within the statutory exception there are no formal requirements. A lease for one year, created orally, will be a legal lease if it

---

[16] See *Mikeover Ltd v. Brady* (1989) 21 H.L.R. 513. (An unfortunate decision on the facts.)

takes effect in possession. The exception relates only to the creation of such a lease. If it is intended, subsequently, to assign such a lease then a deed must be used.[17]

2. Equitable tenancies. A purported grant of a lease which does not comply with the required formality is not wholly ineffective. If, as is likely, the tenant goes into possession and pays rent then, at common law, this will give rise to an implied periodic tenancy, the period being determined by the frequency with which the rent is paid.[18] Of more significance, however, the transaction may give rise to an equitable tenancy.

If L purports to grant a seven year lease to T, but does not use a deed, then there cannot be a legal seven year lease in existence. By means of a fiction, however, this transaction is regarded as a contract to create a legal tenancy.[19] The fiction is clear. L purported to grant a lease. He did not promise to create one in the future. Nevertheless, the fiction is well established. This contract for the creation of a seven year lease is, in principle, specifically enforceable. Applying the maxim that equity looks on that as done which ought to be done, this transaction is effective to create a seven year equitable lease.

The leading case is *Walsh v. Lonsdale.*[20] L, by a document in writing, purported to grant a seven year lease of a mill to T. It was a term of the lease that T should pay the rent a year in advance. T went into possession and paid rent on a quarterly basis for a year-and-a-quarter. L then demanded a year's rent in advance but T refused to pay, whereupon L seized T's goods in lieu of such payment and T sued for trespass. The basis of T's argument was that the remedy of distress, the seizing of goods, was a legal remedy. At law, he was a yearly tenant and, as such, able to terminate the lease upon the giving of six month's notice to quit.[21] The provision requiring the payment of a year's rent in advance was inconsistent with this and, therefore, illegal. As a statement of the legal position this was accurate. It ignored, however, the view of equity. In equity, there was a specifically enforceable contract to grant a seven year lease. Looking upon that which ought to be done as already having been done, equity took the view that there was in existence a valid seven year equitable lease, the terms of which were those set out in the lease. In equity, what L had done was perfectly lawful and T's action was dismissed.

[17] *Crago v. Julian* [1992] 1 W.L.R. 372.
[18] *Post,* p. 124.
[19] *Parker v. Taswell* (1858) 2 De G. & J. 559.
[20] (1882) 21 Ch.D. 9.
[21] *Post,* p. 124.

Walsh v. Lonsdale provides an excellent example of the principle that where law and equity conflict, equity prevails. It also seems, at face value, to establish that an equitable lease is as good as a legal lease. This, for a number of reasons, is not so.

1. Enforceable contract. The basis of the equitable lease is that there is an enforceable contract to create a lease. This raises two issues. First, there must be a contract and, secondly, that contract must be enforceable. As to the first point, until 1989, this was no problem. Prior to the coming into force of section 2 of the Law of Property (Miscellaneous Provisions) Act 1989, the effect of an informal grant of a lease was that, under *Parker* v. *Taswell*, the informal grant was seen as a contract to create a lease. Whether or not it was enforceable depended, then, upon whether section 40 of the Law of Property Act 1925 had been satisfied. This meant either the existence of an adequate memorandum or a sufficient act of part performance. The latter would almost always be present as the tenant had gone into possession: a universally recognised act of part performance. Nowadays, however, matters are more complicated. A contract for the sale of land must be in writing. Unless the informal grant complies with section 2 of the 1989 Act, there is no contract to grant a lease and the basis of *Walsh v. Lonsdale* breaks down. If the "tenant" goes into possession and pays rent, this cannot be part performance of a non-existent contract. It is true that the occupier will have estoppel rights but it is not inevitable that the court will enforce the agreement actually made by the parties, as would have been the case before this Act was passed.[22] This is an undesirable complication.

2. Specific performance. Once one has established the existence of an enforceable contract to grant a lease, for there to be an equitable lease, the remedy of specific performance must remain available. While this remedy is usually available for a contract to create a lease, the remedy is a discretionary one and circumstances may arise when it ceases to be available. In *Bell Street Investments Ltd v. Wood*,[23] the landlord had created a seven year lease of a yard but had not used a deed. The yard was in a dilapidated condition owing, in part, to various breaches of covenant by the tenant. In possession proceedings brought by the landlord, one of the issues to be determined was the status of the tenant. Clearly there was no legal seven year lease as

---

[22] See *United Bank of Kuwait v. Sahib* [1994] *The Times*, July 7 (equitable mortgage); *Morritt v. Wonham* [1993] N.P.C. 2; M.P. Thompson [1994] Conv. 233.
[23] [1970] E.G.D. 812. See, also, *Warmington v. Miller* [1973] 2 All E.R. 372.

there was no deed. Neither was there an equitable lease, however. Because the tenant had behaved inequitably, by being in breach of covenant, he ceased to be entitled to the equitable remedy of specific performance, the effect of which was that there was no equitable lease. It was held that, as the tenant was in possession of the property paying rent, he was, by implication, a legal periodic tenant.

3. *Other distinctions.* In addition to the need for specific performance to remain available for there to be an equitable tenancy in existence, there are other reasons why an equitable lease is not as good as a legal lease. First, an equitable lease is not a conveyance and, so, certain easements which can be implied on a conveyance of property[24] are not implied on the creation of an equitable lease. Secondly, on an assignment of the lease or the reversion, covenants in the lease will not automatically bind the assignee, as there is a lack of privity of estate.[25] Thirdly, an equitable lease is not secure against third parties in the same way as a legal estate is.

In the case of a legal lease, a purchaser of the reversion will be bound by it. In unregistered land, a purchaser will be bound because the lease is a legal estate; in registered land, the lease will, if for less than 21 years, be an overriding interest.[26] An equitable lease is not, however, automatically binding upon a purchaser. Where title is unregistered the lease should be protected by registration of a C(iv) land charge. It is an estate contract. If title is registered, an equitable lease is not an overriding interest[27] and should, therefore, be protected on the register. In both cases, however, if the tenant has gone into possession his postition will be secure. If title is unregistered, the tenant can fall back on the legal periodic tenancy that will arise by implication; if title is registered, the equitable tenancy will become an overriding interest under section 70(1)(g) of the Land Registration Act 1925.

TYPES OF TENANCIES

There are various types of tenancies which will be considered in turn.

1. **Fixed term tenancies.** This, as the name suggests, is a tenancy the length of which has been agreed in advance. It does

---

[24] *Post*, pp. 143–146.
[25] *Post*, p. 130.
[26] L.R.A. 1925, s.70(1)(k).
[27] *City Permanent B.S. v. Miller* [1952] Ch. 584.

not matter what length the term is. A tenancy for a week is just as valid as a tenancy for 1,000 years. All that is necessary is for the start and the finish to be ascertainable before the lease takes effect.[28] Thereafter, each party is bound by the lease for the rest of its duration. This is so, unless there is a clause in the lease permitting either side to determine the lease prior to its expiry (a break clause) or if the landlord is able to forfeit the lease for breach of covenant.

A lease need not take effect in possession. A lease granted in 1995 to take effect in 1997 is termed a reversionary lease. Such a lease, if granted at a rent or in consideration of a fine must take effect in possession not more than 21 years from the date of the grant. Similarly, in the case of a contract to grant a lease, it must begin not more than 21 years from the date of the contract.[29]

2. Periodic tenancies.   A periodic tenancy is one which continues from period to period until terminated by either party by the service of a notice to quit. Such tenancies can be created expressly, for example by the grant of a lease from year to year, or can arise by implication.

A periodic tenancy is implied when a tenant is let into possession and pays rent. One then calculates the period by reference to how the payment of rent is measured. If the rent was £104 per annum, payable at £2 per week, a yearly tenancy would be created. If, however, the rent is simply £2 per week, then a weekly tenancy is created.[30] The tenancy will then continue, potentially indefinitely, period being added to period, until either side serves on the other a valid notice to quit.[31] A periodic tenancy is quite different in nature from a lease which gives the tenant the right to renew the lease at the end of the term. Such a lease will terminate unless the tenant takes an active step to renew it. A periodic tenancy will continue indefinitely unless either side takes an active step to terminate it.

The period is important in that it governs how much notice to quit must be given by either side to terminate the lease. The general rule is that, to terminate a yearly tenancy, six month's notice to quit must be given. In the case of a monthly tenancy and a weekly tenancy the period of notice is the full period of the tenancy, that is a month and a week, respectively.[32] In the

---

[28] *Harvey v. Pratt* [1965] 1 W.L.R. 279.
[29] L.P.A. 1925, s.149(3).
[30] See *Ladies' Hosiery & Knitwear Ltd v. Parker* [1930] 1 Ch. 304.
[31] A clause which seeks to prevent one side serving a notice to quit is void: *Centaploy Ltd v. Matlodge Ltd* [1974] Ch. 1.
[32] For the details of this, see Megarry, *Manual of the Law of Real Property*, (7th ed.), pp. 315–318.

case of dwellings, the minimum period for a notice to quit has been statutorily prescribed and is four weeks.[33]

3. Tenancy at will. A tenancy at will involves a situation where a tenant is let into possession as a tenant but the tenancy can be determined at the will of either party. The usual context for such a tenancy is when a purchaser is allowed into possession of the vendor's property, rent free, prior to completion.[34] When rent is paid and accepted a periodic tenancy will normally arise by implication unless it is clear from the circumstances that this is not intended by the parties.[35]

4. Tenancies at sufferance. A tenancy at sufferance occurs when a tenant holds at the end of the tenancy without the landlord's approval or disapproval.[36] Such a tenancy is not really a tenancy at all. It merely serves to indicate that the occupier did not enter as a trespasser and is not holding over with the consent of the landlord. It can be terminated at will.

5. Tenancies by estoppel. On the grant of a tenancy, both landlord and tenant are mutually estopped from denying the validity of the transaction. It is no defence for a tenant sued by the landlord for breach of a covenant to repair to argue that the landlord did not have title to the land. This is so unless the lease has been determined by the true owner of the land: a process termed eviction by title paramount. If the landlord does not have title to the land, the lease is termed a tenancy by estoppel and is perfectly enforceable as between the parties to the lease.[37] If the landlord subsequently acquires the freehold, the estoppel is said to be fed and the tenant is automatically clothed with a legal lease.[38]

RIGHTS AND DUTIES CREATED BY THE LEASE

A lease, while being an estate in land, is also a contractual relationship. Included in the lease will be a number of contractual terms, called covenants, setting out the respective obligations of landlord and tenant. In addition, certain covenants are implied by law. In general terms, the parties are free to include

---

[33] Protection from Eviction Act 1977, s.3A; Housing Act 1988, ss.31, 32.
[34] *Hagee (London) Ltd v. A.B. Erikson & Larson* [1976] Q.B. 209.
[35] *Javad v. Aqil* [1991] 1 W.L.R. 1007.
[36] For the position when a tenant holds over after the expiry of a notice to quit, see Megarry, *op. cit.*, p. 319.
[37] See, generally, *Cuthbertson v. Irving* (1859) 4 H. & N. 742 at 754, 755.
[38] *Macley v. Nutting* [1949] 2 K.B. 55.

whatever terms they see fit. This section seeks to deal with some of the more important covenants commonly found in leases.

1. Quiet enjoyment.   A covenant which is implied by law, on the part of the landlord, is that the tenant shall enjoy quiet enjoyment. This covenant extends to acts by the landlord and his agents and will afford no remedy to the tenant if he is evicted by title paramount.[39] The covenant protects the tenant from physical interference with his enjoyment of the property and will extend to acts of harassment by the landlord.[40] If the action of the landlord constitutes the tort of trespass, the tenant can, in principle, obtain exemplary damages.[41] In such circumstances, if the tenant is a residential occupier, the landlord may also incur criminal liability.[42]

2. Rent.   A lease will normally require the tenant to pay rent. In the case of a long lease, it is usual for the landlord to include a rent review clause. This enables the quantum of rent to be reviewed at regular periods, it being normal for there to be provision for binding arbitration in the event that the parties cannot agree. The obligation to pay rent may be determined by the contractual doctrine of frustration, for example if the tenanted property is destroyed by fire, but this doctrine will only apply very rarely to the landlord and tenant relationship.[43] Even if the landlord is in breach of his own obligations under the tenancy, this will not relieve the tenant from his obligation to pay rent except, perhaps, if the landlord's breach is so serious as to amount to a fundamental breach of contract, entitling the tenant to repudiate the lease.[44]

3. Repair.   It is, in general, open to the parties to agree between themselves as to who is to be responsible for repairs to the property. This is qualified to an extent in the case of residential property. If property is let as a furnished dwelling, there is an implied obligation on the landlord that the property is fit for human habitation at the outset of the lease.[45] This obligation does not extend, however, to ensuring that the property remains fit for human habitation.[46] The statutory obligation with respect

[39] *Jones v. Lavington* [1903] 1 K.B. 253.
[40] *Kenny v. Preen* [1963] 1 Q.B. 499.
[41] *Drane v. Evangelou* [1978] 1 W.L.R. 455.
[42] Protection from Eviction Act 1977, s.1; Housing Act 1988, s.29.
[43] *National Carriers Ltd v. Panalpina* [1981] A.C. 675.
[44] *Hussein v. Mehlman* [1992] 32 E.G. 59.
[45] *Smith v. Marrable* (1843) 11 M. & W. 5.
[46] *Sarson v. Roberts* [1895] 2 Q.B. 395.

to this matter is redundant because the rent limits laid out in the Act are so low that no lease is likely to be within them.[47]

(1) Short leases. In the case of a lease of a dwelling-house, not exceeding seven years, section 11 of the Landlord and Tenant Act 1985 imposes certain repairing obligations on the landlord. These obligations, which cannot be contracted out of, impose responsibilty on the landlord in respect of the structure and exterior of the house, including drains, gutters and external pipes; the installations in the house for the supply of water, gas, electricity and sanitation; and the installations in the house for space and water heating. For liabilty to arise, the landlord must have notice of the defect in question.[48] The obligations are also limited by the corresponding duty imposed upon the tenant to use the premises in a tenant-like manner. This entails the tenant doing small jobs around the house, such as unblocking the sink, that a reasonable tenant would do.[49]

Guidance as to what comes within the ambit of this statutory obligation was given in *Re Irvine's Estate* v. *Moran*,[50] where the view was expressed that a separate garage and a back yard would not be within the covenant but that items such as windows, frames and sashes would. To be part of the structure of the house, the matter in question need not be load bearing but should properly be regarded as an integral part of the property. On this basis, outside decoration is within the landlord's responsibility as such work is necessary to protect window frames from rotting.

Although the covenant is wide, it does not necessarily give a tenant a remedy simply because the house is unfit for human habitation. In *Quick* v. *Taff-Ely B.C.*,[51] a house suffered severe condensation as a result of the inadequate design of the window frames. The Court of Appeal held that the windows were not in a state of disrepair; they were simply inadequate for their purpose. The condensation, while so bad as to make living in the house virtually impossible in winter, had not caused damage to the structure of the house with the result that the landlord was not in breach of its statutory obligation. In contrast, in *Stent* v. *Monmouth D.C.*,[52] a house had been built in such a way that water came into the house underneath the front

---

[47] Landlord and Tenant Act 1985, s.8 (£80 p.a. in London; £52 p.a. elsewhere.)
[48] *O'Brien* v. *Robinson* [1973] A.C. 912.
[49] *Warren* v. *Keen* [1954] 1 K.B. 15 at 20, *per* Denning L.J.
[50] (1990) 24 H.L.R. 1.
[51] [1986] Q.B. 809. See, also, *Post Office* v. *Aquarius Properties Ltd* [1987] 1 All E.R. 1005 (porous floor).
[52] (1987) 19 H.L.R. 269.

door. While reluctantly accepting that a front door which did not perform the function of keeping out the rain was not, in consequence, in a state of disrepair, the Court did hold the landlord liable, both to replace the door and for the consequent damage, on the basis that the door, itself, had become damaged as result of the flooding and so was in disrepair.

(2) Express covenants. Except where the matter is regulated by statute, the responsibility for repairs to the property is a matter of negotiation. Various expressions can be used in imposing a repairing obligation, such as "tenantable repair", or "good repair", but the use of such terminology does not alter the extent of the obligation.[53] One potential trap which should be noticed, however, is that if the covenant is to keep the property in good repair, then the obligation extends to putting the property into a state of repair, if it was not in such a condition at the commencement of the lease.[54]

The main bone of contention in construing covenants to repair is when what is asserted to be a repair is so extensive that, if done, it would amount to giving back a property quite different from that which was the subject matter of the lease. The distinction is between repair on the one hand and renewal or improvement on the other. In making this distinction, much will depend upon the facts of an individual case. The matter is essentially one of degree.[55] Various factors are relevant when making this assessment. These include the cost of the repair; the length of the lease; the condition of the property at the outset and who has to perform the work.[56] The fact that the work involved amounts to the correction of an inherent defect in the design of the building, such as rectifying damage resulting from a failure to fit expansion joints into a building, will not mean that the work is not a repair.[57]

In the case of leases of more than seven years of which there are more than three years left to run, a landlord must comply with the procedure laid down by section 1 of the Leasehold Property (Repairs) Act 1938, the effect of which is to confer additional rights upon the tenant.[58]

(3) Implied covenants. In certain circumstances a covenant to repair will be implied at common law to give business officacy

---

[53] *Anstruther-Gough-Calthorpe v. McCosker* [1924] 1 K.B. 221.
[54] *Proudfoot v. Hart* (1890) 25 Q.B.D. 42.
[55] *Ravenseft Properties Ltd v. Davstone (Holdings) Ltd* [1980] Q.B. 12.
[56] *Holding and Management Ltd v. Property Holding Plc* [1980] 1 All E.R. 938 at 945.
[57] *Ravenseft Properties Ltd v. Davstone Holdings Ltd, supra.*
[58] See Megarry, *op. cit.*, p. 347.

to the transaction. In *Liverpool C.C. v. Irwin*,[59] the council was the landlord of a block of flats, the tenants being subject to various obligations. It was held by the House of Lords that the landlord was under an implied obligation to take reasonable care to keep the common parts of the building in a state of repair.

4. Assignment and sub-letting. A tenant, as holder of a legal estate, has the right to assign the lease or to create a sub-lease. It is common for a lease to restrict this right. Such a restriction can be absolute or qualified. An absolute covenant against assignment simply prohibits the tenant from assigning the lease. A qualified covenant prohibits the tenant from assigning or subletting without the landlord's consent. The latter covenant is regulated by statute.

In the case of a qualified covenant, it is provided by section 19 of the Landlord and Tenant Act 1927 that the landlord's consent is not to be unreasonably withheld. The tenant's position has been strengthened by section 1 of the Landlord and Tenant Act 1988, which imposes an obligation upon the landlord to give his consent unless it is reasonable not to do so; and if consent is refused, or conditions attached to the giving of consent, he must give written reasons for the decision and this must be done within a reasonable time. The burden of proof on these matters lies on the landlord and a failure to meet these requirements sounds in damages.[60]

In assessing the reasonableness, or otherwise, of the landlord's refusal the courts will take account of those actually given. For the landlord to establish that his refusal was reasonable, it will normally be necessary for him to rely on some characteristic of the tenant or his proposed use of the property.[61] Unless the premises fall within the "small premises" exception in the Act, any refusal of consent grounds stipulated in the Race Relations Act 1976 is unreasonable.[62]

THE ENFORCEABILITY OF COVENANTS

As the landlord can assign his reversion and the tenant can, usually, assign his lease an important issue to consider is the enforceability of the covenants in the lease. This entails consideration being given to the position of the original parties to the lease and then to the position of assignees.

---

[59] [1977] A.C. 239.
[60] Landlord and Tenant Act 1988, s.1(5), 4.
[61] See *Viscount Tredegar v. Harwood* [1929] A.C. 72.
[62] Race Relations Act 1976, ss.1–3, 21, 24.

1. The original parties. As between the original landlord and the original tenant, there exists privity of contract. The effect of this is, as between themselves, unless the lease contains a provision to the contrary, each party can sue and be sued upon all the covenants contained within the lease. This is so notwithstanding that either, or both of them, have parted with their interest in the property, although, in the latter instance it is difficult to envisage a situation where damages would be other than nominal.

The continuing liability of the parties to the original lease can cause considerable hardship to tenants. If, for example, there is an original grant of 21 year lease of commercial premises and the tenant assigns the lease three years later, he will remain liable to the original landlord for the duration of the lease. If the assignee becomes insolvent, the landlord is likely then to look to the original tenant for payment. The rent due may by this time have risen from that originally agreed, owing to the operation of a rent review clause and the tenant will be liable for the increased rent.[63] The Law Commission has recommended that this rule be abolished.[64]

2. Assignees. The mutual liability of the original parties to the lease stems from the doctrine of privity of contract. The position of assignees of the lease and the reversion is based upon the doctrine of privity of estate. The basis of this doctrine is that there exists the relationship of landlord and tenant between the parties involved in the dispute relating to the covenant. If this is the case then, if the covenant touches and concerns the land then the covenant is mutually enforceable. If there is no privity of estate, then it is possible for an assignee to acquire the benefit of a particular covenant. The burden of a covenant may also affect a person not privy to its creation, if it is within the equitable rules relating to the enforcement of restrictive covenants.[65] Apart from these two exceptions, if there is neither privity of contract nor privity of estate between the parties, covenants will not be enforceable.

(1) Privity of estate. Privity of estate, as outlined above, involves the relationship of landlord and tenant between the two parties in question. If there is a lease between L and T and T assigns his lease to A, L is now A's landlord and privity of estate exists between them. Similarly, if L assigns his reversion to R, privity

[63] *Centrovincial Estates Plc v. Bulk Storage Ltd* (1983) 46 P. & C.R. 393.
[64] (1988) Law Com. No. 174.
[65] *Post,* Chapter 10.

of estate exists between R and A. If A then assigns the lease to A2, although there is now privity of estate between R and A2, there is neither privity of estate nor privity of contract between R and A. A is no longer liable for breaches of covenant committed after he assigns the lease.

If the original lease is between L and T and T creates a sub-lease in favour of S-T, then S-T's landlord is T. There is no privity between L and S-T and L cannot, therefore sue S-T in respect of any breach of covenant. In practice, this is rarely a problem as T will be liable to L and, in his own interest, T will ensure that the terms of the sub-lease are in similar terms to that of the headlease, in order that T, to avoid being liable, himself to L, will enforce the covenants in the sub-lease.

(2) Touch and concern the land. Not all covenants in leases will run with the lease. Some covenants are personal to the parties. In order for the benefit of the covenant to run, the covenant must touch and concern the land or, in more modern parlance, affect the landlord in his capacity as landlord and the tenant in his capacity as tenant.[66] A recent attempt was made in *P. & A. Swift Investments v. Combined English Stores Group Plc*[67] to define the nature of such covenants. A covenant by the tenant will touch and concern the land if (i) it is beneficial only to the reversioner for the time being; (ii) it affects the nature, quality, mode of user or value of the reversioner's land; and (iii) it is not expressed to be merely personal in nature; and a similar test is used in the case of covenants by the landlord. Despite the existence of this test, however, it is widely accepted that the distinction between covenants that do touch and concern the land and those that do not is, largely, arbitrary.[68] Because of this, it is normal practice simply to list, as examples, those covenants which do and those which do not touch and concern the land.[69]

(3) Assignment of the lease. When it is the lease that is assigned the principles relating to the running of covenants derive from *Spencer's Case*.[70] Because this was a common law rule, certain consequences follow. First, the lease must be a legal lease. The doctrine of privity of estate does not apply to equitable leases.[71] Secondly, there must be a legal assignment of the whole term. If there is a merely a sub-lease, there is no privity between the

---

[66] *Breams Property Investment Ltd v. Stroulger* [1948] 2 K.B. 1.
[67] [1989] A.C. 632 at 642.
[68] See (1988) Law Com. No. 174 at p. 17, advocating abolition of the distinction.
[69] See Megarry, *op. cit.*, p. 352.
[70] (1583) 5 Co.Rep. 16a.
[71] *Elliott v. Johnson* (1866) L.R. 2 Q.B. 120. See further, Megarry, *op. cit.*, p. 359.

landlord and the sub-tenant and the covenants do not run. A squatter does not acquire the tenant's lease by assignment and, again there is no privity of estate.[72]

The original tenant will remain liable to the original landlord throughout the duration of the lease. An assignee will only be liable for breaches committed while there is privity of estate between him and the landlord, subject to the limited exception introduced in respect of dwellings by section 3(3)(a) of the Landlord and Tenant Act 1985.[73] It is normal, on an assignment of a lease, for the assignee to covenant to indemnify the original tenant against liability for breaches of covenant committed after the assignment and for a chain of such indemnity covenants to be built up on further assignments.

(4) Assignment of the reversion. When the landlord sells the reversion, the original common law position was that, subject to certain exceptions, neither the benefit nor the burden of covenants contained in the lease passed to the assignee. This position was altered by statute, the relevant provisions now being sections 141 and 142 of the Law of Property Act 1925. The position arrived at is broadly similar to that under *Spencer's Case*, but there are some differences.

First, it would seem that, provided the covenant touches and concerns the land and that the rule relating to privity of estate is satisfied, then the benefit and burden of covenants will pass with the reversion in respect of any lease.[74] In the case of an equitable tenancy, the covenants will run with the reversion.

A second point to be made concerns remedies for breaches of covenant occurring prior to the assignment. On an assignment of the reversion, the assignee acquires the benefit of all covenants touching and concerning the land. This means that it is the assignee who acquires the right to sue for breaches of any covenant made by the tenant. Even after assignment, however, the original landlord remains liable to the original tenant for breaches of covenant committed while he was in possession of the land.[75]

THE TERMINATION OF LEASES

The final matter to consider in this Chapter is the termination of leases. It should be stressed at the outset that this section deals

---

[72] *Tichborne v. Weir* (1892) 67 L.T. 735. *Post*, p. 222.
[73] A term inserted into the Act by Landlord and Tenant Act 1987, s.50.
[74] L.P.A. 1925, s.154.
[75] See *City and Metropolitan Properties Ltd v. Greycroft Ltd* [1987] 1 W.L.R. 1085.

with the termination of leases under the general law. In many instances, the tenant will enjoy security of tenure conferred upon him by statutory provision. Unless the lease can be terminated under the general law, such provisions do not come into play. In other words, the statutory provisions impose additional hurdles for the landlord to surmount before he can actually obtain possession of the land. First he must establish that the original lease that was created has come to an end. There are nine ways in which a lease may come to an end.[76] This section will confine itself to the most important of those methods.

1. Expiry. This is applicable to a fixed term lease. At the end of the agreed period, the tenancy automatically terminates by a process termed effluxion of time. In many cases, the tenant will be given a statutory right to remain in the property.

2. Notice. In the case of a fixed term lease, unless there is clause contained in the lease which allows either party to bring the lease to a premature end, neither side can serve an effective notice on the other to bring the lease to an end. In the case of periodic tenancies, these leases will continue until either landlord or tenant brings it to an end by the service of a notice to quit. The length of that notice to quit will be governed by the duration of the period.[77] Where there is a joint tenancy, service of a notice to quit by just one of the joint tenants will be effective to end the tenancy.[78]

3. Forfeiture. The process of forfeiture involves the landlord terminating the lease in consequence of some act of default by the tenant. Forfeiture can occur in one of three situations. First, the landlord has an implied right to forfeit the lease in the event of the tenant denying the landlord's title. Secondly, if the obligations of the tenants are expressed as conditions, in the sense that the continuation of the lease is dependent upon the tenant performing certain duties, the landlord can terminate the lease upon breach of those conditions. Thirdly, and most importantly, the landlord can forfeit the lease by relying on a forfeiture clause in the lease.

Virtually all leases contain a list of things that the tenant must do or refrain from doing. If the tenant is in breach of one of these obligations, or covenants, then the landlord's remedy lies

---

[76] See Megarry, *op. cit.*, pp. 323–335.
[77] *Ante*, p. 144.
[78] *Hammersmith and Fulham L.B.C. v. Monk* [1992] 1 A.C. 478.

in damages. He is limited to that remedy, unless the lease also contains a clause entitling him to determine the lease in the event of a breach of covenant by the tenant. All well-drawn leases will contain a forfeiture clause. Various issues arise when a landlord seeks to forfeit a lease. These are when a breach of covenant has been waived; the procedure to be adopted to effect a forfeiture and the jurisdiction of the courts to grant the tenant relief from forfeiture.

1. *Waiver.* The landlord will lose his right to forfeit the lease if he has waived the breach of covenant complained of. Waiver may be express but can also be implied. A landlord will be regarded as having waived a breach if, with knowledge of the breach, he does some unequivocal act recognising the continuing existence of the lease.

Both elements must be present for waiver to have occurred and their establishment can create difficulties. A landlord will be treated as having knowledge of matters known to his agents.[79] Mere suspicion of a breach is said not to be enough to constitute knowledge,[80] yet in *Van Haarlam v. Kasner*,[81] a landlord was considered to have notice of a tenant's breach of covenant not to use premises for illegal or immoral purposes on that basis that he had notice of the tenant's arrest on spying charges: a decision which seems to go too far.

Difficulty can also arise in determining if the landlord has unequivocally recognised the continuing existence of the lease. The clearest case of waiver occurs when the landlord demands rent from the tenant falling due after the breach. Even if the demand was made due to a clerical error by the landlord's agent, this will amount to waiver.[82] Difficulties can arise in the event of negotiations between landlord and tenant after a breach of covenant by the tenant. Such conduct is capable of constituting a waiver but will not do so if the landlord, while negotiating, does so against a background of threatened proceedings for forfeiture.[83] It is an area where the landlord must tread carefully.

Waiver by the landlord operates only to cause him to lose the right to forfeit the lease. It does not prevent him from obtaining damages for breaches of covenant.[84] Furthermore, the waiver extends only to exisiting breaches of covenant and will not prevent the landlord from seeking to forfeit the lease for future, or continuing, breaches of covenant.

---

[79] See *Metropolitan Properties Co. Ltd v. Cordery* (1979) 39 P. & C.R. 10.
[80] *Chrisdell Ltd v. Johnson* (1987) 54 P. & C.R. 257.
[81] [1992] 2 E.G.L.R. 59.
[82] *Central Estates (Belgravia) Ltd v. Woolgar (No. 2)* [1972] 1 W.L.R. 1048.
[83] *Expert Clothing Service & Sales Ltd v. Hillgate House Ltd* [1986] Ch. 340.
[84] See *Greenwich L.B.C. v. Discreet Selling Estates Ltd* (1990) 61 P. & C.R. 405.

2. *Forfeiture proceedings.* When forfeiting the lease, the landlord will normally issue a writ seeking possession of the property. It is possible, also, to forfeit the lease by actually taking possession of the property but this procedure is extremely unwise in the case of residential property because of the existence of legislation protecting residential tenants.[85] In addition, to forfeit the lease, a landlord will have to follow the statutory procedure and the court may grant the tenant relief from forfeiture.

(i) NON-PAYMENT OF RENT

It is unfortunate that a different procedure pertains if the landlord seeks to forfeit the lease for non-payment of rent and if the forfeiture is in respect of breach of some other covenant. To forfeit a lease for non-payment of rent, the landlord must make a formal demand for payment. This entails the landlord demanding the exact sum due, on the day it falls due, at such convenient time before sunset as to allow the tenant to count out the exact sum due before sunset. To avoid this technicality, it is normal for a lease to absolve the landlord from the need to make a formal demand for rent. He is also exempted from the need to make a formal demand, if half a year's rent is in arrear and no goods are available to the landlord to sell to clear off the arrears.[86]

Once the landlord has instituted forfeiture proceedings for non-payment of rent, the tenant may seek relief against forfeiture. Under the Common Law Procedure Act 1852, if, before trial, the tenant pays off the arrears and costs, the possession proceedings must be stayed. If possession has been granted, the tenant may apply for relief against forfeiture within six months of the execution of the judgment.[87] The criteria that the court will apply are that the arrears have been paid, the tenant has repaid any expense incurred by the landlord and it was just and equitable to grant relief.

(ii) OTHER BREACHES OF COVENANT

In the case of breaches of covenant other than the covenant to pay rent, the landlord must comply with the procedure laid down by section 146 of the Law of Property Act 1925. To forfeit the lease, the landlord must serve upon the tenant a notice. This notice must specify the particular breach which is complained of; must, if the breach is capable of being remedied, require the

---

[85] Criminal Law Act 1977, s.6.
[86] Common Law Procedure Act 1852, s.210.
[87] Common Law Procedure Act 1852, s.210; County Courts Act 1984, s.138.

breach to be remedied; and, if desired, require the tenant to pay compensation in respect of the breach.

The main difficulty regarding the operation of the section has been to determine whether or not a breach is capable of being remedied. If the covenant is a positive one, that is a covenant requiring the tenant to do something, such as repair the property, there is no difficulty. When the covenant prohibits the tenant from doing something, however, and the tenant has done that thing, the question has arisen as to whether what has been done is capable of being undone. Put another way, is the covenant capable of being remedied?

This issue has proved to be controversial and so, from the landlord's point of view, much the safest course of action is for the landlord to require the breach of covenant to be rectified, if it is capable of being remedied. If he fails to adopt this course of action, a notice which does not require the tenant to remedy the breach may still be regarded as adequate if it is regarded as not being remediable. Such a view is likely to be taken if the breach of covenant causes some kind of stigma to be attached to the property, such as where the property has been used for the purposes of prostitution.[88]

After the tenant has been given a reasonable time to comply with the notice, and he has not done so, the landlord may proceed to enforce the forfeiture. While the landlord is proceeding to enforce the forfeiture, the tenant may apply to the court for relief. It is then a matter for the discretion of the court whether relief will be granted. Relevant factors will include the seriousness of the breach and whether there is any stigma attaching to the property. The court will, however, have regard to the value of the lease. Thus in *Van Haarlam v. Kasner*[89] the tenant was in breach of a covenant not to use the property for illegal or immoral purposes, he having been convicted of spying and sentenced to 10 years imprisonment. There was, also a deportation order made at his trial, to take effect upon his release. Harman J. would nevertheless have granted relief against forfeiture. The lease was for 80 years and had been bought by the tenant for £36,000 four or five years previously. To have granted forfeiture would, in the judge's opinion, have amounted to a double punishment depriving the tenant of a valuable asset.

If the landlord has forfeited the lease by taking possession without a court order the court can grant relief, the House of

---

[88] See, *e.g.*, *Rugby School (Governors) v. Tannahill* [1935] 1 K.B. 87.
[89] [1992] 2 E.G.L.R. 59. See, also, *Ropemaker Properties Ltd v. Noonhaven Ltd* [1989] 2 E.G.L.R. 50.

Lords in *Billson v. Residential Apartments Ltd*[90] managing to construe the words "is proceeding" in section 146(2) of the Act to mean "has proceeded". Where, however, the court has made a forfeiture order and the landlord has taken possession under that order, the tenant can no longer seek relief.

4. Surrender. Surrender involves the tenant giving up the lease to the landlord who accepts this action. A surrender should be by deed but a surrender in writing will probably suffice in equity, if done for consideration. If the tenant gives up possession, and this is accepted by the landlord, then this should operate, at law to effect a surrender, both parties being estopped from denying the surrender. It is sometimes a term of a lease that, if the tenant wishes to assign the lease, he must first offer to surrender it to the landlord. Such a clause is perfectly enforceable but will not bind an assignee unless protected by registration.[91]

5. Merger. Merger is effectively the opposite of surrender and will occur if the tenant acquires the freehold reversion. As the tenant cannot be his own landlord, the lease is said to merge in the reversion.

[90] [1992] 2 A.C. 494.
[91] *Greene v. Church Commissioners for England* [1974] Ch. 467.

CHAPTER NINE

Easements

The previous Chapters have principally been concerned with ownership of land. The next three Chapters relate to interests in other people's land. The generic description of this topic is incorporeal hereditaments. The main, but not the only, species of this genus are easements and restrictive covenants, which will be discussed in this Chapter and the succeeding one. Thereafter, attention will be paid to the subject of licences. In the interest of space, the topics of rentcharges and *profits à prendre* will not be considered in any detail.

THE NATURE OF AN EASEMENT

The general characteristic of an easement is that it is a right over someone else's property. A classic example is a right of way over a neighbour's land. There are numerous examples of such rights; a right of light, a right to hang washing on a neighbour's land and even the right to use a neighbour's lavatory have all been held to be easements. What is necessary to do is identify the characteristics that a particular right must possess before it can be admitted to the class of right termed an easement.

The principal features of an easement were articulated, judicially, in *Re Ellenborough Park*.[1] where the Court of Appeal accepted that the right of neighbouring landowners to walk in a park could exist as an easement.

1. Dominant and servient tenement. For a right to exist as an easement, there must be two plots of land, or tenements,

---

[1] [1956] Ch. 131, 163, *per* Sir Raymond Evershed M.R., accepting as correct the classification in Cheshire, *The Modern Law of Real Property* (7th ed.) p. 456.

involved. The land which enjoys the benefit of the right in question is termed the dominant tenement and the land which is subject to the right, the servient tenement. If a person who claims to have a right over someone else's land does not, himself, own land, then he may have a licence over that person's land. Alternatively the right in question may be a public right over the land. What it cannot be is an easement. This rule is sometimes expressed in terms that an easement cannot exist in gross.

2. The right must accommodate the dominant tenement. To exist as an easement, it is necessary, but not sufficient, for the person claiming the land, himself, to own land. The right in question must confer a benefit on the land. Put another way, the person benefitted must be benefitted in his capacity as owner of the land and not merely in a personal capacity. To comply with this requirement, it is not essential that the two pieces of land are physically adjoining; the greater the distance of physical separation, however, the harder it will be for this criterion to be met.[2]

Whether a right accommodates the dominant tenement will be largely a matter of fact in any given case, the essential test being to determine whether the right makes occupation of the dominant tenement more convenient. Depending upon the use of that tenement, an easement can exist to benefit business activity. In *Moody v. Steggles*,[3] the dominant tenement was a pub. The right to place a sign in respect of the pub was recognised as an easement. Conversely, in *Hill* v. *Tupper*[4] a landowner failed in his claim that the right to put pleasure boats on a river was an easement. The right claimed did not accommodate the dominant tenement. The difference in the two cases would seem to be that, in the former case, the right was to the advantage of the existing business use of the land, whereas, in the latter, the right would have represented the business, itself. While the existence of the right would have been an advantage to the landowner, it did not benefit the land, itself.

3. The tenements must be owned by different people. Because an easement is a right over another person's land, it follows from this that the two tenements must be owned by different people. If one person owns a house and a nearby field, and uses the field as a shortcut, there is no easement. This right

[2] See *Bailey v. Stephens* (1862) 12 C.B. (N.S.) 91 at 115.
[3] (1879) 12 Ch.D. 261.
[4] (1863) 2 H. & C. 121.

exercised by the landowner over his own land is frequently referred to as a "quasi-easement" and, as will be seen, can become important.[5]

The rule that the two tenements must not be owned by the same person admits of one qualification. This is that the same person is also in possession of the two plots. If a person owns the freehold of two plots of land and lets one of the properties, there is no reason why the tenant cannot possess an easement over the landlord's other land. This easement will only continue, of course, for the duration of the lease.

4. The right must be capable of being the subject matter of a grant. An easement is capable of existing as a legal interest in land and, as such, must be capable of being created by deed. This entails that there must be both a capable grantor and a capable grantee. In addition to this, the right claimed must be sufficiently definite. This requirement has defeated a claim to an easement entitling a landowner to a good view,[6] and a claim to right of an undefined passage of air.[7]

In considering this final criterion, certainty has not been the only matter to which the courts have had regard. It is commonly said that the right must also be in the nature of an easement. There exist, here, competing pressures. One pressure is for the law to be able to adapt to changing social circumstances. It is therefore, desirable for new rights to be recognised as being capable of existing as easements. An example of this liberating process is *Re Ellenborough Park*, itself, where the right of nearby residents to walk in a park was recognised as an easement. In similar vein has been the recognition of the right to park a car as being capable of existing as an easement.[8] The competing pressure, articulated in the nineteenth century, is the unwillingness of the law to allow individuals to devise and attach novel types of rights to land.[9] Were the law to allow this, this would have potentially adverse consequences on the ability to buy and sell the land in the future.

Balancing these two factors, one can identify various matters which will cause a court to be reluctant to admit a new right to the rank of an easement. First, the right claimed must not be too extensive in nature. So, in *Copeland v. Greenhalf*,[10] a person's

[5] *Post*, pp. 146, 147.
[6] *William Aldred's Case* (1610) 9 Co. Rep. 57b.
[7] *Harris v. De Pinna* (1886) 33 Ch.D. 231.
[8] *Newman v. Jones* [1982] March 22, *unrep.* (Megarry V.-C.); *Patel v. W.H. Smith (Eziot) Ltd* [1987] 1 W.L.R. 853 at 859.
[9] *Keppell v. Bailey* (1833) 2 My. & K. 517 at 533 *per* Lord Brougham L.C.
[10] [1952] Ch. 488.

claim to an easement to store vehicles on an adjoining land-owner's land failed, because, on the facts, what was being claimed amounted to joint user of the land; this was too extensive a right to exist as an easement. Secondly, with the exceptions of the, long established easement of light, the effect of which is to stop the servient landowner from building upon his own land in such a way as to block the flow of light, and an easement of support for buildings,[11] an easement restrictive of the servient owner's use of his own land is unlikely to be recognised as an easement. On this basis, the claim to a right to have one's property protected from the weather failed.[12] Such negative obligations can be attached to land but this has developed through the law of restrictive covenants, to be considered in the next Chapter. Finally, with the exception of the easement of fencing to keep in livestock,[13] the existence of which is considered to be anomalous, a right will not be recognised as an easement if it involves the expenditure of money by the owner of the servient tenement.

These limitations apart, provided that the right claimed exhibits the characteristics of easements, as outlined above, new rights, not previously held to be easements, can be held to have this status.

LEGAL AND EQUITABLE EASEMENTS

An easement may be either legal or equitable. To be legal, it must satisfy the requirements of section 1(2) of the Law of Property Act 1925 which is to say it must exist for the equivalent of either a fee simple absolute in possession or a term of years absolute. It follows from this, that an easement for life is necessarily equitable.

An easement can be created in one of three ways: by statute, by deed or by prescription. Of these three methods, the most important are the last two. Easements that are created by statute tend to involve local Acts of Parliament creating a particular right, such as a right of support.

If a deed is not used, the intended grant may not be entirely ineffective. A contract to create an easement will, if specifically enforceable, create an equitable easement. Whereas a legal easement will automatically bind a purchaser of the servient

---

[11] The right to support for the land, itself, is a natural right. Rights to the support of buildings must be acquired.

[12] *Phipps v. Pears* [1965] 1 Q.B. 76. See *post.*, pp. 151, 152.

[13] See *Crow v. Wood* [1971] 1 Q.B. 77. This easement derives from the enclosure of animals and it is highly unlikely that the existence of an easement of fencing outside this context will be recognised.

land, this is not necessarily the case if the easement is merely equitable. If title is unregistered then a purchaser will not be bound unless the equitable easement has been registered. If, however, title is registered then the easement is likely to take effect as an overriding interest and, therefore, bind a purchaser.[14]

CREATION OF EASEMENTS

Legal easements are often created by the parties themselves. To do this, a deed is essential. The usual, although not invariable, occasion when this occurs is when one person sells a piece of land and retains another piece. In this circumstance, it is important to know whether the vendor has retained any rights over the land which he has sold or, alternatively, has given the purchaser rights over the land which he has retained. The former process is known as reservation and the latter is termed a grant. In either case this may be express or implied.

1. Express reservation.   If the vendor of land wishes to retain rights over the land which he is selling, it is usually essential to do so expressly. The law is very reluctant to imply any rights in favour of the vendor. If for example, A owns a house and a field and sells the field to B, A may wish to retain the right which he previously enjoyed, as owner of that field, to have a means of access across it. The only person who can grant A such a right is B. Until 1926, in a case such as this, B would have, formally, to grant A the right in question. This was inconvenient. To avoid this inconvenience, section 65 of the Law of Property Act 1925 provides that the reservation of the right will operate as a regrant without the need for the purchaser to execute the conveyance by way of regrant. So, in the example above, if A, when conveying the land to B had, in the conveyance, reserved to himself a right of way across the field this would be sufficient to create a legal easement over the field, without B needing to execute the conveyance. Instead of expressly reserving the right, if A, instead, conveys the field subject to the right of way, this will, also, be sufficient to create an easement in his favour.[15]

2. Implied reservation.   When a person grants land to another, the law is extremely reluctant to imply rights in his favour over that land. In the present context, easements over the land will, in the absence of an express reservation, be implied in two situations.

[14] *Ante*, p. 52.
[15] L.P.A. 1925, s. 65(2); *Wiles v. Banks* (1984) 50 P. & C.R. 80.

(i) Necessity. It may happen that when a person sells off part of his land and retains another plot that he has so arranged matters that that land is now landlocked; there is no means of access to it or from it. In such circumstances, the court will imply an easement of necessity in his favour. For this to occur, the case must be one of real necessity; the lack of a convenient means of access will not be sufficient. In *Titchmarsh v. Royston Water Co.*[16] access to the land was only possible by means of a road which was in a cutting some 20 feet below the land itself. While access was clearly inconvenient, it was not impossible and, as a result, there was no easement of necessity. This tough line has been followed consistently.[17]

The basis upon which the courts will imply an easement of necessity is that this is taken to be the intention of the parties; it is not supposed that either grantor or grantee intended the grantor to be marooned on his own land. If, however, it is clear that there is no intention to grant an easement then the courts will not invoke the doctrine of public policy in order to hold that an easement of necessity has been created.[18]

(ii) Implied intention. The court will imply the reservation of an easement in favour of the grantor of land if satisfied that this is what the parties intended. As is the case with easements of necessity, which operate upon an essentially similar principle, the grantor will not find it an easy task to persuade a court that this was the mutual intention of the parties.[19] A normal situation where such an intention is implied is when a person sells a house and retains the property next door. Mutual easements of support are then normally implied.

3. Express grant. Little need be said about the situation where the one party consciously grants an easement to another. Care should be taken when drafting such a grant to determine the extent of any such easement. For example, it is preferable upon granting a right of way to stipulate whether this includes access by car, or lorry, as well as pedestrian access. Similarly if the right in question is an easement of light, thought should be given to the issue of whether a greater amount of light is necessary than that required for normal domestic purposes, which may be the case if the dominant tenement is to be used as a market garden. What does require rather more discussion is the effect of section 62 of the Law of Property Act 1925.

---

[16] (1899) 81 L.T. 673.
[17] See *M.R.A. Engineering Ltd v. Trimster Co. Ltd* (1987) 56 P. &. C.R. 1; *Manjang v. Drammeh* (1990) 61 P. & C.R. 194.
[18] *Nickerson v. Barraclough* [1981] Ch. 426.
[19] See *Re Webb's Lease* [1951] Ch. 808.

(i) Section 62 of the Law of Property Act 1925. Until the enactment of the Conveyancing Act 1881, it was necessary, when conveying land, expressly to convey with it all appurtenant rights. If land had the benefit of an easement this had to be conveyed together with the land itself. The effect of this was to lengthen conveyances. With a view to shortening the length of conveyances, first section 6 of the 1881 Act and, latterly, section 62 of the 1925 Act made this unnecessary.

Section 62 provides that a conveyance of land shall be deemed to include and shall . . . convey all . . . liberties, privileges, easements, rights, and advantages, whatsoever appertaining or reputed to appertain to the land, or any part thereof or, at the time of the conveyance. . . .

This section, which takes effect subject to the expression of any contrary intention in the conveyance,[20] is obviously sufficient to convey existing easements together with the land. Rather less obviously, it operates, also, to upgrade mere licences into easements. In *International Tea Stores Co. Ltd. v. Hobbs*,[21] a tenant had been given permission by his landlord to use a roadway. Later the landlord sold the property to the tenant. It was held that the licence had become an easement. As the licence was a liberty or privilege existing at the time of the conveyance, the effect of the section was to include in the conveyance of the property words to the effect that the premises were sold together with the right to use the roadway; an express grant of an easement.

This section, which can be something of a trap for an unwary vendor, is subject to a number of conditions.

(A) COMPETENT GRANTOR

For the section to operate, there must be a capable grantor of the easement.[22] In other words, at the time of the conveyance, the vendor must own the land which is to become the servient tenement. The section is only applicable if the vendor is selling off part of his land or selling both parts simultaneously.[23]

(B) RIGHT CAPABLE OF BEING AN EASEMENT

For an easement to be created by virtue of the operation of this section, it is necessary that the right in question is capable of being an easement. It must fulfil the criteria set out in *Re*

---

[20] L.P.A. 1925, s.62(4).
[21] [1903] 1 Ch. 165.
[22] L.P.A. 1925, s.62(5).
[23] See *M.R.A. Engineering Ltd v. Trimster Co. Ltd* (1987) 56 P. & C.R. 1.

Ellenborough Park. In *Green v. Ashco Horticulturist Ltd*,[24] the argument that a licence to use the landlord's passageway whenever it was not inconvenient to the landlord had been upgraded into an easement failed, because the right was of too intermittent a nature to exist as an easement.

(C) THE RULE IN LONG V. GOWLETT

In *Long v. Gowlett*[25] two plots of land had, at one time been in common ownership. The owner of plot 1 used to go onto plot 2 to clear weeds from the river. The person who acquired plot 1 claimed to have acquired an easement to go onto plot 2 to clear weeds. This was rejected. According to Sargent J., before an easement can be acquired under the section then, subject to one exception, there must, prior to the conveyance, be a diversity of occupation. In other words, for an easement to be acquired as a result of section 62, the person must have been in occupation of the dominant land, either as a licensee or a tenant, before that land is conveyed to him by the common owner of the dominant and servient tenements. This rule was confirmed, albeit *obiter*, by the House of Lords in *Sovmots Investments Ltd v. Secretary of State for the Environment.*[26]

The exception to the requirement that there must be a prior diversity of occupation is that the quasi-easement is continuous and apparent. This stems from the case of *Broomfield v. Williams*,[27] where a purchaser acquired under the section an easement of light. Prior to the conveyance the building and adjoining land had been in common ownership. The purchaser of the building acquired an easement of light over the retained land. The point here is that the enjoyment of a right of light as a quasi-easement was visible upon an inspection of the two properties. The fact that there was in existence a quasi-easement was evident and this was sufficient for the right to be upgraded into an easement.

The rationale of the rule in *Long v. Gowlett* is to allow the section to operate in accordance with what might be supposed to be the implied intention of the parties. If a person is allowed into occupation of land prior to a conveyance and allowed to exercise rights over other land owned by the vendor, it is not unreasonable to suppose that that right is to continue after the conveyance. Similarly, if it is evident that the quasi-servient land

---

[24] [1966] 1 W.L.R. 889.
[25] [1923] 2 Ch. 177. For an excellent discussion, see Charles Harpum [1979] Conv. 113.
[26] [1979] A.C. 144.
[27] [1897] 1 Ch. 602.

has been used for the benefit of the quasi-dominant land it is, again, not unreasonable for a purchaser to suppose that he will, on acquiring the quasi-dominant plot, acquire also the right in question. When neither of these factors are present, it would not occur to either party that rights are being created over the land which is to be retained. The rule in *Long v. Gowlett* prevents an easement from being created in these circumstances.

(D) CONVEYANCE

Section 62 will only operate if there is a conveyance. This includes a lease. An equitable lease is not a conveyance and section 62 has no application to equitable leases.

(E) CONTRARY INTENTION

The operation of section 62 can be precluded by the expression of a contrary intention. In situations when the section may be potentially relevant, a vendor should take care to revoke any licences that have been granted and, in the contract of sale, exclude the operation of the section. That exclusion should then be repeated in the conveyance.

2. Implied grant.   There are three situations when the grant of an easement will be implied.

(i) Necessity.   The same principles operate in the context of an implied grant as in the case of an implied reservation.

(ii) Intended easements.   Again, similar principles operate as is the case of implied reservations, save that the task of a grantee in persuading a court that the grant of an easement was intended is possibly a little easier than is the case for a grantor. In *Wong v. Beaumont Property Trust Ltd*,[28] a property had been let as a restaurant. To comply with health regulations, it was necessary for there to be adequate ventilation. An easement to install and use a ventilation duct on the landlord's property was implied. Similarly if the grantee has a right over the landlord's property and an easement is necessary for that right to be utilised, an easement will be implied.[29]

(iii) The rule in Wheeldon v. Burrows.   The rule in *Wheeldon v. Burrows*[30] is similar, albeit not identical, to the operation of

---

[28] [1965] 1 Q.B. 173.
[29] *Pwllbach Colliery Co. Ltd v. Woodman* [1915] A.C. 634 at 646.
[30] (1879) 12 Ch.D. 31.

section 62 of the Law of Property Act 1925. Under the rule, on the grant of the quasi-dominant tenement, the grantee will acquire as an easement all those quasi-easements which were continuous and apparent and necessary for the reasonable enjoyment of the land.

In practice, the second requirement has not been a particular issue; the main matter being to establish that the right is continuous and apparent. This means that there is some visible sign, such as a marked track, that there was in existence a quasi-easement.

The main difference between the rule in *Wheeldon v. Burrows* and the operation of section 62 is that the latter operates only when there is a conveyance. *Wheeldon v. Burrows* will operate at the contract stage. In the case of an equitable lease, any quasi-easements that satisfy the requirements of the rule will become equitable easements.[31]

PRESCRIPTION

The final method by which an easement can be acquired is by prescription. The basis of this is that a right has been openly enjoyed for a long period; the effect of that use being to entitle the person who has enjoyed the right to a legal easement. As one would expect, for an easement to be acquired by prescription, it must exhibit the general characteristics of an easement. A number of issues then arise. These relate to the nature of the user and the length of time that the right has been enjoyed. Unfortunately, as will be seen, the latter issue is complicated by the existence of three separate methods of prescription; an unsatisfactory situation and one which is ripe for reform.

1. Nature of use. To establish a claim to an easement by prescription, the claimant must show user as of right. This is traditionally summed up in a Latin phrase, that the enjoyment of the right must be *nec vi, nec clam, nec precario*; that is use neither by force, by stealth or by permission. So, if the claimant demolishes barriers in order to use a right of way, or if the use is not obvious, as for example if underground rods are used to support a structure, no easement will be acquired.[32] Because the requirement that the user must be as of right, a claim to an easement by prescription will be defeated if it is shown that the right was enjoyed with the permission of the servient owner. If,

---

[31] *Borman v. Griffith* [1930] 1 Ch. 493.
[32] *Newnham v. Willison* (1987) 56 P. & C.R 8; *Union Lighterage Co. v. London Graving Dock Co.* [1902] 2 Ch. 557.

however, it is shown that the servient owner tolerates the use, without expressly consenting to it, this will be sufficient to found a claim to an easement.[33]

The other general requirement to found a prescriptive claim to an easement is that the user must be in fee simple. Any claim to an easement by prescription made by a tenant can only be made on behalf of the owner of the freehold reversion. Similarly, if the servient land is in the possession of a tenant, a claim to an easement by prescription will fail unless the freehold owner was able to prevent the use of the property.

2. Prescription periods.   It is unfortunately the case that there are three basic methods of acquiring an easement by prescription; two deriving from the common law and one from statute.

(1) Prescription at common law.   The common law rule was that, to establish a claim to an easement by prescription, the claimant must show that the right in question had been enjoyed since time immemorial. For historical reasons, the date of legal memory is set at 1189, so that the claimant would have to show use since that time. Clearly such a task would be extremely difficult to accomplish and so, to alleviate the difficulty, the courts were prepared to make the presumption that, if there had been user of the right for a period of 20 years, it had been enjoyed since 1189. This was only a presumption, however, and could be rebutted. If it could be proved that the right could not have been enjoyed since that date, the claim to an easement would fail. This meant that it became virtually impossible to establish a prescriptive claim to an easement of light. If the building had been erected after that date, then it could be established that there had in fact been no exercise of the right since 1189.

(2) Lost modern grant.   The extreme difficulty in establishing a prescriptive claim to an easement at common law led to a judicial modification of the rule. This involved the entirely fictitious doctrine of a lost modern grant. The basis of this doctrine was that if a right had been enjoyed for a prolonged period, now 20 years, the court would presume that the right had been granted at some time in the past but that that grant had been lost.[34] This existence of this fiction was endorsed by the House of Lords in *Dalton v. Angus*.[35]

---

[33] *Mills v. Silver* [1991] Ch. 271.
[34] See *Bryant v. Foot* (1867) L.R. 2 Q.B. 161 at 181 *per* Cockburn C.J.
[35] (1881) 6 App. Cas. 740.

Because the doctrine is entirely fictitious, it is entirely irrelevant that evidence exists that no grant was actually made.[36] A claim to an easement on this basis will only be defeated if it is shown that it was impossible for a grant to have been made because, for example, there was nobody during the relevant period with power to make such a grant. Other than this restriction on the fiction, if the claimant can adduce evidence of 20 years user of the right, and this does not have to be 20 years user immediately connected with the adjudication of the claim,[37] then the claim will succeed. It seems also to be the case that rather stronger evidence of user is required than is the case at common law and that the doctrine of lost modern grant can only be prayed in aid when a claim at common law has failed.

(3) Statutory prescription. A legal doctrine which is based squarely on a fiction, as is the case with the doctrine of lost modern grant, is inherently unattractive. It would, of course, be possible to replace by a statutory alternative. While there is in existence the Prescription Act 1832, this does not replace the two common law doctrines but will operate in tandem with them. Moreover, the Act is not particularly well drafted and is complicated by the separate treatment meted out to easements of light which are subject to a different regime from other easements and must, in consequence, be treated separately.

(A) Easements other than Light

To acquire an easement under the Act, it must be shown that there has been either 20 or 40 years continuous enjoyment of the right next before some action. The reason for there being alternative periods will be considered shortly. The latter requirement means that, subject to the degree of interruption permitted under the Act, the requisite period of user must occur prior to the matter being litigated. If, for example, a particular right had been openly used for 25 years but that user had been discontinued two years prior to the action, a claim under the Act will fail. As noted previously, it would be open to the claimant, in these circumstances, to seek to employ the doctrine of lost modern grant in order to claim an easement.[38]

In determining whether there has been 20 years user prior to the action, section 4 of the Act requires the court to disregard an interruption[39] unless it has been acquiesced in or submitted to

---

[36] *Tehidy Estates Ltd v. Norman* [1971] 2 Q.B. 528.
[37] See *Mills v. Silver* [1991] Ch. 271.
[38] See *Mills v. Silver, supra.*
[39] Complicated provisions exist in respect of deductions of time in the event of limitation of the capacity of the servient owner. Prescription Act 1832, ss.6, 7. See Megarry, *Manual of the Law of Real Property* (7th ed.), pp. 393–395.

for one year. This means that a claim to an easement can be made under the Act even when there has not been the full 20 years user. If a person has used a right for 19 years and one day and that use is then interrupted then, provided that the action is brought precisely 364 days after the interruption, the claim to easement will succeed; the two periods will be added together to make up the requisite 20 years. The action cannot be brought before this time as, taking the two periods together, there will not have been 20 years user. It cannot be brought after that date, because delay for a further day will defeat the claim, as the interruption will have lasted for a year.[40]

(i) The different time periods. Section 2 of the Act, in setting out the prescription periods, stipulates two different periods: 20 years and 40 years. The distinction that is then made is that a prescriptive claim based upon 40 years prior to the action will only be defeated if it was shown that it was enjoyed by written consent or agreement. This provision needs a little explanation.

Under the general law relating to prescription, the use must be as of right. It must be *nec vi, nec clam, nec precario*. These general rules pertain in respect of prescription under the Act but the last criterion, *nec precario*, is modified in respect of the 40 year period. The effect can be summarised as follows. If prior to user for 20 years, permission was given verbally to use the particular right that use will be regarded as *precario* and no easement will be acquired. If, on the other hand, the verbal permission was given prior to 40 years use, the effect of the Act is to modify the normal rule concerning the acquisition of of easements and an easement will be acquired. It is only if the permission was in writing that the claim to the easement would be defeated. The final scenario is where permission was given to use the particular right and this permission is repeated over the years. In this case, an easement will not be acquired whether the user is for 20 years or for 40 years. The user has not been as of right.[41] The provision relating to the longer period effectively allows the first, verbal, permission to be disregarded. It will not affect the position if permission is given periodically.

(B) Easements of Light

Easements of light are governed, pricipally, by section 3 of the Act. If enjoyment of access to light has been enjoyed for 20 years, without interruption, that right will become absolute

[40] See *Reilly v. Orange* [1955] 1 W.L.R. 616.
[41] *Gardner v. Hodgson's Kingston Brewery Co. Ltd* [1903] 2 A.C. 229.

unless it was enjoyed with written permission. As is the case with prescription in respect of other rights, the use must be next before the action. The same rule applies, also, with respect to interruptions. There are, however, some important differences between a prescriptive right to light and to other easements.

(i) Interruption. Whereas it is easy to obstruct a right of way being exercised, it is rather more difficult to do this in the case of light. While it may be possible to build in such a way as to the block the flow of light over the servient land, this may not always be the case. The building may be prevented by planning legislation. Alternatively, the servient owner may not want to build but may also be concerned to prevent the acquisition of an easement of light. To alleviate this difficulty, a procedure exists under the Rights to Light Act 1959 whereby the owner of the servient land can register a notional obstruction to the flow of light and this will be sufficient to amount to an interruption of the user.

(ii) Written consent. In the case of easements of light, there is only one relevant period of time: 20 years. A claim to an easement of light by prescription will fail if, and only if, it was permitted in writing. The wording of section 3 does not insist that the user has been of right. It is sufficient if access to the light was actually enjoyed. The ordinary rules are, therefore, largely abrogated. Thus if an annual payment is made for enjoyment of the right to light, this will not, after 20 years, prevent the right maturing into an easement.[42]

(iii) No grant. The easement of light does not rest upon any presumed grant. The section provides for the right to become absolute after the expiry of the relevant period. This has been held to mean that, unlike other cases of prescription, a tenant can acquire an easement of light by prescription.[43]

ACCESS TO NEIGHBOURING LAND

As has been seen, an easement to protect property against the weather does not exist. Given modern housing conditions, this was not without its problems, in that it may be necessary to go on to a neighbour's land in order to effect repairs and maintenance. To meet this problem, the Access to Neighbouring Land Act 1992 was passed. A landowner may apply to a court for an

---

[42] See *Plasterers' Co. v. Parish Clerk's Co.* (1851) 6 Exch. 630.
[43] *Morgan v. Fear* [1907] A.C. 429.

access order, under section 1 of the Act, to enable access to adjoining or adjacent land. The court will make such an order if satisfied that a landowner needs to go onto that land to do work reasonably necessary for the protection of his own land, and the work can only be done, or would be substantially more difficult to do, without entering the servient land. The access order will be binding upon a purchaser of the servient land if protected by registration: in the case of unregistered land by the registration of a writ or order affecting land and in the case of registered land by the registration of a notice or a caution.[44]

---

[44] Access to Neighbouring Land Act 1992, ss.4, 5.

CHAPTER TEN

Covenants Between Freeholders

In a previous Chapter, the enforceability of covenants between landlord and tenant and their respective successors in title was considered. This Chapter is principally concerned with the enforcement of covenants between freeholders, although some of what is said may have relevance to landlords and tenants.

People at large are generally aware that if they wish to develop their land, or make significant alterations to their house, then planning permission is needed. Applications for planning permission are publicised and people who may be affected are given an opportunity to make representations. The law governing this area of law is extensive and complex and no attempt will be made here to enter into any discussion of it. Perhaps less well known is that private arrangements can be made between landowners which affect the way that certain land may be used. These arrangements, which take the form of covenants, may affect not only the parties that make them but can also affect successors in title. They can operate to prevent development of land, even when planning permission has been granted by the requisite authority and can, in effect, represent a form of private planning law, operating in tandem with regulations affecting the public control of land. It is with these covenants that this Chapter is concerned.

PRIVITY OF CONTRACT

As a general rule, landowners are free to enter any contractual relations that they wish. If A, the owner of a house, covenants with B, his neighbour, to decorate the outside of B's house each year, this is a fully binding contract and, if A does not carry out the work, he can be sued. Similarly, if B covenants with A that he will only use his house as a private residence, this obligation is fully enforceable as between A and B. The questions of principal concern to a Land Lawyer are whether, if A sells his land to C and B sells his land to D, C and D can sue and be sued on the covenants which were made by A and B, their predecessors in title. Put another way, the respective issues are whether the benefit of either or both covenants run and whether the burden of the covenants run. These questions raise separate issues and will be addressed shortly. First, however, attention must be paid to the extended notion of privity of contract which operates in this area.

1. Statutory extension of privity.   A key statutory provision in this context is section 56(1) of the Law of Property Act 1925, which enables a person who is not actually a party to the covenant to acquire the right to sue upon it. The section provides that:

> A person may take an immediate or other interest in land, or other property, or the benefit of any condition, right of entry, agreement over or respecting land or other property, although he may not be named as a party to the conveyance or other instrument.

The meaning of this section has proved to be somewhat controversial. In particular, it was, at one time, used as authority in an attempt to do away with the common law rule of privity of contract, at least in so far as it affected property.[1] This expansive view of the meaning of the section did not, however, survive the decision of the House of Lords in *Beswick v. Beswick*.[2] Although that case did not resolve all the difficulties surrounding the section, it is tolerably clear, in the context of covenants affecting land, how it operates.

In the case of covenants affecting land, the section will allow a person to be regarded as being privy to the covenant, and therefore able to sue upon it, although not actually a party to it. The only person who can call on section 56 is someone with whom the conveyance purports to grant some thing or with whom some agreement or covenant is purported to be made.[3] It is not sufficient if the covenant simply seeks to confer a benefit

---

[1] See *e.g. Drive Yourself Car Hire Co (London) Ltd* v. *Strutt* [1954] 1 Q.B. 250 at 274 *per* Denning L.J.

[2] [1968] A.C. 58.

[3] *White v. Bijou Mansions Ltd* [1937] Ch. 610. See, also, *Re Ecclesiastical Commission for England's Conveyance* [1936] Ch. 430.

upon someone. Section 56 will operate if the covenant between A and B expresses itself to be made, also with C; it will not if the covenant is expressed to be for the benefit of C. Accordingly, for section 56 to be applicable, the persons in question must be existing and ascertainable at the time when the covenant was made. A covenant which purports to be made with future owners of land is unaffected by section 56.

THE TRANSMISSION OF COVENANTS

Once one has established who is a party to a particular covenant, the next important issue is to consider the circumstances when the benefit of the covenant is acquired by a successor in title to the covenantee and when a successor in title to the covenantor is subject to the burden of the original covenant. It will usually be necessary to consider these questions separately. If the issue in a given case is whether A can sue B on a covenant, to which neither of them were original parties, one must consider separately the questions of whether the benefit of the covenant passed to A and whether the burden of the covenant has passed to B. It is also necessary to distinguish between the approach taken at law and in equity.

COMMON LAW

1. The burden. It is a general common law principle that only a party to a contract can be sued upon it. The law relating to landlord and tenant comprises a substantial exception to this principle, the burden of certain covenants running on the basis of privity of estate.[4] Other than that, however, the rule is largely inviolate. There is no question of the burden of a covenant running at law so as to affect a successor in title.[5]

2. The benefit. The common law has never had any difficulty, however, with the benefit of covenants of contractual rights being transmitted. Contractual rights, such as a debt, can be assigned to others. In the case of covenants affecting land, the benefit of covenants can pass to a successor in title without express assignment. The leading case is *Smith & Snipes Hall Farm Ltd v. River Douglas Catchment Board*.[6] The defendants cove-

---

[4] *Ante*, pp. 130–132.
[5] *Austerberry v. The Corporation of Oldham* (1885) 29 Ch.D. 750. See, also, *Rhone v. Stephens* [1994] 2 W.L.R. 429. *Post*, p. 158.
[6] [1947] 2 K.B. 500.

nanted with various freeholders that they would maintain the banks of the Eller Brook. One of the landowners then conveyed land to the first plaintiff, expressly with the benefit of the covenant. The first plaintiff then let the land to the second plaintiff. The river burst its bank causing extensive flooding and the action was brought by both plaintiffs for damages.

The Court of Appeal held that the plaintiffs had acquired the benefit of the covenant. The benefit of the covenant would run with the land if the following criteria were met. First, for the covenant to run at law, the successor in title must have a legal estate in land, albeit not necessarily the same estate as the covenantee.[7] Secondly the covenant must touch and concern the land, a matter clearly satisfied on the facts of the case. Thirdly, the land to be benefited must be reasonably identifiable and, finally, the benefit must be intended to run.

This last requirement was held to be satisfied owing to the effect of section 78 of the Law of Property Act 1925. This section, which has become controversial in the context of the running of the benefit of covenants in equity,[8] provides that:

> A covenant relating to any land of the covenantee shall be deemed to be made with the covenantee and his successors in title and the persons deriving title under him or them, and shall have effect as if such successors and other persons were expressed.

The effect of the section was held to be that the defendants' covenant was read as if it said that the covenant was made with the covenantees and their successors in title and this, together with the other criteria having been satisfied, meant that the benefit of the covenant ran with the land. It was further held to be immaterial that the covenantor did not possess any land. In so far as the running of the benefit is concerned, this is not a relevant consideration.[9] In addition, where one is concerned with the running of the benefit of the covenant, it does not matter if the covenant is positive or negative; a matter of considerable significance when attention is turned to the running of the burden.[10]

A further, more recent, example of the benefit of a covenant running at law, this time in the context of landlord and tenant, is provided by *P. & A. Swift Investments (A Firm) v. Combined*

---

[7] See, also, *Williams v. Unit Construction Co. Ltd* (1955) 19 Conv.(N.S.) 262.

[8] *Post*, pp. 161, 162.

[9] *Smith & Snipes Hall Farm v. River Douglas Catchment Board, supra*, at pp. 517, 518, *per* Denning L.J.

[10] *Post*, pp. 157, 158.

English Stores Group Plc.[11] In this case the defendant had stood surety for the rent payable by the tenant to the original landlord. The landlord assigned the reversion to the plaintiff and the tenant was, subsequently, unable to pay the rent and so the plaintiff sued the defendant upon the contractual guarantee that had been given to the original landlord. The issue in the case was whether the benefit of that contract had run with the reversion without any express assignment.

Because there had never been any relationship of landlord and tenant between the plaintiff and the defendant the rules concerning the running of covenants in leases were irrelevant. The House of Lords, nevertheless, held the surety liable deciding that, because the covenant touched and concerned the land, the benefit of it ran at common law to the successor in title of the covenantee. The covenant touched and concerned the land because, first, it was only of benefit to the holder of the reversion for the time being, it being of no use to him after he had parted with the reversion; secondly, it affected the nature, quality or mode of user of the land or its value and, finally, it was not expressed to be personal to the original parties to the covenant.[12]

At common law, therefore, the position is that the benefit of certain covenants can run with the covenantee's land but the burden cannot. In equity, however, a quite different attitude was taken to the question of the running of the burden.

EQUITY

As has just been seen, the common law position was that, while the benefit of certain covenants could run with the covenantee's land, the burden of the covenant would not run with the land of the covenantor. Equity, however, took a different approach to this matter, the starting point being the decision in *Tulk v. Moxhay*,[13] a case which represents the origin of the development of a new property right: the restrictive covenant.

1. The burden. In *Tulk v. Moxhay*, Tulk, in 1808, sold a vacant plot of land, in Leicester Square, to Elms, who covenanted on behalf of himself, his heirs and assigns that he would, at all times keep and maintain the said piece of ground in an open state, uncovered with any buildings. The land then passed through a number of pairs of hands until it was conveyed to

---

[11] [1989] A.C. 632.
[12] *ibid.* at p. 642 *per* Lord Oliver.
[13] (1843) 2 Ph. 773.

Moxhay, who admitted that he had notice of the covenant. He then threatened to build on the land, in disregard of the covenant, and Tulk sought an injunction to restrain him from so doing. The injunction was granted.

In granting the injunction, the reasoning of Lord Cottenham L.C. was quite general. He said:

> "That the question does not depend on whether the covenant runs with the land is evident from this, that if there was a mere agreement and no covenant, this court would enforce it against a party purchasing with notice of it; for if an equity is attached to the property by the owner, no one purchasing with notice of that equity can stand in a different situation from the party from whom he purchased."[14]

It should be observed that Lord Cottenham is not making the decision on the basis that this type of covenant is an interest in land, the burden of which affects successive owners of that land; to the contrary, the basis of the decision is that if a purchaser takes the land with notice of a prior undertaking relating to that land, then it is unconscionable for him to act in a way inconsistent with that undertaking. Put in that way, all sorts of different obligations could be entered into which could affect successive owners of the land and this is something to which the law has traditionally been opposed; the reason being that, to allow this to happen, could render land unsellable. So, although *Tulk v. Moxhay* is the foundation of the modern law, the basis of the decision has been modified considerably, that modification being based by close analogy with the law of easements, the end result being that restrictive covenants can be seen as being a form of equitable negative easement.

RESTRICTIVE COVENANTS

1. Negative covenants.   Taken at face value, there is nothing in Lord Cottenham's judgment which draws any distinction between positive covenants, such as a covenant to maintain a building, and negative covenants, such as a covenant against building. The conscience of a purchaser would, seemingly, be equally affected by either type of covenant. For a while, no distinction was drawn between positive and restrictive covenants, both being enforced against purchasers with notice.[15]

---

[14] *ibid.* at p. 778.
[15] See *Morland v. Cook* (1868) L.R. 6 Eq. 252; *Cooke v. Chilcott* (1876) 3 Ch.D. 694.

Such a distinction was made, however, in the leading case of *Haywood v. Brunswick Permanent B.S.*,[16] where it was held that only negative, or restrictive, covenants were capable of running with the land and, therefore, binding a successor in title to the covenantor.

The limiting of *Tulk v. Moxhay* to restrictive covenants has meant that it is difficult to make a positive covenant binding as a proprietary interest. This has caused problems and will be considered below. The status of the rule was recently confirmed, however, by the House of Lords in *Rhone v. Stephens*,[17] where it was held that a covenant to maintain a roof was not binding upon a successor in title to the covenantor. In reaching this conclusion, great stress was put upon a dominant theme in Property Law: the need to maintain certainty, Lord Templeman said:

> "It is plain from the articles, reports and papers to which we were referred that judicial legislation to overrule the *Austerberry* case would create a number of difficulties, anomalies and uncertainties and affect the rights and liabilities of people who have for over 100 years bought and sold land in the knowledge, imparted at an elementary stage to every student of the law of real property, that positive covenants affecting freehold land are not directly enforceable except against the original covenantor."[18]

2. Land to be benefited. For the burden of a covenant to run, the covenantee, or his successor in title must have land to be benefited. This requirement, which parallels the requirement that there is a dominant tenement in the case of easements, was not an essential element in the judgment in *Tulk v. Moxhay* but was an incidental fact. Tulk did, in fact, own other land in the vicinity of the plot which had been sold. The need for there to be, effectively, a dominant tenement was established in *Formby v. Barker*[19] and confirmed in *London C.C. v. Allen*.[20] The latter case involved a local authority and caused certain problems in relation to the enforcement of covenants by such bodies. For this reason, the rule has been modified by statute, in respect of such authorities,[21] but the general rule remains the same.

---

[16] (1881) 8 Q.B.D. 403.
[17] [1994] 2 W.L.R. 429.
[18] *ibid.* at p. 436.
[19] [1903] 2 Ch. 539.
[20] [1914] 3 K.B. 642.
[21] Housing Act 1985, s.609; Town and Country Planning Act 1990, s.106(3).

Allied to the rule that the covenantee must have land to be benefited, that land should be sufficiently proximate to the burdened land, in fact, to benefit from it. This requirement is, in substance, the same as the rule in the law relating to easements that the right must accommodate the dominant tenement.

3. The burden must be intended to run. It is not compulsory that restrictive covenants entered into by two parties must necessarily create a property right. The parties must intend this to occur. This factor is governed by section 79 of the Law of Property Act 1925, which provides that a covenant relating to any land of a covenantor or capable of being bound by him, shall, unless a contrary intention is expressed, be deemed to be made by the covenantor on behalf of himself, his successors in title and the persons deriving title under him or them, and, subject as aforesaid, shall take effect as if such successors and other persons were expressed.

The expression "relating to the land" is the familiar concept that the covenant must touch and concern the land. Provided that the other criteria, discussed above, are met, the covenant will run with the land unless the covenantor opts out.

4. Equitable right. The restrictive covenant is a property right which has been developed in equity. Unlike legal rights, it does not automatically bind purchasers of the burdened land. It is dependent for its enforceability on the doctrine of notice. That doctrine has, of course been much affected by registration. It is better to treat separately unregistered and registered land.

(a) Unregistered land. A restrictive covenant is, with two exceptions, registrable as a Class D(ii) land charge. If registered, all subsequent purchasers will be deemed to have notice of it and will, therefore be bound by it. Conversely, a failure to register means that it will be void against a purchaser for money or money's worth.[22] Covenants created before 1925 and covenants between landlord and tenant are not registrable. Their enforceability will depend upon the old doctrine of notice.

(b) Registered land. A restrictive covenant is a minor interest and must be protected by registration, either by a notice or a caution.

A second feature of restrictive covenants being the creation of equity is that only equitable remedies are available to enforce them. This means that the remedy which is sought will either be

---

[22] *Ante,* pp. 41, 42.

an injunction to restrain an apprehended breach of covenant or a mandatory injunction to undo what has been done.[23] The court has jurisdiction, in appropriate cases, to award damages in lieu of an injunction.[24]

RUNNING OF THE BENEFIT

As is the case at law, equity also developed rules governing the running of the benefit of a restrictive covenant. In practice, these rules are more important than their common law counterparts because if a person is seeking to enforce a covenant, the burden of which has run in equity, he must rely upon the equitable rules to show that the benefit of the covenant has passed to him.[25]

In equity, the benefit of a covenant can run in one of the three ways enumerated in *Renals v. Cowlishaw*.[26] These are:

(i) Annexation;
(ii) Assignment; and
(iii) A Scheme of Development.

These three methods will be considered in turn.

1. Annexation. Annexation involves the permanent attachment of the benefit of a covenant to the land in question. Once attached, the benefit will automatically pass to successors in title without it being specifically mentioned. It was previously the case that the law concerning what amounted to annexation was highly complex, with meticulous attention being paid to the precise wording used to determine whether the requisite intention to annex the benefit of the covenant had been shown.[27] It was also necessary for the land which was to be benefited to be clearly identified. Furthermore, there was the additional complication that once the benefit had been annexed, it was regarded as being annexed to the land as a whole, so that if only a part of the land was sold, the benefit of the covenant would not pass.[28] Happily a good deal of the complexity attached to this part of the law was, in respect of covenants entered into

[23] See *Wakeham v. Wood* (1982) 43 P. & C.R. 40.
[24] Supreme Court Act 1980, s.50, replacing the jurisdiction introduced by the Chancery Amendment Act 1858. See *Wrotham Park Estate Co. v. Parkside Homes* [1974] 1 W.L.R. 798.
[25] See, *e.g.* Re *Union of London & Smith's Bank Ltd's Contract, Miles v. Easter* [1935] Ch. 611.
[26] (1878) 9 Ch.D. 125.
[27] See, *e.g.*, *Rogers v. Hosegood* [1900] 2 Ch. 388.
[28] *Re Ballard's Conveyance* [1937] Ch. 473.

after 1925,[29] swept away as a result of the Court of Appeal decision in *Federated Homes v. Mill Lodge Properties Ltd.*[30]

One of the issues in *Federated Homes* was whether the benefit of a covenant restricting the amount of building which could be carried out on a neighbouring plot had been annexed to land and could, therefore, be enforced. Despite the fact that there were no express words of annexation in the conveyance creating the covenant, the Court of Appeal held that it had been. It was held that section 78 of the Law of Property Act 1925 had the effect of annexing the benefit of the covenant. Section 78, it will be recalled, provides that a covenant relating to the land of the covenantee shall be deemed to be made with the covenantee and his successors in title and persons deriving title under him. Brightman L.J. held that the effect of the section, in respect of covenants which relate to the covenantee's land, was to annex the covenant. He further held that the covenant was annexed to each and every part of the land, thereby removing the difficulty adverted to earlier.

The decision in *Federated Homes*, although advocated by some writers in the past,[31] attracted a critical reaction,[32] strong exception being taken to the interpretation of section 78 that, provided the covenant touched and concerned the land, and that there was some identification of the land to be benefited, the benefit would become annexed to that land without the need for clear words of annexation. In defence of the decision, however, it can be pointed out, as Brightman L.J., himself did, that the benefit of covenants will, owing to the operation of the section, run at law without the need for the intention to be expressed that the benefit would run,[33] and these decisions have not been criticised on this basis. The decision should be welcomed for having consigned to history some of the arcane learning that surrounded this area of the law.

Another criticism levelled at *Federated Homes* was that, unlike section 79 of the Act, which concerns the burden of covenants, section 78 does not include any statement that the section only operates subject to the expression of a contrary intention. So, it was argued, if the covenant in question touched and concerned the land, the effect of section 78 was to make annexation of the benefit of the covenant compulsory. This fear was dispelled in

---

[29] For the position with regard to pre-1926 covenants, see *Shropshire C.C. v. Edwards* (1982) 46 P. & C.R. 270.

[30] [1980] 1 W.L.R. 594.

[31] See, *e.g.*, H.W.R. Wade [1972B] C.L.J. 157.

[32] See, *e.g.*, G.H. Newsom (1981) 97 L.Q.R. 32.

[33] [1980] 1 W.L.R. 598 at 605, referring to *Smith & Snipes Hall Farm v. River Douglas Catchment Board; Williams v. Unit Construction Co. Ltd, supra.*

Roake v. *Chadha*.[34] In this case, the covenant was expressed "not to enure for the benefit of any owner or subsequent purchaser of the . . . estate unless the benefit of the covenant shall be expressly assigned." It was held that this statement was sufficient to prevent the annexation of the covenant.

To sum up the present position, the benefit of a restrictive covenant will be annexed to the land if it touches and concerns the land and there is no expression of a contrary intent. It is probably also still necessary that the covenant identifies the land to be benefited.

2. Assignment.   Where the benefit of a covenant has not been annexed at the time of its creation, it is possible for the benefit to be assigned together with the land. For assignment to take place in equity, the assignment of the covenant must be coupled with a transfer of the land and the assignment must be simultaneous with the transfer of the land.[35] The assignment must identify the land to be benefited, although this requirement is satisfied if the land can be identified from surrounding circumstances.[36]

Once the benefit of the covenant has been assigned, the better view is that this should operate as a "delayed annexation", so that the benefit of the covenant should pass automatically on the next transfer of the land.[37] Such authority as there is, however, is against this view and so it appears to be necessary for there to be an express assignment of the covenant each time the land is transferred, so that there is an unbroken chain of assignments from the covenantee to the person seeking to enforce the covenant.

3. Schemes of development.   The final method of ensuring that the benefit of a covenant runs with the land is to establish a scheme of development. The essence of a scheme is that land, at one time owned by a common vendor, is divided up into lots and then sold to various different purchasers. It can then become important that the covenants entered into, which will have been created for the benefit of the estate, are mutually enforceable between the owners of the different plots. While the existing rules could have been employed to achieve this end, a different set of rules was devised, the result being that, when a scheme is established, a local law is created with respect to this area of land. It should also be borne in mind, however, that it

---

[34] [1984] Ch. 40.
[35] *Re Union of London and Smith's Bank Ltd's Conveyance* [1933] Ch. 611.
[36] *Newton Abbot Co-operative Soc. Ltd v. Williamson & Treadgold Ltd* [1952] Ch. 286; *Marten v. Flight Refuelling Ltd* [1962] Ch. 115.
[37] P.V. Baker (1968) 84 L.Q.R. 22.

has been said of this branch of the law that "It may be, indeed, that this is one of those branches of equity which work best when explained least."[38]

(a) Origins of the doctrine.   At the outset of the development of this branch of the law, the courts adopted quite stringent criteria in determining whether a scheme of development had been created. This involved satisfying each of the four criteria laid down in *Elliston v. Reacher*.[39] These were:

   (i) The land must have been disposed of by a common vendor;

  (ii) Prior to the sale, the land must have been laid out in lots subject to the reciprocal obligations;

 (iii) The common vendor must have intended the benefit of the covenants to be for the benefit of all owners of lot and not merely for himself; and

 (iv) The land must have been bought on the footing that the restrictions were to be enforceable by the owners of other lots.

(b) A more relaxed approach.   In more recent times, there has been a tendency to relax the criteria laid down in *Elliston v. Reacher* and hold there to be a scheme of development to be in existence when one, or other, of these criteria had not been met.[40] Nowadays, the courts will need to be satisfied as to two things. First, that the area affected by the scheme is properly identified.[41] Secondly, and of cardinal importance, that it was clearly intended to set up a reciprocal scheme of enforcement. To establish such an intention, it helps if the land is laid out in lots, this giving rise to a presumption that there is such a reciprocal intention,[42] but that intention can also be established by extrinsic evidence; the identical nature of the covenants being a strong pointer to there being such an intention.[43] No such intention to set up a reciprocal scheme will be found unless the existence of such a scheme is brought to the attention of prospective purchasers.[44]

---

[38] *Brunner v. Greenslade* [1971] 1 Ch. 993 at 1006, *per* Megarry J.

[39] [1908] 2 Ch. 374.

[40] See, generally, Gray, *Modern Elements of Land Law* (2nd ed.) pp. 1162–1164.

[41] See *Lund v. Taylor* (1975) 31 P. & C.R. 167.

[42] See *Brunner v. Greenslade* [1971] Ch. 993.

[43] See *Baxter v. Four Oaks Properties Ltd* [1965] 1 Ch. 816; *Re Dolphin's Conveyance* [1970] Ch. 654.

[44] See *Jamaica Mutual Life Assurance Society v. Hillsborough Ltd* [1989] 1 W.L.R. 1101.

DISCHARGE OF COVENANTS

Covenants may have been attached to land many years previously, and still be binding upon purchasers of that land, and yet serve little purpose in modern society. Indeed, their continued enforcement may, in fact, be detrimental to the common good, for example, by preventing a socially desirable development of the land. To prevent covenants from having this undesirable effect there is a statutory jurisdiction, afforded to Lands Tribunals to modify or discharge restrictive covenants, with or without compensation.

Applications may be made to the Lands Tribunal under section 84 of the Law of Property Act 1925[45] for a covenant to be modified or discharged. The grounds upon which such an order can be on one of four grounds:

(i) That the covenant has become obsolete;

(ii) That the continued enforcement of the covenant would be obstructive to some public or private use of the land and that the covenant confers not practical benefit or is contrary to the public interest;

(iii) With the consent of all persons of full age entitled to the benefit have, either expressly or by implication, agreed to the modification; and

(iv) Discharge or modification would confer no injury on the person entitled to the benefit.

POSITIVE COVENANTS

As has been seen, the burden of covenants between freeholders does not run at all at law and, in equity, only the burden of restrictive covenants will run. The upshot of this is that one cannot directly make positive covenants run in so far as freehold land is concerned. This has caused practical problems in that it may be very desirable for positive obligations, such as a covenant to repair, or to maintain the common parts of building, to bind successive owners of land. For this reason, certain types of property are held on long leases, so that such covenants can be made to bind successors in title on the basis of privity of estate.[46] While some of the problems caused by the rule preventing the running of positive covenants may be alleviated to a limited extent by the enactment of the Access to Neighbouring Land Act 1992, the need has been felt, for some considerable

---

[45] As amended by L.P.A. 1925, s.28.
[46] *Ante,* pp. 130–132.

time, for the law to be reformed to enable positive covenants to run with freehold land. To this end, reports have been published recommending such reform[47] including, most radically, the proposal to establish a new form of land ownership termed commonhold.[48] To date, however, none of these proposals have been implemented. So far as freeholders are concerned, therefore, it remains difficult to make positive covenants enforceable against successors in title to the covenantor. It cannot be done directly, although there are a number of devices, of varying degrees of reliability, to achieve this end, indirectly.

1. Chain of covenants. One, not very effective, method of seeking to impose continuing liability in respect of positive covenants is to use a chain of covenants. If A covenants with B to maintain a fence between their two properties, A will be liable, in damages to B for any failure to maintain the fence. This liablility remains even after A has sold and conveyed the land to C. On the occasion of that conveyance, A can obtain a covenant from C that C will indemnify A against any liability in respect of the covenant pertaining to the fence. When C conveys the land to D, a similar indemnity covenant is entered into between A and D. And so on. To enforce the covenant, B sues A, who in turn sues C, who, in turn sues D. In time this chain will break down and, as a result, this method is unsatisfactory.

2. Enlargement of a lease. In the case of certain long leases, the tenant has the right, under section 153 of the Law of Property Act 1925 to enlarge the lease into a freehold. If this is done the freehold takes effect subject to the same terms as did the lease. Positive covenants contained in the original lease will then be binding upon the freeholder. This method is regarded as artificial and does not appear to have been tested in the courts.

3. Rentcharges. A rentcharge is an annual payment charged upon land. This is enforced by attaching a right of entry to the rentcharge, the effect of which is that the holder of the rentcharge can re-enter the land upon non-compliance with the terms of the rentcharge. The rentcharge can be imposed to secure the performance of various positive covenants. A failure to comply with these covenants will enable the owner of the rentcharge to enter the land and perform the covenants, charging the cost of this to the freeholder. Although the creation of new rentcharges was stopped by the Rentcharges Act 1977, this

---

[47] See (1965) Cmnd. 2719; (1984) Law Com. No. 127.
[48] (1987) Cmnd. 179 (the Aldridge Committee).

type of rentcharge was expressly exempted from the operation of the Act.

4. Benefit and burden. In *Halsall v. Brizell*,[49] a purchaser of land was given the right to use various roads on an estate, it being a requirement of this that he made a contribution to the upkeep of the roads. It was held that, so long as he intended to avail himself of that right, he must take subject to the correlative burden. From this basis, the principle was extracted in *Tito v. Waddell (No. 2)*[50] that, if one took the benefit of a conveyance, one must take subject to all burdens attached to it. This principle, termed the "pure principle" of benefit and burden would, if accepted, have operated effectively to remove the bar on the running of positive covenants. In *Rhone v. Stephens*,[51] the House of Lords refused to accept the existence of such a wide principle. The doctrine of benefit and burden was limited to situations when the two obligations were reciprocal, the enjoyment of the right being conditional upon the performance of the obligation. It must be open to the person to forego the right and thereby free himself from the corresponding burden.

The rejection of the "pure principle" confirms the well-established position that, as between freeholders, it remains very difficult to make the burden of positive covenants run with the land.

---

[49] [1957] Ch. 169. See, also, *E.R. Ives Investment Ltd v. High* [1967] 2 Q.B. 379.
[50] [1977] Ch. 106 at 289–311, *per* Megarry V.-C.
[51] [1994] 2 W.L.R. 429 at 437.

CHAPTER ELEVEN

Licences and Estoppel

In the previous Chapter, the development of a new proprietary interest, the restrictive covenant, was described. The present Chapter is concerned with an attempt, ultimately unsuccessful, to develop another such right, the contractual licence. It will also consider the closely related doctrine of estoppel.

THE NATURE OF A LICENCE

The classic definition of a licence was given in the seventeenth century by Vaughan C.J. He said in *Thomas* v. *Sorrell*[1] that "A dispensation or licence properly passeth no interest nor alters or transfers property in anything, but only makes an action lawful, which without it had been unlawful."

This statement is not totally accurate but can be taken as a useful starting point in a consideration of the subject of licences. The essential nature of a licence is that it is a personal permission given to a person, the licensee, to do something on another person's, the licensor's, land. Licences fall into four basic categories, all of which must be considered. The two fundamental questions which must be addressed in each case are the effect of the licence between the original parties and the effect, if any, of that licence on successors in title.

1. Gratuitous licences. This type of licence is, as the name makes clear, a licence given without consideration. Examples would include inviting friends around for dinner, or allowing a

---

[1] (1673) Vaugh. 330 at 351.

neighbour's child to come into the garden to collect a football inadvertently kicked over the fence. Because these licences are given without any consideration, it is open to the licensor to revoke them at any time. The only restriction on his ability to do so is the requirement that the licensee is given a reasonable period of time in which to vacate the property. Once that period has elapsed the erstwhile licensee will become a trespasser. Because a licensor can always revoke such a licence, it necessarily follows that a purchaser from him cannot be in any worse position. A gratuitous licence cannot, therefore, bind a purchaser.

2. Licence coupled with a grant. This type of licence is one which is appurtenant to a property right, such as the right to remove game or minerals from another person's land. Such a right will be meaningless unless there is also the right to go on to that land. The licence is inextricably linked with the property right and will, therefore, be irrevocable and bind purchasers to the same extent as the property right in question.

3. Contractual licences. Numerous examples of contractual licences exist. A ticket to the theatre or cinema, or the reservation of a hotel room are instances of contractual licences. In the case of contractual licences, two questions arise. These are the enforceability of the licence as between the contracting parties and the enforceability of the licence against successors in title of the licensor. These issues will be addressed shortly.

4. Licences by estoppel. Estoppel is a flexible equitable doctrine of considerable antiquity. The essence of the doctrine, as it applies to Land Law, is that one person, A, has the expectation that he either has, or will acquire, rights over B's land. He then relies upon that belief in circumstances when it would be unconscionable for B to deny some efficacy to that expectation. The court then has a discretion as to how the equity which has arisen should be satisfied. The issues of how the equity arises, how it is satisfied and the effect of it on third parties will, again, be considered shortly.

CONTRACTUAL LICENCES

The four different types of licence having been sketched, one can now address the characteristics of the two most contentious types of licence, starting with the contractual licence. It is necessary, first, to consider the effect of the licence between the parties themselves and then examine their potential proprietary effect.

1. Revocability of contractual licences. The question as to whether a contractual licence can be revoked has had a somewhat chequered history. The common law position was robust. In *Wood v. Leadbitter*,[2] the plaintiff had bought a ticket to attend Doncaster races but was evicted by the defendant, on the instruction of the stewards, no more force than was reasonably necessary being used to eject him from the ground. His action for trespass and false imprisonment failed, it being held that, because a contractual licence did not create an interest in land, it was always revocable and that, once it had been revoked, the defendant was entitled to use reasonable force to remove a trespasser from his land.

A rather different approach was taken in *Hurst v. Picture Theatres Ltd*,[3] where a person who had bought a theatre ticket was forcibly removed from the hall before the performance had finished. The majority of the Court of Appeal upheld an award of damages for assault. One reason given for the decision that the licence could not be revoked was that this was licence coupled with a grant, the property right in question being the right to watch the performance. This is clearly wrong and has had no lasting impact. The second reason given, however, is the basis of the modern law. *Wood v. Leadbitter* was seen as case decided entirely at common law. As a result of the Judicature Act, the court should now have regard to equity as well as to law. The view was taken that equity would have granted an injunction to restrain the breach of contract. Because the eviction was unlawful, the defendant was not allowed to use force to effect that eviction and damages were, therefore, payable for assault.

As matters developed, the view was taken in *Millenium Productions Ltd v. Winter Garden Theatre (London) Ltd*[4] that whether or not a contractual licence was revocable was a matter of the construction of the contract. Although the actual decision in the case was reversed by the House of Lords, this view received *obiter* approval.[5] Unfortunately, an earlier Court of Appeal decision, where the old common law approach seemed to have re-emerged was not referred to in the judgments. In *Thompson v. Park*,[6] a schoolmaster had a licence to share a school with another teacher, the plaintiff. Upon being evicted the defendant forcibly re-entered the school in circumstances which,

---

[2] (1835) 13 M. & W. 838.
[3] [1915] 1 K.B. 1.
[4] [1946] 1 All E.R. 678 at 685.
[5] *Winter Garden Theatre (London) Ltd v. Millenium Productions Ltd* [1948] A.C. 173 at 202, *per* Lord Uthwatt.
[6] [1944] K.B. 408.

according to Goddard L.J., would have made him "guilty at least of riot, affray, wilful damage, forcible entry and, perhaps, conspiracy."[7] The plaintiff was then granted an injunction requiring the defendant to vacate the school.

In holding for the plaintiff, two reasons were advanced. One was that, given the conduct of the defendant, and the impossibility of ordering two people who were at loggerheads to share the same building, he was not, as a matter of the court's discretion, entitled to equitable relief. This is uncontroversial. Rather more controversial was the reiteration of the common law rule laid down in *Wood v. Leadbitter*, that it was always open to a licensor to terminate a contractual licence.

This conflict of judicial opinion caused difficulty but, in *Hounslow L.B.C. v. Twickenham Garden Developments Ltd*,[8] after an extensive review of the authorities, Megarry J. decided to follow the views expressed in the *Winter Gardens* case and held that, whether or not a contractual licence could be revoked, was a matter of construing the particular contract in question and, as a matter of construction, some contractual licences are irrevocable. This was, in turn, confirmed in *Verrall v. Great Yarmouth B.C.*,[9] where the Court of Appeal upheld the award of specific performance of a contract to use a conference hall. *Thompson v. Park* was held to be bad law. The conclusion is that certain contractual licences can, as between the parties themselves, be irrevocable. This will depend upon each particular contract. So in one case, a contractual licence was held to irrevocable for as long as the licensee continued to pay the licence fee;[10] in another, the licence could be revoked upon the giving of 12 months notice.[11]

2. The effect on third parties. The traditional view of a licence is that it created a personal right in favour of the licensee but that it did not create an interest in land. This view was adopted by the House of Lords in *King v. David Allen & Sons, Billposting Ltd*.[12] King contracted with David Allen that the latter would have the right to fix posters on the wall of King's cinema for a period of four years. King then leased the cinema to a third party and he refused to permit David Allen to fix the posters on the wall. David Allen then sued King for breach of contract. In holding King liable, an essential part of the reasoning was that

---

[7] *ibid.* at p. 409.
[8] [1971] Ch. 233.
[9] [1981] Q.B. 202.
[10] *Hardwick v. Johnson* [1978] 1 W.L.R. 683.
[11] *Chandler v. Kerley* [1978] 1 W.L.R. 693.
[12] [1916] 2 A.C. 54. See, also, *Clore v. Theatrical Properties Ltd* [1936] 3 All E.R. 483.

the tenant was not bound by the licence. If he was bound, David Allen could continue to fix his posters on the wall and King would not have been in breach of contract.

(a) The development of a new interest in land?   Nothwithstanding this decision a different view was expressed in the controversial case of *Errington* v. *Errington*.[13] A father bought a house and gave permission to his son and daughter-in-law to live in it, provided that they paid the mortgage instalments. When they had paid the mortgage in full, he further promised to convey the house to them. The father then died and his widow, who was his entitled to the house under his will, sought to evict the daughter-in-law, her son having left the property. The action failed, the Court of Appeal holding the widow to be bound by the licence.

In reaching this conclusion, Denning L.J. referred to the cases concerning the revocability of licences and observed that, because of the intervention of equity, certain licences could not be revoked. He then went on from this to say:

"[The] infusion of equity means that contractual licences now have a force and validity of their own and cannot be revoked in breach of contract. *Neither the licensor nor anyone who claims through him can disregard the contract except a purchaser for value without notice.*"[14]

In the italicised part of this passage, Denning L.J. makes a leap from holding that, if a contactual licence between A and B is irrevocable, it becomes an equitable interest in land. This is similar in approach to that taken by Lord Cottenham in *Tulk* v. *Moxhay*,[15] when considering the enforceability of covenants, but the main difficulty in the present context was that there was binding authority, not cited in *Errington*, to the opposite effect. A more substantive objection to the decision is that its effect was to create a new interest in land that was not registrable. This prompts the standard conveyancing objection that the creation, or recognition, of a new type of property right undermines the security of conveyancing transactions and necessitates inquiries over and above the normal searches in the appropriate register.

Despite the controversial nature of the reasoning in *Errington*, it was continued in *Binions* v. *Evans*,[16] a case where the merits lay entirely with the licensee but considerable difficulty was

---

[13] [1952] 1 K.B. 290.
[14] *ibid*. at 299, italics supplied.
[15] *Ante*, p. 157.
[16] [1972] Ch. 359.

encountered in reaching a solution in her favour.[17] Mr Evans was a long-standing employee of Tredegar Estate and lived, with his wife, in a cottage owned by the Estate. On his death, the Estate entered into an agreement with Mrs Evans that she could stay in the cottage, rent free, for the rest of her life, in return for keeping it and the garden in good order. Tredegar Estate then sold the cottage to Mr and Mrs Binions. The contract of sale expressly provided that the sale was to be subject to Mrs Evans' right of occupation and the purchase price reflected this agreement. They then sought to evict Mrs Evans from the house.

Megaw and Stephenson L.JJ. held that the agreement between the Estate and Mrs Evans had created a life estate and the land was subject to a settlement within the meaning of section 1 of the Settled Land Act 1925. As Mr and Mrs Binions had notice of this, they were bound by her interest. As Lord Denning M.R., dissenting on this point, pointed out, however, the effect of this finding was that Mrs Evans, as tenant for life, should have the legal estate vested in her and would then acquire the wide range of powers, including the power of sale, conferred by the Act on the tenant for life.[18] This was regarded as an undesirable outcome. Instead, Lord Denning repeated his views first stated in *Errington* to the effect that a contractual licence of this type was an interest in land. As an alternative basis for his decision, he also held that, as Mr and Mrs Binions had bought the cottage expressly subject to Mrs Evans' rights it would be inequitable for them to go back on that agreement and a constructive trust should be imposed to protect Mrs Evans.

Lord Denning's views on contractual licences, while remaining controversial, began to have an impact, being applied in other cases, at times with evident reluctance. Thus in *Re Sharpe*,[19] Browne-Wilkinson J. felt moved to describe the emergent doctrine in unenthusiastic terms. He concluded that the line of cases in the Court of Appeal had established that licences conferred some sort of equity or equitable interest under a constructive trust. He went on to say that

> "I do not think that the principles lying behind these decisions have been fully explored and on occasion it seems that such rights are found to exist simply on the ground that to hold otherwise would be a hardship on the plaintiff."[20]

In similar vein, he concluded by expressing

[17] See R.J. Smith [1973] C.L.J. 123.
[18] *Ante*, pp. 78, 79.
[19] [1980] 1 W.L.R. 219.
[20] *ibid.* at p. 223.

"the hope that in the near future the whole question can receive full consideration in the Court of Appeal, so that, in order to do justice to the many thousands who never come to court at all but who wish to know with certainty what their proprietary rights are, the extent to which these irrevocable licences bind third parties."[21]

(b) The return to orthodoxy. The misgivings expressed by Browne-Wilkinson J. were fully vindicated and the hoped for review of the law occurred in *Ashburn Anstalt v. Arnold.*[22] The review in this case was technically *obiter* but is nevertheless authoritative. Fox L.J., giving the judgment of the Court of Appeal concluded that the statement by Denning L.J. in *Errington* was inconsistent with earlier Court of Appeal decisions and with *King v. David Allen* in the House of Lords. It was held, therefore, that statements that contractual licences amounted to a new equitable interest in land were wrong or, as subsequently described, a heresy.[23]

In reaching this conclusion, the Court of Appeal nevertheless concluded that the actual decision in *Errington* was correct. Various bases were offered for the decision. First, the agreement in question amounted to an estate contract which would have binding upon the mother, who was not a purchase for value. Secondly, it was considered that the licence in question may have been protected by estoppel which, as will be seen, is generally regarded as being binding upon a purchaser. Finally, the view was expressed that, by paying the mortgage instalments, the couple could have acquired a beneficial interest under a trust which would have been binding upon a purchaser.[24]

(c) Constructive trusts. Attention was also given in *Ashburn Anstalt* to the role of the constructive trust in this context. One of the grounds for Lord Denning's decision in *Binions v. Evans* was that, because Mr and Mrs Binions had agreed to take subject to the rights of Mrs Evans, a constructive trust should be imposed upon them to give effect to that undertaken. This was also regarded with a lack of enthusiasm. The Court was anxious that

---

[21] *ibid.* at p. 226.

[22] [1989] Ch. 1. This aspect of the case is unaffected by the subsequent overruling of this decision by the House of Lords in *Prudential Assurance Co. Ltd v. London Residuary Body* [1992] 2 A.C. 386.

[23] *I.D.C. Group Ltd v. Clark* [1992] 1 E.G.L.R. 187 at 189, *per* Browne-Wilkinson V.-C.

[24] [1989] 1 Ch. 1 at 17.

a constructive trust of land should not be too lightly imposed because the effect of so doing would be to upset titles. It was held that a constructive trust should only be imposed when a purchaser expressly undertakes to give effect to a particular interest.[25] It is not sufficient to give rise to a constructive trust that the purchaser merely agrees to take subject to a particular right.

(d) Tort. The impositon of a constructive trust, even in the limited circumstances envisaged in *Ashburn Anstalt*, has been criticised, partly on the basis that it is unclear as to the nature of the beneficial interest which the licensee has under the trust.[26] An alternative approach to this issue is to take up a suggestion of Megaw L.J. in *Binions* v. *Evans* and rely on the tortious doctrine of interference with contractual relations.[27] Under this doctrine, if there is contract between A and B and C, with knowledge of that contract, induces A to break it, C is liable in tort to B. An injunction can be granted to restrain C from doing this. In a case such as *Binions v. Evans*, if Mr and Mrs Binions were allowed to evict Mrs Evans, the result would be to cause Tredegar Estate to be in breach of contract with her. As the couple had actual knowledge of her contractual right to stay in the cottage, there seems to be no reason, in principle, why they should not be restrained by injunction from doing this. This solution would have the merit of avoiding the imposition of an ill-defined constructive trust which may, in the future, adversely affect successors in title to Mr and Mrs Binions, while at the same time meeting the justice of the case. As yet, however, there has been little judicial discussion of the potential use of this tort.

(e) Conclusion. The development of the law of contractual licences represented an, ultimately unsuccessful, attempt to create a new interest in land. This could be seen to have been motivated by two considerations: the desire to reach what was perceived to be a fair result in an individual case and a desire to give effect to informal transactions. The competing interest is the weight given to certainty and security in conveyancing transactions; a concern which appeared to weigh heavily with Browne-Wilkinson J. in *Re Sharpe*. The curtailment of the reasoning which originated in *Errington* does not, however, close the door on similar developments. Many of the cases concerning licences do so in situations of considerable informality where it

---

[25] Applying *Lyus v. Prowsa Developments Ltd* [1982] 1 W.L.R. 1044.
[26] M.P. Thompson [1988] Conv. 201 at 205–206.
[27] [1972] Ch. 359 at 371.

is frequently difficult to establish a contract. Rather greater scope exists for arguing such cases on the basis of estoppel where the courts are considerably less reluctant to recognise that an interest in land has been created.

ESTOPPEL

Equitable estoppel is a doctrine of considerable antiquity and is widely perceived as taking one of two forms. In the general law of contract, it is seen principally as a defensive doctrine, operating to modify the doctrine of consideration to provide partial defences to actions for breach of contract.[28] In the law of contract, this branch of estoppel, known as promissory estoppel, is traditionally viewed as being a shield and not a sword. Although this view has been challenged,[29] this is not of major importance in the context of land law. In land law, the view that equitable estoppel can directly found a cause of action has long been uncontroversial and the doctrine is generally known as proprietary estoppel.

1. The origins of the doctrine. Although cases of proprietary estoppel can be traced back into the seventeenth century,[30] it is preferable to start a discussion of the doctrine with one of the leading nineteenth century cases. In *Plimmer v. The Mayor of Wellington*,[31] the plaintiff's predecessor in title had built a jetty on his land. Later, at the request of the Government, this jetty was, at considerable, expense, extended by building on their land. The land in question then passed to the defendant and the issue was whether the plaintiff had an interest in land sufficient to qualify him for compensation under the relevant statute.

The Privy Council upheld his claim. It was held that the Government had actively encouraged the jetty owner to extend the structure, clearly in the belief that he was acquiring some interest in the property. In the circumstances, it would be quite inequitable for him to be denied some relief in equity. It was held that he was entitled to an indefinite licence to occupy the land which, it was held, was a sufficient interest in the land to entitle the plaintiff to compensation when the land was subsequently acquired.

There are a number of features about this case which deserve emphasis. First, it was a case where the plaintiff had been

---

[28] *Central London Property Trust Ltd v. High Trees House Ltd* [1947] K.B. 130.
[29] M.P. Thompson [1983] C.L.J. 257.
[30] See *Hobbs v. Nelson* (1649) Nels. 47.
[31] (1884) 9 App.Cas. 699.

encouraged to do work on the implicit understanding that he would acquire an interest in the land. In such cases, it is often easier to establish an estoppel than it is in cases where one person is under a mistake as to what the true position is and acts on the faith of that belief. In such circumstances, it can be more difficult to establish that it is inequitable for the other person to deny him some relief. Secondly, it was expressly found that the full nature of the plaintiff's expectation had never been articulated. This was not considered to be a problem and is one factor which distinguishes estoppel from contract. In the case of contract, it is essential that just what it is that the parties have agreed is certain. As was made clear in *Plimmer*, this is not the case in estoppel cases.[32] Thirdly, and linked to the second point, unlike the law of contract, the remedy available to satisfy the equity that has arisen is a matter for the discretion of the court. As Sir Arthur Hobhouse put it in *Plimmer*, "the Court must look at the circumstances of each case to decide in what way the equity must be satisfied."[33]

These three points were made more succinctly by Scarman L.J., in *Crabb v. Arun D.C.*,[34] and are common to all estoppel cases. For him the three questions to be answered in an estoppel case are

"First, is there an equity established? Secondly, what is the extent of the equity if one is established? And, thirdly, what is the relief appropriate to satisfy the equity?"

These questions will be considered in turn.

2. Establishing an equity. At the risk of overgeneralisation, estoppel cases can be divided into two main categories. The first is where one person, A, encourages another person, B, to believe that he either has, or will acquire, rights over A's land. If B then relies on that belief, or expectation, it is inequitable for A to deny B some remedy. A must bear some degree of responsibility for B's act of reliance. The second type of case is more difficult. In this case C believes he has rights over D's land and acts in reliance on that belief. D, however, has not necessarily caused C to make this mistake. The question that then arises is as to the circumstances in which C can obtain a remedy against D.

A good example of the second type of situation is provided by the leading case of *E.R. Ives Investment Ltd v. High*.[35] Mr

---

[32] *ibid.* at p. 713, *per* Sir Arthur Hobhouse.
[33] *ibid.* at p. 714.
[34] [1976] Ch. 179 at 193.
[35] [1967] 2 Q.B. 379.

Westgate and Mr High were neighbours. Mr Westgate con-
structed a block of flats on his land only for it to be discovered
that the foundations encroached onto Mr High's land. The two
of them agreed that, in return for Mr Westgate being allowed to
keep the foundations on Mr High's land, the latter should have
a right of way over Mr Westgate's land. This agreement, which
was a contract to create an easement, should have been registered as a land charge but was not. The effect of this was that,
unbeknown to the parties concerned, when Mr Westgate sold
and conveyed his land to the Wrights, Mr High's right of way
was void against them for non-registration. All concerned were
oblivious to this. Mr High then built a garage in such a way that
the only access to it was over the Wrights' land. The Wrights
were perfectly well aware of this and, indeed, complimented
him on his work. When the yard over which the right of way
was re-surfaced, Mr High contributed to the cost of the work.
The Wrights then conveyed their land to Ives Investment,
expressly subject to Mr High's right of way. Ives Investment
sought to restrain him from exercising the right.

In deciding in favour of Mr High, one of the grounds for the
decision was estoppel. It was held that when building the
garage, Mr High was acting on the expectation that he had a
right of way over the Wrights' land. Although they did not
create that belief, in the circumstances of the case, it would have
been inequitable for them to have denied him some right over
their land. An equity had arisen and this equity was, in turn,
binding upon Ives Investment; the latter point being one which
will be further developed below.

At one time, particularly where the latter type of case was
concerned, it was thought that, to raise an equity, the court must
have regard to the so-called five *probanda*.[36] This is no longer the
case. In *Taylors Fashions Ltd v. Liverpool Victoria Trustees Co. Ltd*,[37]
Oliver J. conducted an extensive review of the authorities and
concluded that the underlying theme of equitable estoppel was
that it was unconscionable for one party to deny the other a
remedy. To establish this degree of unconscionability one must
show that the party claiming the equity has acted on the faith of
an expectation in such circumstances that it would be detrimental to him for that expectation to be left unsatisfied. There must
be a link between the expectation and the reliance, although
there is authority for the view that in cases of actual encouragement, or direct representation, reliance will be assumed unless it
can be proved to the contrary, thereby reversing the normal
burden of proof.[38]

---

[36] *Willmott v. Barber* (1880) 15 Ch.D. 96 at 105, 106.
[37] [1982] Q.B. 133n.
[38] *Greasley v. Cooke* [1982] 1 W.L.R. 1306.

The notion of reliance is central to any right arising due to the operation of estoppel. That reliance must also be to the detriment of the person seeking the right. The idea of detriment is sometimes misunderstood to mean that what the person does in reliance on the expectation is to his disadvantage. This is not so. The element of detriment, or disadvantage, arises when the expectation acted upon is not fulfilled. Thus in *Ives v. High* it was not the building of the garage which was, itself, detrimental; what would have amounted to detriment would have been the denial of the right of way which was the expectation which had been acted upon.

In terms of what constitutes reliance, this will commonly involve expenditure. This is not, however, a pre-requisite. Other conduct can also constitute reliance. In *Maharaj v. Chand*,[39] for example, a woman had been told, in effect, that, if she moved into her partner's house, he would see that she always had a roof over her head. In reliance on that, she gave up secure rented accommodation of her own. This was held to be a sufficient act of reliance to raise an equity in her favour.

Reliance on its own is not sufficient. The other party must, in some way, bear responsibility for that reliance. In situations where a person makes a representation, such as "you can have a right of access",[40] or "the house is your's"[41] finding this responsibility presents no problem. In cases where the parties are both, initially mistaken as to the legal position, the situation is more difficult. The *Taylors Fashions* case is instructive.

Somewhat simplified, the facts were that there were two plaintiffs each having leases of commercial property owned by the defendant. An important factor in both leases was the existence of an option to renew a lease which, unknown for some considerable time to any of the parties involved, was void against the defendant for non-registration. The main issue in the litigation was whether, by operation of estoppel, the respective plaintiffs could, nevertheless, proceed on the basis that the option was binding upon the defendant. The second plaintiff succeeded but the first plaintiff did not. The difference between the cases was that the entire history of the transactions involving the second plaintiff had proceeded upon the basis that the option was valid. The lease with the defendant had been designed to synchronise with the first plaintiff's lease, on the basis that the option was valid. Although the defendant had not encouraged that belief, the parties being mutually mistaken with

[39] [1986] A.C. 898.
[40] See *Crabb v. Arun D.C., supra.*
[41] See *Pascoe v. Turner* [1979] 1 W.L.R. 431.

regard to this, because it had been involved with the acts of reliance, it would be unconscionable, as against that plaintiff to deny the validity of the option. With respect to the first plaintiff, the act of reliance relied upon was the installation of a lift, allegedly in reliance on the expectation that the option was valid. This argument failed on two grounds. First, the installation of the lift was entirely explicable on the basis of the original term agreed and it could not be shown that it was done because of an expectation that the lease was renewable. There was no proof of reliance. Secondly, even if reliance could have been proved, no equity would have arisen against the defendant. As the premises were under the exclusive control of the plaintiff, there was nothing that the defendant could have done to prevent the installation of the lift. The defendant was not involved in any way with the alleged act of reliance. For an estoppel to arise, there must be some responsibility or element of mutuality in the claimant's act of reliance.

2. The extent of the equity.   This second aspect of estoppel, identified by Scarman L.J., means, simply, the extent of the expectation. Where there has been an actual representation, then the extent of any equity is defined by that. In the absence of a representation, where the parties have proceeded on the basis of unarticulated intentions, then the court can only proceed on the basis of what could reasonably be inferred the expectation was.

3. Remedies.   The third element in an estoppel case is to determine how the equity that has arisen should be satisfied. What must be stressed is that the claimant does not have a right to have the expectation fulfilled. As was made clear in *Plimmer's* case, it is for the discretion of the court as to how the discretion is to be exercised.

The most extensive remedy that can be granted is to satisfy the expectation in full. Such a course was adopted in *Pascoe v. Turner*,[42] where a man purported to give a house and its contents to his partner. She relied upon what he had said by spending several hundred pounds on repairs and improvements to the house. He, subsequently sought to evict her. The Court of Appeal ordered him to convey the house to her. This, as was recognised by Cumming-Bruce L.J., was an extreme solution. Relevant factors which were considered were their respective financial positions, he was wealthy and she was not, and any lesser remedy was likely, in the circumstances of the case, likely to lead to him pestering her in the future; something considered to be less likely if a once and for all solution was achieved.

[42] *Supra.* See, also, *Dillwyn v. Llewelyn* (1862) 4 De G.F. & J. 517.

It should not be thought from this case that the court will always satisfy the expectation in full. This was made clear in *Crabb v. Arun D.C.*,[43] where the plaintiff had relied upon a representation by the defendant that he could have a right of way over the defendant's land. Although the Court of Appeal ordered the defendant to grant him an easement, all three members of the court made clear that, had it not been for the obstructive and unco-operative behaviour of the defendant over a prolonged period, any such remedy would only have been granted on terms that the plaintiff paid something for the right.

Because it is a matter for the court's discretion as to how the equity is to be satisfied, cases can serve only as illustrations. There are, nevertheless, certain identifiable factors to which the courts will have regard. One such matter is the respective conduct of the parties. If, as in *Crabb v. Arun D.C.*, it is the person against whom the claim is being made who has behaved badly, then this can increase the relief granted to the claimant. The converse is also true. If the claimant behaves badly this will effect the remedy available and, in extreme cases, can cause a court to refuse to grant any remedy at all.[44]

The element of misconduct aside, a principal concern of the courts is to protect the occupation right of the claimant, most estoppel cases involving occupation rather than claims in the nature of an easement. Various methods have been employed to this end, a common element being that the courts will seek to arrive at a solution that does not result in the licensee becoming a tenant for life under the Settled Land Act 1925. To this end, the conferment of a right to remain in property until money spent on improvements to a house were reimbursed is one option,[45] as is simply dismissing an action for possession.[46] More imaginatively, in *Griffiths v. Williams*[47] the court, in satisfying the equity which had arisen, prevailed upon the parties to agree to the creation of a long lease, which was non-assignable, at a nominal rent, determinable upon death. This solution protected the occupation rights of the claimant without bringing into play the provisions of either the Settled Land Act 1925 or the Rent Acts. As has been justifiedly said, the area of estoppel is one where equity is seen at its most flexible.[48]

---

[43] [1976] Ch. 179.
[44] *J. Willis & Son v. Willis* [1986] 1 E.G.L.R. 62. *Cf. Williams v. Staite* [1979] Ch. 291. See M.P. Thompson [1986] Conv. 406.
[45] *Dodsworth v. Dodsworth* [1973] E.G.D. 233.
[46] *Williams v. Staite, supra.*
[47] [1978] E.G.D. 919.
[48] *Crabb v. Arun D.C., supra*, at p. 189, *per* Lord Denning M.R., citing Snell's *Equity* (27th ed.) p. 568. See now (29th ed.) p. 577.

This flexibility, which is a valuable part of the doctrine in the present context, may be less welcome in other affected areas. Prior to the enactment of the Law of Property (Miscellaneous Provisions) Act 1989, contracts for the sale or dispositions of interests in land were enforceable if either there was an adequate note or memorandum of the contract, or a sufficient act of part performance.[49] In either case, the actual agreement entered into by the parties would be enforced by the courts. The effect of section 2 of the 1989 Act is to abolish the doctrine of part performance. Cases which, before 1989, would have been part performance cases will now become estoppel cases. While the courts may decide to satisfy the equity that has arisen by enforcing the oral agreement between the parties, equally they might not.[50] It can be argued that the introduction of uncertainty into this area is one of the less welcome aspects of the new statutory regime which governs the area of formalities.

ESTOPPEL AND THIRD PARTIES

The final issue to be considered is the effect of estoppel rights upon third parties.[51] It is sensible, in discussing this matter, to distinguish between cases when a court has decided how the equity has arisen and cases where it has not. In the former case, the binding effect of the estoppel right will depend principally upon what order the court has made to satisfy the equity. If it has ordered that a property right be granted to the claimant then, according to general principles, a purchaser will be bound by that right. The position where the nature of the right has not been determined requires a little more discussion.

Until it has been decided what remedy is appropriate to satisfy the estoppel, the claimant has an indeterminate equity. In principle, such an equity is capable of binding a purchaser. Where title is unregistered, this equity is not registrable as a land charge[52] and so its enforceability is dependent on the old doctrine of notice. Where title is registered, there seems to be no reason, in principle, why such a right should not be protected by the registration of a caution although, given that such rights tend to arise very informally, it is unlikely that that course of action will have been adopted. The enforceability of the right will depend, then, upon whether the right takes effect as an overriding interest which it will under section 70(1)(g) of the

---

[49] L.P.A. 1925, s. 40(1)(2).
[50] See *e.g. Morritt v. Wonham* [1993] N.P.C. 2.
[51] See Simon Baughen (1994) 14 L.S. 147.
[52] *E.R. Ives (Investment) Ltd v. High* [1967] 2 Q.B. 379.

Land Registration Act 1925, if the claimant is in actual occupation of the land in question.

There have been a number of cases where the estoppel right has been inforced against successors in title of the person against whom the right originally arose. In all of these cases, the person had either inherited the property, and was not, therefore, a purchaser for value,[53] or was a purchaser for value but had actual notice of the estoppel claim.[54] In all of these cases, there was no indication that the court exercised its discretion in any way differently against the successor in title than it would have done against the person against whom the estoppel had arisen. In cases where the successor in title does not fall into one of those two categories, it is possible that this may be a factor to which the court will have regard in deciding how the equity that has arisen should be satisfied.[55]

It is quite clear that equitable estoppel has grown considerably in importance in recent years. In virtually all cases, the parties involved could, upon receipt of legal advice have ordered their affairs in such a way as to preclude subsequent legal difficulties. For example, in *Ives v. High*, the intentions of the original parties could easily have been effected by the grant of a legal easement, thereby avoiding the problems that were to occur subsequently. The development of estoppel to situations of this nature shows the willingness of the courts to adapt and develop the law to safeguard the interests of those who have proceeded in a highly informal manner and has also shown a willingness to allow purchasers to be affected by such rights. In the not so distant past, the latter development would probably not have occurred because of the great emphasis placed upon the conveyancing interest of certainty of title. The development of estoppel shows a willingness, also evidenced in *Williams & Glyn's Bank Ltd v. Boland*,[56] to protect the rights of people who have acquired rights informally. The decreased emphasis placed on the conveyancing dimension is also evidence of the force of the competing pressure: security of occupation rights.

---

[53] *Inwards v. Baker* [1965] 2 Q.B. 29.
[54] *E.R. Ives Investment Ltd v. High, supra; Williams v. Staite, supra.*
[55] See the observations in *Re Sharpe* [1980] 1 W.L.R. 219 at 226, *per* Browne-Wilkinson J. See, also, M.P. Thompson [1985] C.L.J. 280 at 295–299.
[56] [1981] A.C. 487.

CHAPTER TWELVE

Mortgages

The essence of a mortgage is that a creditor obtains security for a loan. The mortgage confers a proprietary right upon the mortgagee, which can be transferred to third parties. Equally, the mortgage is capable of binding purchasers of the freehold. As a matter of terminology, the person who borrows money and creates the mortgage is termed the mortgagor and the lender, who owns the mortgage, is termed the mortgagee.

Although property other than land is capable of being mortgaged, the main context of mortgages is that of land. In particular, the normal method of financing the purchase of a house is to borrow much of the purchase price, that debt being secured by a mortgage against the house, usually in favour of a building society, and to repay the loan over a prolonged period of time, 25 years being a not uncommon period. The house can, also, be used as security for future borrowing. This can be done by increasing the size of the existing mortgage, or, alternatively, by creating a second mortgage over the property.

Over the course of the past few decades, there has been a considerable expansion in the incidence of home ownership. This has been encouraged by central government, the two most important incentives being the existence of tax relief on the interest element of mortgage repayments[1] and the introduction, by the Housing Act 1980[2] of the right to buy council houses. The outcome of this expansion of home ownership is that over two thirds of the housing stock is now in owner-occupation.[3] The

---

[1] The extent of such relief is being scaled down: see Finance Act 1994, s.81(3), inserting a new s.369 into the Income and Corporation Tax Act 1988.
[2] The provisions are now contained in the Housing Act 1985, Part V.
[3] Social Trends (1994), p. 112.

downside of this, however, is that, in 1993, over 350,000 mortgages were more than six months in arrears and that the 1990s has seen a huge rise in the number of mortgage repossession actions, the peak year being 1991, when there over 142,000 such actions brought.[4]

On any view, therefore, the law relating to mortgages vitally affects millions of people in this country. This Chapter is concerned to analyse the rights and duties of the parties to a mortgage. It is unfortunately the case, however, that despite recommendations for reform,[5] the substantive law remains based upon rules and concepts developed centuries ago, leading to the depressing comment, itself made early this century, that "No one . . . by the light of nature ever understood an English mortgage of real estate."[6] Before seeking to analyse the nature of an English mortgage, it may be helpful to describe, briefly, the two types of mortgage most commonly encountered.

TYPES OF MORTGAGE

1. Repayment mortgages. Under a repayment mortgage, a sum of money is borrowed and it is agreed that it will be paid over a prolonged period, say 25 years. The interest payable on a loan over that period is calculated and a monthly instalment rate is calculated which will be sufficient to pay off interest and capital at the end of the mortgage period. At the outset, the monthly repayments consist almost entirely of interest and the capital indebtedness is only very gradually reduced. As time goes on, the amount of capital repayment gradually increases until, towards the end of the term, the repayments represent almost entirely capital payments. As mortgage tax relief is directed at payments of interest, that relief will progressively decline over the years.

2. The endowment mortgage. The main alternative to the repayment mortgage is the endowment mortgage. Under this scheme, there is no repayment of capital until the end of the mortgage period. The only payments made to the mortgagee are in respect of interest. The mortgagor is, also, required to take out an endowment policy, which is assigned to the mortgagee, and is scheduled to mature at the end of the mortgage period and produce a lump sum sufficient to pay off the capital amount

---

[4] Lord Chancellor's Department, Judicial Statistics (1993) p. 41.
[5] (1991) Law Com. No. 204.
[6] *Samuel v. Jarrah Timber and Wood Paving Corporation Ltd* [1904] A.C. 323 at 326, *per* Lord Macnaghten.

that was borrowed. In some cases, the lump sum produced is designed to exceed the amount which had been borrowed. Such a policy is termed a "with profits" policy.

THE NATURE OF A MORTGAGE

The traditional method of creating mortgage of land was for the mortgagor to convey the land to the mortgagee as security for the loan and a date would be set for repayment. If repayment was made on that date, the property would be reconveyed to the mortgagor. If on that date, however, the mortgagor did not repay the money which he had borrowed, then he lost the right to have the land conveyed back to him. Moreover, he remained liable to repay the debt. This represented an obvious source of injustice and, as was to be expected, equity intervened to temper the harshness of the law.

1. The equitable right to redeem. As part of its aim to modify the common law, equity took the view that, even when the contractual date for redemption of the mortgage had passed, the mortgagee retained good security for his loan. Consequently, it was prepared to allow the mortgagor to repay the debt, and thereby redeem the mortgage, after the contractual date of redemption had passed. This right, which remains relevant today, is termed the equitable right to redeem.

2. The equity of redemption. In addition to the development of the equitable right to redeem the mortgage, equity went further; a consequence of taking a wholly different, and more realistic, view of the nature of a mortgage transaction than did the common law. At law, the owner of the land was the mortgagee. In the eye of equity, however, the mortgagee was merely a secured creditor. Equity took the view that, subject to the mortgagee's rights as a secured creditor, the true owner of the land was the mortgagor. To reflect this view, the sum total of the mortgagor's rights in the property, which consist of the rights of an owner minus the rights of the mortgagee, is termed the equity of redemption. The equity of redemption, which includes the equitable right to redeem, comes into being from the date that the mortgage was created. The equitable right to redeem arises only when the contractual date of redemption has passed.

The equity of redemption or, as it is commonly abbreviated, the equity, is frequently a valuable asset. If, for example, a house worth £70,000 is subject to a mortgage of £40,000, the equity in the house is worth £30,000 and that can be used as security for further borrowing. If, on the other hand, as a result of falling house prices, the house is now worth only £50,000 but the original mortgage was for £60,000, the house is said to have a negative equity of £10,000.[7] The incidence of negative equity has been a considerable social and economic problem which has, in recent times, affected many people.

THE CREATION OF MORTGAGES

Prior to the 1925 legislation, a mortgage was created by conveying the land to the mortgagee. In the light of the approach of equity to mortgages, this practice totally failed to reflect the reality of the transaction. The method of creating legal mortgages was altered in 1925.

1. Legal mortgages. After 1925, it is no longer possible to create a legal mortgage by transferring the relevant estate to the mortgagee. In the case of freehold land, a legal mortgage can be created in only two ways. Under section 85 of the Law of Property Act 1925, a mortgage of an estate in fee simple can only be created by:

(i) a demise for a term of years absolute, subject to a provision for cessor on redemption; and
(ii) a charge by deed expressed to be by way of legal mortgage.

It is further provided by section 85(2) that any purported conveyance of the fee simple by way of mortgage shall operate to create a 3,000 year lease subject to cessor on redemption.

In the case of a mortgage of leasehold property, similar provisions exist so that a mortgage is created either by the creation of a sub-lease, at least one day shorter than the head lease, in favour of the mortgagee, or by a deed expressed to be by way of legal mortgage.[8] Again, any purported assignment of the lease to effect a mortgage will take effect as a sub-lease 10 days shorter that the lease which was purported to be assigned.[9]

(i) Charge by way of legal mortgage. The charge by way of legal mortgage is the form of mortgage most commonly used, a principal reason for this being that it is more readily com-

---

[7] See Dorling, Gentle and Cornford, *Housing Crisis: Disaster or Opportunity* (1992) University of Newcastle upon Tyne, C.U.R.D.S, Discussion Paper No. 96.
[8] L.P.A. 1925, s.86(1).
[9] L.P.A 1925, s.86(2). See *Grangeside Properties Ltd* v. *Collingwood Securities Ltd* [1964] 1 W.L.R. 139.

prehensible to the mortgagor than is the creation of a long lease in favour of the mortgagee. The effect of such a charge is that, in the case of freehold mortgages, the mortgagee is given the same rights and powers as if he had been granted a 3,000 year lease of the property and, in the case of the mortgage of a leasehold estate, a sub-lease one day shorter than the headlease.[10]

The effect of the post-1925 method of creating mortgages has two principal consequences. First, the purchaser retains ownership of a legal estate. A fee simple subject to a 3,000 year lease is, however of little value. As before, the principal rights of the mortgagor rest in his ownership of the equity of redemption. Secondly, the mortgagee is treated, also, as having a legal estate in land. This means that he is a purchaser of a legal estate for money or money's worth with the result that any interests dependent for their protection against purchasers upon registration, will be void as against a mortgagee if not registered.

2. Equitable mortgages.   An equitable mortgage can be created in one of two ways.

(a) Equitable interest.   First, if the mortgagor has only an equitable interest in the property, then he can create only an equitable mortgage. This can be done in the pre-1925 method of assigning the equitable interest to the mortgagee, with provision being made for its reassignment on the repayment of a loan. A deed is not essential to create a mortgage of this type, although, if the mortgagee is to have the power of sale, it is necessary to use a deed.[11] If a deed is not used, the assignment must be in writing signed by the mortgagor, or his authorised agent, who must be appointed in writing or by will.[12]

(b) Deposit of title deeds.   A traditional method of creating an equitable mortgage was, for the purpose of securing a loan, to deposit the title deeds with the creditor. This was seen as a contract to create a mortgage and the deposit of title deeds was then viewed as an act of part performance by both sides. As there existed a specifically enforceable contract to create a mortgage, equity, as ever, viewing as done that which ought to be done, regarded the transaction as an equitable mortgage. This method of creating a mortgage has been recognised for centuries.[13]

---

[10] L.P.A. 1925, s.87.
[11] *Post*, p. 205.
[12] L.P.A. 1925, s.53(1)(c).
[13] See *Russel v. Russel* (1793) 1 Bro.C.C. 269.

Owing to the enactment of section 2 of the Law of Property (Miscellaneous Provisions) Act 1989, however, it seems that an equitable mortgage cannot any longer be created in this way. Unless there is writing signed by both parties, there is no contract to create a mortgage and there cannot be part performance of a non-existent contract. The theoretical basis of the equitable mortgage by deposit of title deeds has been removed. Although it was thought that this method of creating a mortgage may have survived the passing of the Act, being regarded as *sui generis*, it was confirmed in *United Bank of Kuwait Plc v. Sahib*,[14] that this was not the case. It remains arguable, however, that, in circumstances where an equitable mortgage may have been created in the past, similar rights will be held to have arisen through estoppel.

3. Registered land. A mortgage of registered land is effected by a registered charge. Such a charge does not create a legal mortgage until it is registered.[15] Until so registered, the mortgage is effective only in equity and can be overridden as a minor interest.[16] Upon registration of a legal charge in the charges register, the mortgagee is issued with a charge certificate and the mortgagor's land certificate is lodged at the Land Registry.

RIGHTS OF THE MORTGAGOR

This section is concerned with the respective rights and obligations of the parties to a mortgage. It does not purport to be exhaustive; instead, the issues of most practical relevance will be addressed, considering, first, the rights of the mortgagor.

1. No clogs on the equity of redemption. The equity of redemption was a concept developed both to have regard to the true nature of a mortgage transaction and also to protect the mortgagor against the oppression allowed by the common law. Consistent with this second motivation, equity was jealous to see that the mortgagor's rights were not whittled down by terms inserted in the mortgage agreement. To this end, the doctrine developed that there should be no clogs or fetters on the equity of redemption.

In approaching this area, it is well to point out that some of the cases are difficult to reconcile with each other. This stems

---

[14] [1994] *The Times*, July 7. See M.P. Thompson [1994] Conv. 465.
[15] *Grace Rymer Investments Ltd v. Waite* [1958] Ch. 831.
[16] L.R.A. 1925, s.106, as substituted by Administration of Justice Act 1977, s.26.

from there being two competing pressures at work, each of which being afforded different importance at different times in history. These pressures are the protection of the mortgagor, on the one hand, and the doctrine of freedom of contract on the other. In modern times, as will be seen, it is the second of these two pressures that has been given priority.

(i) Restriction on right to redeem. Clogs can be broadly divided into three types of case. The first relates to restrictions on the mortgagor's right to redeem the mortgage. An early example is provided by *Howard v. Harris*.[17] In this case, the mortgage agreement provided that the mortgage could be redeemed only by the mortgagor or his heirs male. As the effect of this clause was to prevent the mortgagor from assigning his interest in land, this was an unacceptable restriction on the right to redeem and was struck out as being a clog on the equity of redemption.

A more modern example is provided by *Fairclough v. Swan Brewery Co. Ltd.*[18] The property that was mortgaged was a 20 year lease. It was a term of the mortgage that redemption could not occur until there would only be six weeks left on the lease. Despite this clause, the mortgagor was permitted to redeem at an earlier date. It was said that

> "equity will not permit any device or contrivance being part of the mortgage transaction or contemporaneous with it to prevent or impede redemption . . . . [A] mortgage cannot be made irredeemable."[19]

This case does not decide that a long postponement of the right to redeem will always be regarded as a clog and, therefore, void. In *Knightsbridge Estates Trust Ltd v. Byrne*,[20] a company had created a mortgage over freehold property, it having been agreed that repayment of the loan would be by 80, six-monthly instalments. In other words, there could be no redemption of the mortgage for 40 years. This was upheld, the court being unwilling to upset a freely entered commercial contract. What distinguished the case from *Fairclough* was that the right to redeem had not been rendered illusory. The property was freeehold and not leasehold. Secondly, the term was not unconscionable. The case represents, also, the emerging trend of attaching greater importance to freedom of contract than to the protection of the mortgagor.

---

[17] (1681) 1 Vern. 33.
[18] [1912] A.C. 565.
[19] *ibid*, at p. 570, *per* Lord Macnaghten. See, also, *Re Wells* [1933] Ch. 29 at 52.
[20] [1939] Ch. 441, affirmed, on other grounds, [1940] A.C. 613.

(ii) Options to purchase. A second type of clog on the equity of redemption is the grant to the mortgagee of an option to purchase the mortgaged property. Such a clause was struck out, albeit with a distinct lack of enthusiasm, in *Samuel v. Jarrah Timber and Wood Paving Corporation Ltd,*[21] where a mortgage of stock also gave the mortgagee an option to purchase that stock within a period of 12 months from the date of the mortgage. Because this term was in the mortgage, it was held to be a clog, even though there was nothing oppressive about it. Nevertheless, it was, according to the Earl of Halsbury, "contrary to a principle of equity the sense or reason of which I am unable to appreciate."[22]

For such an option to be struck out as a clog, it is vital that it is granted by the mortgage agreement itself. If it is given in a separate transaction, even if a mere 12 days from the date of the mortgage, then the option will be upheld.[23] The rule that it will be struck out if it is contained in a mortgage is, however, firmly established with the result that perfectly fair, and freely entered into, bargains may be upset because of a rule of equity,[24] developed in very different times, when mortgagors needed that protection to protect them from oppression.

(iii) Collateral advantages. Typically, a mortgagee will seek more than mere security in return for the loan. In modern times this relates primarily to the charging of interest. In the developing law of mortgages, however, it was by no means uncommon for other advantages to be secured by the mortgagee. This was particularly so if the mortgagee was a brewery who would seek to tie the mortgagor to buying its product, a clause known as a *solus* agreement. Latterly, similar issues have arisen with regard to petrol companies. It is in the sphere of collateral advantages that the attitude of the courts has changed the most.

The traditional approach was to differentiate between advantages which would last only until the mortgage was redeemed and those which were sought to be extended over a more prolonged period. In *Noakes v. Rice,*[25] the mortgagor of a public house agreed with the mortgagor that he would buy the latter's beer for the duration of his lease. This was struck out. The effect of the clause was that what was a free house prior to the mortgage would, on redemption of the mortgage, be a tied house. This was a clog on the equity of redemption. In contrast,

---

[21] [1904] A.C. 323.
[22] *ibid.* at p. 325.
[23] *Reeve v. Lisle* [1902] A.C. 461.
[24] See *Lewis v. Frank Love Ltd* [1961] 1 W.L.R. 261.
[25] [1902] A.C. 24.

in *Biggs v. Hoddinott*,[26] the mortgagor was precluded from redeeming the mortgage for a five year period and had to buy the mortgagee's products during that period. It having been held that the period of postponement of the right to redeem was valid, the tie limited to that period was also valid.

This essential distinction was upheld by a bare majority of the House of Lords in *Bradley v. Carritt*,[27] where after redemption of a mortgage of shares, a clause requiring the mortgagor to employ the mortgagee as a broker was struck down as being a clog on the equity of redemption. A major turning point in the development of this branch of the law occurred in *Kreglinger v. New Patagonia Meat & Cold Storage Co. Ltd*.[28] The case involved a mortgage entered into by a wool company, one of the terms of which was that the mortgagee should have, for a period of five years, a right of pre-emption in respect of sheepskins. Because the mortgage could be redeemed before the five years had passed, the right could continue after redemption. It was nevertheless upheld.

Although it is possible to distinguish *Kreglinger* from *Bradley v. Carritt*, it is quite evident from the speeches in *Kreglinger* that the House of Lords were keen to limit the role of the doctrine of clogs and fetters. Thus, Lord Mersey was moved to liken the doctrine to "an unruly dog which, if not securely chained to its own kennel is prone to wander into places where it ought not to be."[29] The case involved an entirely normal commercial contract which the House of Lords were anxious to uphold. To that end, it was held that there was now no rule in equity that the mortgagee cannot stipulate in the mortgage deed for a collateral advantage which will continue beyond redemption. Such a clause will only be struck out if it is unfair and unreasonable; it operates in the nature of a penalty clogging the equity of redemption; or it is inconsistent with or repugnant to the contractual or the equitable right to redeem.

Subsequently the courts have, in considering clauses in mortgages, emphasised the need for the mortgagor to show that a particular clause is unconscionable before it will be struck out as being a clog. This was successfully done in *Cityland and Property (Holdings) Ltd v. Dabrah*,[30] where, at a time when the base lending rate was 7 per cent p.a., the interest rate in this mortgage was 19 per cent p.a. If there was default, the effective

[26] [1898] 2 Ch. 307.
[27] [1903] A.C. 307.
[28] [1914] A.C. 25. The speech of Lord Parker contains a valuable review of this area of the law.
[29] *ibid.* at p. 46.
[30] [1968] Ch. 166.

rate of interest would have been 57 per cent. This was regarded as a penal rate of interest and an annual rate of interest of 7 per cent was substituted for the agreed rate.

For a mortgagor successfully to challenge a clause in a mortgage, it is not enough to show that it is unreasonable. It must be unconscionable. This was stressed in *Multiservice Book-binding Ltd v. Marden*,[31] where a clause in a commercial mortgage linking repayment over a 10 year period to the value of the Swiss franc was upheld, despite the effect of the depreciation on the value of sterling having the effect that this had caused the level of indebtedness to rise substantially. The mortgagee had driven a hard bargain but not an unconscionable one.

(iv) The Consumer Credit Act 1974. The issue of unconscionable mortgage terms is now less likely to be considered as part of an equitable jurisdiction but to be decided under the terms of the Consumer Credit Act 1974. Under the provisions of the Act, mortgages for less than £15,000, unless within the class of exempt agreements, are governed by regulatory provisions concerning the mortgagor's right to redeem and requiring him to be informed of his rights under the Act.

The court is empowered under sections 137-140 of the Act to re-open extortionate credit arrangements. This applies only to mortgages by individuals and applies to all such mortgages.

(v) Restraint of trade. The issue of *solus* agreements contained in mortgages was considered by the House of Lords in *Esso Petroleum Ltd v. Harper's Garage (Stourport) Ltd*.[32] Two mortgages were involved. In the case of one, the mortgagor had entered a *solus* agreement for five years; in the case of the other the period was 21 years. The first tie was upheld but not the second. This was decided on the basis of the common law doctrine of restraint of trade and not on the basis of clogs and fetters. As Diplock L.J. put it, in the Court of Appeal,

> "I am not persuaded that mortgages of land are condemned today to linger in a jurisprudential cul-de-sac built by the Courts of Chancery before the Judicature Acts from which the robust doctrines of the common law are excluded."[33]

The use of the doctrine of restraint of trade does seem a better way of resolving such disputes than the somewhat anachronistic doctrine of clogs and fetters which, in truth, seems to have

[31] [1974] Ch. 84.
[32] [1968] A.C. 269.
[33] [1966] 2 Q.B. 514 at 577, 578.

outlived its usefulness and is now more likely to upset a reasonable commercial contract than to prevent oppression.

2. Power to lease. A mortgagor is empowered by section 99 of the Law of Property Act 1925 to grant certain leases, which will be binding upon the mortgagee. This is subject, however, to this right not having been excluded in the mortgage. In practice, it is the normal practice for the mortgagee to exclude the power of leasing. The effect of a lease created, notwithstanding the exclusion of the power to do so, will be considered below.

3. Redemption. Ordinarily, it is the mortgagor who will redeem the mortgage. If that is not the case, then the effect of redemption will be to transfer the mortgage to the person who has redeemed it.[34]

The mortgagor has the unfettered right to redeem on the contractual date of redemption and need not give notice of his intention to do so. If, as is commonly the case, the mortgagor wishes to redeem the mortgage after the contractual date of redemption, that is, he is relying on the equitable right to redeem, then, unless the mortgage deed contains a provision to the contrary, he must give the mortgagee notice of his intention to redeem, a period of six months, or payment of six months' interest in lieu, being regarded as sufficient. Where the equitable right to redeem is being relied upon the doctrine of consolidation may apply. The effect of this complex doctrine being that the mortgagor may be prevented from redeeming a particular mortgage unless he also redeems other mortgages in favour of the mortgagee.[35]

RIGHTS OF THE MORTGAGEE

Having considered the main rights of the mortgagor, attention can be turned to the rights of the mortgagee. There are a number of rights that the mortgagee has. It is not proposed to discuss all of these rights; instead, attention will be confined to the principal rights and remedies which are relevant to the enforcement of the mortgagee's security.

POSSESSION

The most effective method for the mortgagee to enforce his security is either to sell the mortgaged property or to foreclose

---

[34] L.P.A. 1925, s.115(2).
[35] See Megarry, *Manual of the Law of Real Property* (7th ed.), pp. 460–463.

on the mortgage. The former means of enforcement is of
overwhelmingly greater significance than the latter. In order to
sell the property, it is usually essential for the mortgagee first to
obtain possession; it is very unlikely that a purchaser will be
found, if the mortgagee has not first acquired possession. The
possession action is, therefore, very often associated with the
sale of the property.

In considering the possession action, various matters arise.
The first concerns the respective rights of the mortgagor and the
mortgagee. The second concerns the rights of third parties, who
may assert that they have rights binding upon the mortgagee,
the effect of which being that the mortgagee is not entitled, as
against them, to possession of the property. Related to this
second general issue is the methods by which the mortgagee can
ensure that he is not bound by such rights; a problematic area
which involves the law relating to undue influence.

1. The right to possession. It is historically inaccurate to
regard the taking of possession by a mortgagee as being a
remedy. It is the exercise of a right. The basis of this right is that
the fee simple was conveyed to the mortgagee who, accordingly,
had the right to possession. It remains true, today, that the
mortgagee is entitled to possession. This was put in charac-
teristically pungent terms by Harman J., who said:

> "the right of a mortgagee to possession in the absence of
> some contract has nothing to do with default on the part of
> the mortgagor. The mortgagee may go into possession before
> the ink is dry on the mortgage unless there is something in
> the mortgage, express or implied, whereby he has contracted
> himself out of that right."[36]

Of course, in most cases, the mortgagee will not want to
exercise this right. If the mortgagor was in default, however, or
if, for some other reason, the mortgagee wished to take possession, the mortgagor had no defence. To provide a mortgagor of
residential property at least a degree of protection the mortgagee's rights have been curtailed by statute.

(i) Administration of Justice Acts. Under section 36 of the
Administration of Justice Act 1970, when a mortgagee under a
mortgage of land, which consists of or includes a dwelling-
house, brings an action in which he claims possession of the
mortgaged property, the court is empowered to adjourn the

---

[36] *Four Maids Ltd v. Dudley Marshall Ltd* [1957] Ch. 317 at 320.

proceedings; stay or suspend execution of the judgment or order; or postpone the date for delivery of possession for such period or periods as it thinks reasonable. The court may exercise these powers if it appears that the mortgagor is likely to be able within a reasonable period to pay any sums due under the mortgage or remedy any default consisting of a breach of any other obligation arising under or by virtue of the mortgage.

While the aim of this section seemed to be tolerably clear — to provide a temporary respite for a mortgagor who had fallen into arrears under the mortgage — the drafting of the section led to difficulties. The first problem was relatively minor; whether a court could grant relief to a mortgagor who was not in default. Taking the view that it would be absurd that a mortgagor, who was in default under the mortgage, should be in a better position than one who was not, the Court of Appeal held, by a majority, in *Western Bank Ltd v. Schindler,*[37] that it did have jurisdiction in these circumstances. The problem which emerged in *Halifax B.S. v. Clarke,*[38] however, was very much more serious.

In this case, there was a provision in the mortgage, termed a default clause, whereby, if the mortgagor defaulted on two monthly mortgage instalments, the whole amount that had been borrowed became repayable from that time. The reason for such a clause was simply to ensure that the statutory power of sale arose[39]; it was not actually envisaged that the whole sum borrowed would be paid there and then, thereby redeeming the mortgage. The effect of the clause was that, although the arrears amounted only to £72.97, the amount owing under the mortgage was £1,420.58. The key question that arose was to decide which was the relevant sum for the purposes of section 36 of the Act. It was held that the latter sum was the one to which regard should be had and, as there was no prospect of that sum being repaid within a reasonable period, the court had no power under the Act to postpone possession proceedings.

This unfortunate decision meant that for a significant number of mortgagors, the Act provided no protection. To rectify this situation, section 8 of the Administration of Justice Act 1973 was enacted with a view to reversing the effect of the decision in *Clarke.* Unfortunately this section was, also, badly drafted leading to further problems which, happily have now been resolved. Section 8 has to be read together with section 36. It provides that:

> where the mortgagor is entitled to pay the principal sum
> secured by instalments or otherwise to defer payment of it in

[37] [1977] Ch. 1.
[38] [1973] Ch. 307.
[39] See *post*, p. 206.

whole or in part, but provision is made for earlier payment in the event of default by the mortgagor or of a demand by the mortgagee or otherwise, then, for the purposes of section 36 of the Administration Act 1970 . . . a court may treat as due under the mortgage on account of the principal sum due under the mortgage on account of the principal sum secured and of interest on it only such sums as the mortgagor would have been expected to pay if there had been no such provision for earlier payment.

While the general intention of the section is, again, clear — default clauses are to be ignored and regard had simply to the arrears which have accumulated — its construction has proved to be difficult; the main difficulty being to determine what, if anything, is meant by the expression "is to be permitted to defer payment".[40]

In *Habib Bank Ltd v. Tailor*,[41] Mr Tailor had a bank overdraft secured by a mortgage on his house. It was a term of the loan that it would be repaid upon demand. When Mr Tailor exceeded his agreed overdraft limit, the bank called in the loan and sought possession under the mortgage. Mr Tailor argued that the loan was for an indefinite period and the effect of its being called in was such that the case came within section 8 of the 1973 Act. The court should, it was further argued, exercise its discretion on the basis that he should be allowed a reasonable period to pay off the sum by which his present indebtedness exceed the agreed overdraft limit. This was rejected and section 8 held was held to be inapplicable to the present situation. The phrase "is to be permitted . . . otherwise to defer payment" must refer to a date from which payment was to be deferred. This could mean either from the date of the mortgage or, alternatively, the date when the money became payable. The former construction was considered to be untenable and so the second date was accepted as being the relevant time for the purpose of the Act. As there was no provision to defer payment from the date of the demand for payment, which was what the mortgage envisaged, section 8 did not apply and so the issue was whether Mr Tailor could repay the whole overdraft within a reasonable time. As he could not, possession was ordered.

The potential difficulty with this decision is that its effect might have been to exclude endowment mortgages from the protection given by section 8.[42] This is because the capital sum is

[40] For an excellent discussion, see Stephen Tromans [1984] Ch. 91.
[41] [1982] 1 W.L.R. 1218.
[42] See Tromans *op. cit.*

repayable at the end of the agreed mortgage period; there is no provision for the deferment of payment after that date. If the money becomes payable before that date because of some default in payments, then section 8 would not seem to apply. This potential difficulty was sidestepped in *Bank of Scotland v. Grimes*,[43] a case concerning an endowment mortgage over a period of 25 years, where the mortgagor had defaulted on payments with the result that the whole sum borrowed became repayable. The Court of Appeal felt unable to give any meaning to the phrase "permitted to defer payment". The view was taken that, as a matter of commonsense, a mortgage where payment is not expected for 25 years is one where the mortgagor is permitted to defer payment. *Tailor* was distinguished as being a case where, given the nature of the transaction, repayment upon demand was genuinely envisaged, whereas, in the instant case, it was not. The upshot is that, except in cases where the sum borrowed is expected to be repaid upon demand, by a process of benevolent construction, the provisions of the two Acts will apply to all types of mortgage commonly used to finance the purchase of a house.

(ii) Spouses.　Under section 1(5) of the Matrimonial Homes Act 1983, the mortgagor's spouse is entitled to make the mortgage payments. The spouse may also take advantage of the provisions of the Administration of Justice Acts. To do so, the spouse will need to be made a party to the possession proceedings. Such an application may be made when notice is served of the initiation of possession proceedings. The difficulty facing the spouse in this regard is that notice of such proceedings need only be served if the rights conferred by the Act have been protected in the appropriate manner by registration.[44] It may well be the case that this will not have been done in that, unless the spouse is in receipt of legal advice, perhaps because there is a matrimonial dispute between the couple, the spouse is unlikely to know about the registration provisions.

(iii) Exercise of discretion.　In deciding whether or not to postpone the granting of possession, clearly, much will depend upon the facts of each case. Some general principles have, however, emerged. First, there should be no open-ended postponement of a possession order. A finite period must be stipulated by the end of which the arrears should be paid off, together with the payments normally expected.[45] Secondly, the

---

[43] [1985] Q.B. 1179.
[44] Matrimonial Homes Act 1983, s.8(2)(3).
[45] *Royal Trust Co. of Canada v. Markham* [1975] 1 W.L.R. 1416.

expectation of being able to pay off the instalments must be realistic and not based upon the hope of a legacy[46] or of being able to secure highly paid employment.[47] In keeping with that approach, the Court of Appeal has laid down that, in the exercise of discretion, it is improper either to make an order which would clear the arrears and meet the ongoing liability under the mortgage, if the mortgagor's resources would not enable him to meet the terms of the order or, conversely, to make an order which he can afford but which will not be sufficient to pay off the arrears within the stipulated time period.[48] In making a judgment about the ability of the mortgagor to meet the terms of the order, regard will not be had to the existence of any counterclaim against the mortgagee, the two actions being seen as independent.[49] Finally, the court may be willing to give the mortgagor a short postponement of a possession order to enable him to seek to sell the property, the reason for this being that it is often easier to sell a house when it is still occupied by the vendor.[50]

THIRD PARTY RIGHTS

In order for the mortgagee to be able to get possession of the mortgaged property, it is essential that his right to possession has priority over the rights of other people in the property. This will involve considering the position of tenants and of co-owners.

1. Tenants. As a matter of general principle, any tenancy granted before the mortgage will be binding on the mortgagee, either, when title is unregistered because it is a legal interest in land, or, if title is registered, because it takes effect as an overriding interest. When the lease is created after the mortgage, various possibilities arise.

Under section 99 of the Law of Property Act 1925, the mortgagor is empowered to grant certain types of lease. This is subject to the power of leasing not being excluded in the mortgage. If the power to grant leases has not been excluded, then any tenancies created by the mortgagor will be binding upon the mortgagee, who will, therefore, as against the tenant, be unable to obtain possession of the property.

---

[46] *Hastings & Thanet B.S. v. Goddard* [1970] 1 W.L.R. 1544 at 1548 *per* Russell L.J.
[47] *Town & Country B.S. v. Julien* (1991) 24 H.L.R. 261. But contrast *Cheltenham & Gloucester B.S. v. Grant* [1994] *The Times*, May 9.
[48] *First National Bank Plc v. Syed* [1991] 2 All E.R. 250.
[49] *Citybank Trust Ltd v. Ayivor* [1987] 1 W.L.R. 1157; *National Westminster Bank Plc v. Skelton* [1993] 1 W.L.R. 72n.
[50] *Target Home Loans Ltd v. Clothier* (1992) 25 H.L.R. 48.

If, as is usually the case, the mortgage excludes the mortgagor's power to create a tenancy then, in the event of the
mortgagor creating a lease, that lease will be perfectly valid as
between the mortgagor and the tenant but will be void as
against the mortgagee, who will be able to get possession[51]; a
situation which can be very hard on the tenant who may well
have no prior notice of the weakness of his position. This is
subject to two qualifications. First, the action for possession
must be genuine and not a collusive action between the mortgagor and mortgagee to effect a Rent Act avoidance scheme.[52]
Secondly, and more importantly, the mortgagee must not adopt
the tenancy. If the mortgagee recognises the validity of the lease,
for example by accepting rent from the tenants, this will cause a
new relationship of landlord and tenant to arise between the
mortgagee and the tenant with the result that the mortgagee will
be unable to recover possession.[53]

2. Co-owners. In recent years, the question of the enforceability of co-ownership rights against mortgagees has been a
central issue in much litigation. This has involved, principally,
the situation where the legal title is vested in one person but
there is co-ownership in equity. The issue which then arises is as
to the enforceability of that equitable right against a mortgagee,
the mortgage having been created by the legal owner. A second
problem occurs when the house is in the joint names of two
people and a mortgage is created for the benefit of one of the co-
owners, the other co-owner having been persuaded to sign the
mortgage deed. In those circumstances, it is possible to argue
that the signature is invalid with the result that the mortgage is
void as against the co-owner.

(1) Enforcing equitable rights. The starting point is the decision
of the House of Lords in *Williams & Glyn's Bank Ltd v. Boland.*[54]
Mr Boland was the sole registered proprietor of a matrimonial
home which he shared with his wife who, it was conceded, was
a beneficial co-owner of it. Without consulting her, and to secure
his overdraft, he mortgaged the house to the bank. The bank
addressed no enquiries to Mrs Boland. When he defaulted on
the mortgage and the bank sought possession, this was
defended by Mrs Boland on the basis that her rights as a
beneficial co-owner were binding upon the bank. This claim was

---

[51] *Britannia B.S. v. Earl* [1990] 1 W.L.R. 427.
[52] *Quennell v. Maltby* [1979] 1 W.L.R. 318.
[53] See *Stroud B.S. v. Delamont* [1960] 1 W.L.R. 431.
[54] [1981] A.C. 487.

upheld in the House of Lords, it being held that her rights as a beneficial co-owner, coupled with her actual occupation of the land, resulted in her having an overriding interest binding upon the bank.

Although the decision turned on the construction of section 70(1)(g) of the Land Registration Act 1925 and, in particular, the meaning of the phrase actual occupation, in most cases the result would be the same where title is unregistered. In the case of unregistered land, the issue as to whether a mortgagee is bound by interests of the type seen in *Boland* is determined by whether or not the mortgagee had notice of the right; the issue is whether it should have been discovered by making reasonable inquiries. In most cases, the questions of whether the person was in actual occupation and whether the right should have been discovered by making reasonable enquiries will yield the same answer.[55]

The decision in *Boland* was highly controversial. From a conveyancing perspective, the decision was unwelcome, the reason for this being that it meant that purchasers had to make more extensive enquiries relating to the rights of occupiers than had previously been thought to have been necessary. Building societies, in particular, were extremely concerned, their nightmare scenario being a situation where a single person approached them for a mortgage but, unbeknown to them, another person was also going to move into the house having contributed to the initial payment, thereby acquiring an interest in it. That interest, it was feared, would then be binding upon the society who, in consequence, would not, in the event of mortgage default, be able to realise its security.

As will be seen, these fears were exaggerated but, in the aftermath of the case, itself, were keenly felt. The matter was referred to the Law Commission, who recommended that rights such as those possessed by Mrs Boland should only be enforceable against a purchaser if they had been protected by registration.[56] Although draft legislation was introduced which sought, in part, to implement this proposal,[57] it did not reach the statute book.

One argument that can adduced against any such legislation is that, by making such rights registrable, in practice, it would mean that a mortgagee would take free from such rights because the co-owner is likely to be unaware of the registration requirement. The problem pertaining to this area is how to

---

[55] See *ante*, p. 56.
[56] (1982) Law Com. No. 115.
[57] Land Registration and Law of Property Bill 1985.

resolve the competing pressures of facilitating conveyancing, on the one hand, and protecting occupation rights, on the other. The task of establishing where a compromise between these two competing tensions has been left to the courts.

3. Limiting *Boland*.   The worries generated by the decision in *Boland* have, to a considerable extent, been assuaged by subsequent case law.

(1) Two legal owners.   A key feature of *Boland* was that the ownership of the legal estate was vested in only one person. An issue to be decided was whether the result would have been different has there been two owners of the legal estate. This was raised in *City of London B.S. v. Flegg.*[58] A property, Bleak House, was transferred to a Mr and Mrs Maxwell-Brown who were the daughter and son-in-law of the Fleggs. The Fleggs were beneficial co-owners of the house. The legal position, therefore, was that the registered proprietors, the Maxwell-Browns, held the property upon trust for sale for themselves and the Fleggs. Without consulting their parents, the Maxwell-Browns mortgaged the house on a number of occasions until, finally, they created one mortgage in favour of the plaintiffs, the money being used to redeem the other mortgages. Following default in payment, the plaintiffs sought possession. The Fleggs argued, unsuccessfully, that they had an overriding interest in the house.

Their argument that, as beneficial co-owners who were in actual occupation of the property, they had an overriding interest was rejected by the House of Lords. The reason was that because there were two trustees for sale, the interests of people with an interest behind that trust were overreached by the mortgage; their interest took effect only against the equity of redemption.

This reasoning is entirely orthodox and is consistent with the theory of the trust for sale; provided that the purchase money is paid to at least two trustees for sale, it does not matter, from the point of view of the purchaser, if there are two or 22 co-owners in equity. Their interests will be overreached.[59] Although this point is, from a theoretical view, entirely sound, one suspects that it might have rather been lost on the Fleggs, however, who might not fully appreciate that they should lose their home, unlike Mrs Boland, because of the slightly different position with regard to the legal ownership. This was one consideration

---

[58] [1988] A.C. 54.
[59] See, *ante*, pp. 89–91.

which led a differently constituted Law Commission, in marked contradistinction to the earlier reaction to *Boland*, to recommend the statutory reversal of *Flegg*[60]; a proposal which, it is suggested, is more compelling in the light of the other, more significant limitation on *Boland*.

(2) Second mortgages. It will be recalled that one of the great fears on the part of building societies, in their reaction to *Boland*, was that they would lend money to finance the purchase of a house and then find themselves unable, later, to enforce their security due to the existence of an overriding interest. It has now become apparent that this fear was misplaced.

In *Bristol & West B.S. v. Henning*,[61] a couple were buying a house together. A relatively small amount of the purchase price was provided by Mr Henning, into whose name the house was conveyed, and the remainder provided, by way of mortgage, by the plaintiffs. It was assumed that Mrs Henning was an equitable co-owner of the house. She knew that the house purchase was being financed through a loan from the plaintiffs but she was not asked by them what, if any, interest she had in the house. When he defaulted on the mortgage, the plaintiffs sought possession and this action was resisted by Mrs Henning. Possession was granted. It was held by the Court of Appeal that, because she knew that the property was being mortgaged, and also knew that the house could not have been purchased without this mortgage, that the intention should be imputed to her that the interest of the building society should have priority to her's.

Although the reasoning in this case has been criticised and, its extension in a later case has produced an, arguably, questionable result,[62] on the facts, the result arrived at appears to be sensible. When a person knows that a house cannot be bought without a mortgage, there seems little to be said for allowing that person to assert prior rights against the mortgagee; particularly when that person has benefited from the mortgage by being able to live in the house which, otherwise could not have been bought.

The practical impact of the decision in *Henning* is considerable. There can be very few situations where a person who is buying a house with a partner, and who will become a co-owner of it, will be unaware that the house is not being bought

---

[60] (1989) Law Com. No. 188. See, especially, paras. 3.4–3.9.

[61] [1985] 1 W.L.R. 778. See, also, *Paddington B.S. v. Mendelsohn* (1985) 50 P. & C.R. 244.

[62] *Equity & Law Home Loans Ltd v. Prestidge* [1992] 1 W.L.R. 137. See M.P. Thompson [1992] Conv. 206.

outright, so that a mortgage is necessary to provide the requisite finance.[63] Even in such a situation, it is unlikely that the person will be in possession of the property prior to the mortgage taking effect.[64] Accordingly, *Boland* is not likely to affect mortgagees in situations where the mortgage is being used to finance the purchase of the home. It will be relevant where the house is being used as collateral for further loans. In such circumstances, there is much to be said for insisting that all other occupiers should be consulted before their home is put at risk by such borrowing. It is this consideration which, it is suggested, adds weight to the proposal of the Law Commission that the decision in *Flegg* should be reversed by legislation.

4. Undue influence. Related problems to those just discussed can arise even when the house is in joint names, legally, and one of the co-owners wishes to mortgage the property for purposes of their own. In such cases, both legal owners must, of necessity, be parties to the mortgage. The potential difficulty for mortgagees is to ensure that the mortgage will be binding upon both parties, that is that they are not affected by any vitiating factor connected with the transaction.

The leading authorities are *Barclays Bank Plc v. O'Brien* and *CIBC Mortgages Plc v. Pitt*.[65] In *O'Brien*, a matrimonial home was in the joint names of husband and wife. He was closely associated with a company and acted as guarantor to the bank of its overdraft. When the overdraft had reached £60,000, the bank sought security for the debt. At this stage it was envisaged that the loan would be outstanding for only about a month. When the house was actually mortgaged, the indebtedness had risen to £135,000 and the mortgage, itself, contained an all monies clause, the effect of which was that the total indebtedness of the company was secured by the loan. When the bank sought to enforce the mortgage, the debt had risen to £154,000. When Mrs O'Brien signed the mortgage, she did not read it. Neither did she read a side letter, which she also signed, which acknowledged that the mortgage had been fully explained to her. The bank official, contrary to the bank's policy, had not explained the mortgage to her. She thought, and this was a view that her husband had encouraged her to hold, that the mortgage was limited to securing a short term loan of £60,000 rather than securing all monies owed by the company. The House of Lords held that the mortgage was not binding upon her.

---

[63] For an example of such a rarity, see *Lloyd's Bank Plc* v. *Rosset* [1991] 1 A.C. 107.
[64] See *Abbey National B.S.* v. *Cann* [1991] 1 A.C. 56.
[65] [1994] 1 A.C. 180 and 200 respectively.

In *Pitt*, the house in question was, again, a matrimonial home. In 1986, it was valued at £270,000 and was subject to a mortgage of £16,700. Mr Pitt wished to borrow £150,000, secured on the house, in order to speculate on the stock exchange. His wife was highly reluctant to do this but, as a result of undue influence, was persuaded to go along with the plan. The finance company was told that the purpose of the loan was to pay off the existing mortgage and buy a holiday home. The loan was agreed and the mortgage created. Some time later, as a result of the stock market crash, his investments became worthless, the house had plummeted in value and the mortgagee sought possession of the house. In this case, the House of Lords held that the mortgage was enforceable against Mrs Pitt.

The two cases were decided upon the same basis. It was held that, as between husband and wife, there exists a relationship of trust. This may also exist between unmarried cohabiting couples, be they heterosexual or homosexual. In a business transaction between the two, this trust may be abused, either by undue influence or some other legal wrong. In such circumstances, the transaction can be set aside. A third party, in these cases, the mortgagees, will take subject to this equity if they have notice, actual or constructive, of it. In *O'Brien*, the transaction in question was one where she was standing as surety for debts which her husband was guaranteeing. On its face, this transaction was not for her benefit and this put the bank upon notice that undue influence or some other legal wrong was present in securing her consent to the transaction. In such circumstances, for the bank to take free from the equity in her favour, they should have advised her of the nature of the mortgage and also recommended that she take legal advice prior to signing it. As the bank had not done either of these things, the mortgage was not binding upon her. In *Pitt*, on the other hand, the loan in question appeared to be a joint application to borrow money for their mutual benefit: principally to buy a holiday home. In these circumstances, there was nothing to put the mortgagee on inquiry that he may have been guilty of some wrongdoing in order to get her signature to the mortgage. Accordingly, no special precautions were necessary before accepting her signature.

These two cases are of considerable importance. Being of recent vintage, their full import has yet to be fully worked out. What is clear is that a vitally important matter is the expressed purpose of the loan. This will cause difficulties, in that situations can be envisaged where it is not clear if the loan is potentially to the wife's disadvantage. This will particularly be the case where the borrowing is for the benefit of a company in which they both may have interests. A counsel of prudence would seem to be sensible in such cases and the wife should be urged to seek legal advice before signing the mortgage. What these cases do demonstrate, however, is the increased importance that the courts attach to the interests of occupiers of property when that property is used as security for loans.

DUTY ON TAKING POSSESSION

When a mortgagee has exercised his right to take possession, he is subject to potential liability imposed by equity. In particular, he is under a liability to account strictly for any profits, such liability being on the basis of wilful default. An example of this principle is provided by *White v. City of London Brewery Co.*[66] The mortgaged property was a public house which was let as a "free house". The mortgagee, who was a brewer, took possession of the property and let it as a "tied house". He was liable to the mortgagor for the additional rent which could have been obtained if it had been let as a "free house."

APPOINTMENT OF A RECEIVER

The potential liability of a mortgagee who takes possession is sufficient to act as a disincentive for him to do so, except as a prelude to selling the property with vacant possession. If it is not envisaged that the property will be sold in the short term but the mortgagee, nevertheless, is anxious to protect his interest, a more attractive alternative to going into possession is to appoint a receiver.

Provided that the conditions stipulated with regard to the power of sale becoming exercisable have been satisfied,[67] the mortgagee may, in writing, appoint a receiver. The advantage of appointing a receiver is that, by section 109(2) of the Law of Property Act 1925, the receiver is deemed to be the agent of the mortgagor. So, although the receiver will collect income derived from the property, which will be used to pay the interest due under the mortgage, the mortgagee will escape the strict liability that would arise if he had taken possession himself. A further advantage is that, if there is a tenant in the property, receipt of rent by a receiver will not, of itself amount to the adoption of the tenancy. Assuming the tenancy to be unauthorised, receipt of rent, directly, by the mortgagee will have that effect.[68]

[66] (1889) 42 Ch.D. 237.
[67] *Post*, p. 206.
[68] See, *ante*, p. 198.

FORECLOSURE

The right of the mortgagor to redeem the mortgage after the contractual date of redemption has passed is a right conferred by equity; it is the equitable right to redeem. What equity has given, it can also take away. Before 1925, when the legal estate was vested in the mortgagee, the effect of foreclosure was simply to extinguish the equity of redemption. After 1925, an order is necessary to vest the fee simple in the mortgagee.

Foreclosure, which can only occur after the contractual date of redemption has passed, involves a two stage process: a foreclosure order *nisi* and a foreclosure order absolute. The former requires the mortgagor to repay the money borrowed, and so redeem the mortgage, within a set period, which is usually six months. A failure to do so will lead to a foreclosure order absolute. Under section 91 of the Law of Property Act 1925, the court may, at the instance of the mortgagee or any person interested, order a sale of the property rather than a foreclosure. As the effect of foreclosure may well be to overcompensate the mortgagee, by vesting in him property worth more than the debt, foreclosure orders are rarely seen today.

SALE

The most potent remedy of the mortgagee is to sell the mortgaged property. This is normally done after possession has been obtained. Various issues arise concerning the sale of mortgaged property. These are determining when the property can be sold, the duties incurred in selling the property and, finally, determining what is to happen to the proceeds of sale. The last matter involves a consideration of the question of priority of mortgages.

1. Power of sale. Because the mortgagee does not own the fee simple, in order to transfer it to a purchaser, the power to do so has to be conferred by statute. The statutory provisions relating to the power of sale are sections 101 and 103 of the Law of Property Act 1925 and it is important to distinguish between them. Section 101 governs when the power of sale arises and section 103 when it is exercisable.

(1) Power arising. The power of sale arises if:

   (i) the mortgage is by deed; and
   (ii) the mortgage money is due.

As all legal mortgages must be made by deed, the first condition is invariably satisfied in the case of legal mortgages.

This is not necessarily the case with equitable mortgages but, to enable the power of sale to arise, it is preferable for a deed to be used.

The second provision, that the mortgage money is due, means that the contractual date for redemption has passed. It is for this reason that mortgages have artificial clauses which either set the date for redemption six months from the date of the mortgage or stipulate that, if there is default in the payment of an instalment, the whole sum borrowed becomes repayable. In the event of instalment mortgages such clauses would seem to be unnecessary because it has been held that, in such cases, the failure to pay an instalment means that the power of sale arises.[69] Such clauses are, nevertheless, common and add to the air of artificiality that attaches to mortgage agreements.

It is essential, so far as the purchaser is concerned, that the power of sale has arisen. If it has not, then all the mortgagee can transfer is his own mortgage. He cannot transfer the fee simple.

(2) Power becoming exercisable. Although the power of sale may have arisen, it is only exercisable if one of the following conditions is satisfied:

    (i)   notice requiring payment of the mortgage money has been served on the mortgagor and default has been made in payment of part or all of it for three months; or

   (ii) some interest under the mortgage is two months in arrear; or

  (iii) there has been a breach of some provision in the mortgage, other than the covenant for the payment of mortgage money or interest.

The consequence of the property being sold when the power of sale is not exercisable is quite different from that which ensues if there is a purported sale before the power of sale has arisen. In the latter case, the purchaser acquires only the mortgage. In the case of a sale when the power of sale is not exercisable then, unless the purchaser actually knows this to be the case,[70] the purchaser will get a good title. Any person who is injured by the improper exercise of the power of sale has a remedy in damages against the person exercising it, that is the mortgagee.

2. Duties on sale. The mortgagor is vitally concerned with how the sale of the mortgaged property is conducted. If the sale

[69] *Payne v. Cardiff R.D.C.* [1932] 1 K.B. 241.
[70] See *Lord Waring v. London & Manchester Assurance Co. Ltd* [1935] Ch. 310 at 318.

realises a sum in excess of what the mortgagee is owed, then the mortgagor is entitled to the balance. The sum represents his equity of redemption. If, on the other hand, there was a negative equity in the house, the purchase will, after the sale, still owe the remaining amount to the mortgagee. Given these considerations, it is not surprising that the mortgagee is subject to some duties. The extent of those duties is, however, tempered by the countervailing interest of the mortgagee to realise his security.

The first point to make is that there must be a genuine sale. Unless authorised by statute or by the court,[71] the mortgagee cannot sell the property to himself, either directly, or through an intermediary as part of a pre-planned arrangement.[72] While it is not prohibited to sell the property to an associated person or organisation, if this is done, then the onus of proof, which is normally on the mortgagor, shifts to the mortgagee and the purchaser to show that the sale was proper.[73]

In deciding to sell the property, the mortgagee owes no duty at all to the mortgagor. He can sell the property at any time, to suit himself, even if the market is in depressed condition and, conversely, will not be liable for not selling the property at a time when market conditions are favourable.[74] When the mortgagee has made a contract of sale, the mortgagor's right to redeem is suspended and the contract has priority over any earlier contract of sale entered into by the mortgagor.[75]

In actually selling the property, the mortgagee is under a duty, which in the case of building societies is statutory,[76] to exercise reasonable care to get the true market price[77] and will be liable in damages for a failure to do so. This liability, which is also owed to any surety of the mortgage,[78] is not discharged simply by putting the property in the hands of a reputable agent. If the agent negligently sells the property at an undervalue, the mortgagee will remain liable to the mortgagor and must then pursue his own remedy against the agent.

In deciding whether the mortgagee is in breach of his duty, much will depend upon the facts of each case. One principle of general application which has emerged, however, is that the

---

[71] See Housing Act 1985, s.452; Sched. 17; *Palk v. Mortgage Services Funding Plc* [1993] Ch. 330.

[72] *Farrar v. Farrars Ltd* (1888) 40 Ch.D. 395 at 409; *Robertson v. Norris* (1858) 1 Giff. 421.

[73] *Tse Kwok Lam v. Wong Chit Sen* [1983] 1 W.L.R. 1349.

[74] *China & South Sea Bank Ltd v. Tan Soon Gin* [1991] 1 A.C. 531.

[75] *Property & Bloodstock Ltd v. Emerton* [1968] Ch. 94; *Duke* v. *Robson* [1973] 1 W.L.R. 267.

[76] Building Societies Act 1986, Sched. 4, replacing earlier legislation.

[77] *Cuckmere Brick Co. Ltd v. Mutual Finance Ltd* [1971] Ch. 949.

[78] *Standard Chartered Bank Ltd v. Walker* [1982] 1 W.L.R. 1410.

property must be properly exposed to the market and not sold on a "crash sale" basis.[79] It may well be the case that if property is advertised for sale on the basis of being a repossessed property, this fact, alone, may constitute a breach of duty by the mortgagee, it being well known that such properties are frequently bought on the basis that they can be bought cheaply.

3. Proceeds of sale.   Although a mortgagee is not a trustee of his power of sale, he is a trustee of the proceeds of sale. After deducting the expenses connected with the sale he must deal with the proceeds in the following way. He will first deduct the money that he is owed. He must then pay any subsequent mortgagees, if any, and the balance is then paid to the mortgagor.[80] The existence of subsequent mortgages will be discovered by searching in the land charges register or the land register, as appropriate.

PRIORITY OF MORTGAGES

The final matter to consider with regard to the law of mortgages is the question of priority. In the case of unsecured creditors, in the event of an insolvency, the creditors are paid from the assets of the debtor in proportion to what each of them are owed. This is not the case with secured creditors. Each secured creditor is paid what they are owed in full, but the order in which they are paid is determined by the priority of their securities. If the property secured is of insufficient value to meet all the claims, then those at the end of the list of priorities will effectively lose their security and will remain unpaid, unless the mortgagor has other assets of sufficient value to meet the amount owed. Even if that is the case, their claim to be paid from those assets will be of no greater weight than that of other creditors. The method of working out priorities is, therefore, important. Unfortunately, the law governing a number of issues which may arise is in a state of some confusion. Moreover, despite the major changes made to the law of mortgages by the 1925 legislation, as will be seen, certain aspects of the pre-1925 law remain relevant. Although difficulties can occur in respect of equitable mortgages,[81] the treatment here will be confined to legal mortgages.

1. Unregistered land.   Before 1925, a mortgage was usually created by the mortgagor conveying the land to the mortgagee.

---

[79] *Predeth v. Castle Phillips Finance Co. Ltd* [1986] 2 E.G.L.R. 144. See M.P. Thompson [1986] Conv. 442.

[80] L.P.A. 1925, s.105.

[81] See Thompson, *Repossession of Property on Mortgage Default*, pp. 92–93.

This could only be done once, so one would not find more than one legal mortgage affecting the property. After 1925, there is no difficulty in creating a succession of legal mortgages and so issues of priority will arise. It is necessary to distinguish between mortgages which are registrable and those which are not.

(1) Deposit of title deeds. A mortgagee is entitled to the title deeds. This type of mortgage is not registrable as a land charge. As a legal interest affecting the land, it has priority over subsequent mortgages. Where difficulties can arise is when the mortgagee subsequently parts with the title deeds. As will be seen, a mortgage which is not protected by deposit of title deeds is registrable. If the mortgagee parts with the title deeds, it is generally accepted that the mortgage does not become registrable; otherwise, the mortgage would oscillate between being registrable or not depending upon the present possession of the deeds. Instead, where there is a mortgage initially protected by deposit of title deeds, and the mortgagee parts with possession of the deeds and a subsequent mortgage is created, the issue of priority between the two mortgages is governed by the pre-1925 law.

Under the pre-1925 rules, a legal mortgage could lose priority to a subsequent equitable mortgage either by a failure to take possession of the title deeds or by subsequently parting with them. It was not sufficient to lose priority, simply, to neglect to take possession of the deeds. The mortgagee had to be shown to be either fraudulent or grossly negligent in failing to take possession of them.[82] Although dicta exist which seem to draw a distinction between an initial failure to obtain the deeds and a failure to retain them, with loss of priority being easier to establish in the former case,[83] the better view is that the principles are the same.[84] It is thought that if, after 1925, a mortgagee negligently parts with the title deeds, and a subsequent legal mortgage is then created, the second mortgage will have priority.

(2) Registrable mortgages. Ordinarily, as a matter of principle, one would expect legal mortgages to rank in order of priority in accordance with the order of their creation. Being legal interests they should bind the world, regardless of notice. In the case of

---

[82] *Colyer v. Finch* (1856) 5 H.L.Cas. 905 at 924.
[83] *Northern Counties of England Fire Insurance Co. v. Whipp* (1884) 26 Ch.D. 482 at 487.
[84] *Oliver v. Hinton* [1899] Ch. 264 at 274.

mortgages there are sound practical reasons why this is not the case.

If one takes as an example a house which is worth £100,000 and subject to a mortgage of £60,000, the house is good security for further lending up to £40,000. A second mortgagee, who is approached, will know of the existence of the first mortgage because the first mortgagee will have possession of the title deeds. Armed with this information, he will discover the amount of the mortgage and decide accordingly how much he is prepared to lend. Because only the first mortgagee will have the title deeds, unless other legal mortgages were made registrable, there is no way that the mortgagee could discover if there was a second, or even a third, mortgage affecting the property. It would, therefore, be very unsafe for him to lend money by way of mortgage. To circumvent this problem, a mortgage which is not protected by deposit of title deeds, termed a puisne mortgage, is registrable as a Class C(i) land charge.

Whereas the consequence of non-registration of a land charge is normally quite clear; it is void for non-registration against a subsequent purchaser,[85] the position is far from clear in the case of mortgages. The reason for this is the existence of two conflicting statutory provisions.

Under section 4(5) of the Land Charges Act 1972, a land charge of Class C . . . shall be void as against a purchaser of the land charged with it, or any interest in such land, unless the land charge is registered in the appropriate register before the completion of the purchase.

Section 97 of the Law of Property Act 1925 provides that: Every mortgage affecting a legal estate in land . . . (not being a mortgage protected by the deposit of documents relating to the legal estate affected) shall rank according to its date of registration pursuant to the Land Charges Act [1972].

The conflict between the two sections is best shown by an example.

> On January 1, a puisne mortgage is created in favour of A.
> On January 8, a puisne mortgage is created in favour of B.
> On January 10, A registers his mortgage.
> On January 12, B registers his mortgage.

According to the Land Charges Act, A's mortgage is void against B for non-registration and so B's mortgage should have priority over that of A. According to the Law of Property Act,

---

[85] *Ante*, pp. 41, 42.

the mortgages rank in order of registration and so A's mortgage should have priority over that of B.

As to which solution should prevail there are two opposing arguments, each of which is persuasive. In favour of the first solution is the argument that something which is void for non-registration should not be capable of resurrection by a subsequent registration. The opposing view is that section 97 deals specifically with the priority of mortgages and, unless allowed to prevail, has no meaning. While appreciating the force of the latter argument, it is thought that the former argument should prevail and that the priority order should be B and then A. Because A had not protected the mortgage by registration, there was nothing that B could have done to ascertain the existence of the mortgage and should, therefore, have a stronger claim to priority than A who neglected to register his mortgage. It does no credit to the law that this important issue remains shrouded in doubt.

2. Registered land. Where title is registered, a mortgage is created by means of a registered charge. Until the charge is registered, the mortgage takes effect as a minor interest. Various situations can arise, which will depend upon whether or not the mortgage is registered as a charge.

(1) Registered charges. According to section 29 of the Land Registration Act 1925, registered charges rank in the order in which they are entered on the register and not the order of their creation.

(2) Protected minor interest. Until the mortgage is registered, it takes effect as a minor interest. This may be protected by the entry of a notice or a caution. The effect of registration of a notice is that the mortgage will take priority over a subsequent interest. In the case of protection by way of a caution, the normal procedure at the registry will ensure that the cautioner will be notified of any proposed dealing with the land and can, therefore, sustain the case to have the mortgage registered as a charge at the resulting hearing. If, for some reason, the registry does not notify the cautioner, then priority will be lost to a subsequently registered charge.[86]

(3) Unprotected interests. Where both mortgages are unprotected, they both take effect in equity as minor interests and the issue of priority is governed by the general rule that the

---

[86] *Clarke v. Chief Land Registrar* [1993] Ch. 294.

first in time will prevail. This is the case, even though the second mortgage is protected by the registration of a notice.[87] In this second situation, an argument could be put that the first mortgagee should lose priority by reason of gross negligence in not registering the mortgage.

3. Tacking. The process of tacking involves a mortgagee granting a further loan to the mortgagee and adding that loan to the amount secured by the existing mortgage. The ability to do this may, of course, affect the rights of any subsequent mortgagee and, consequently, restrictions are imposed on this right. Again, one must distinguish between unregistered land and registered land.

(1) Unregistered land. The right to tack is governed by section 94 of the Law of Property Act 1925 and can be done in three situations.

(A) Consent of Intervening Mortgagee

If there is a mortgage in favour of A, followed by a mortgage in favour of B, A may tack a further loan to the existing mortgage if B consents.

(B) No Notice of Intervening Mortgage

A mortgagee may tack a further loan to an existing mortgage if he has no notice of an intervening mortgage. If the property is mortgaged to A and then to B, A cannot tack if he has notice of B's mortgage. Notice is supplied if either B has registered his mortgage as a land charge, or has possession of the title deeds. If, however, the mortgage in favour of A is to secure further advances then A will not be regarded as having notice of B's mortgage simply on the basis of registration. To avoid this difficulty, B should inform A of the existence of his mortgage.

(C) Obligation to Make Further Advances

If the first mortgagee is, under the terms of the mortgage, obliged to make further advances to the mortgagor, he is entitled to tack the loan to the original mortgage regardless of whether he has notice of a subsequent mortgage.

(2) Registered land. The right to tack is governed by section 30 of the Land Registration Act 1925. Only the registered proprie-

---

[87] *The Mortgage Corporation Ltd v. Nationwide Credit Corporation Ltd* [1993] 4 All E.R. 623.

tor of a charge may tack. If the proprietor is under an obligation, noted on the register, to make further advances, any subsequent registered charge will take subject to any further advance.

If the proprietor has the option of making further advances, but the charge is registered for the purpose of securing further advances, the registered proprietor must be given notice of any entry which would prejudicially affect the priority of any further advances.

CHAPTER THIRTEEN

Limitation

As is the case with other causes of action, actions for the recovery of land are affected by limitation periods. In the context of land, however, the effect of an action being statute barred is more fundamental than is the case with other forms of limitation. This is because the consequence of a right of recovery being statute barred is that, for most practical purposes, the person who was an initial trespasser acquires the rights of owner of the land in question.

OWNERSHIP AND POSSESSION

At the heart of English Land Law is the notion that ownership of the land or, more accurately, estates in land is relative. Although when title is registered, this concept is heavily qualified by the state guarantee of title, the essential premise remains true. Thus, in determining rights to land, a court is not concerned with seeking to establish who is the owner of the land; rather it is concerned to determine which of two rival claimants to it has the better right to possession.

This essential point was made by Lord Mansfield in the eighteenth century when he said "the plaintiff cannot recover but upon the strength of his own title. He cannot found his claim upon the weakness of the defendant's title. For, possession gives the defendant a right against every man who cannot show a good title."[1]

Put in a more modern context, the same point was made in *Ocean Estates Ltd v. Pinder*.[2] The case concerned an action for

[1] *Roe d. Haldane v. Harvey* (1769) 4 Burr. 2484 at 2487.
[2] [1969] 2 A.C. 19. See, also, *Asher v. Whitlock* (1865) L.R. 1 Q.B. 1.

trespass. The defence was that title had been acquired by adverse possession. When this defence failed, an alternative defence was put, which was that the plaintiff's paper title to the land was defective. This defence also failed, the plaintiff having been in possession of the land before the defendant. Lord Diplock, giving the judgment of the Privy Council, said:

"Where questions of title to land arise in litigation the court is concerned only with the relative strengths of title proved by the rival claimants. If party A can prove a better title than party B he is entitled to succeed notwithstanding that C may have a better title than A, if C is neither a party to the action nor a person by whose authority B is in possession or occupation of the land."[3]

The essence of this judgment is that the court is concerned solely to determine the relative strengths of the claims to possession of the parties to the litigation. If A has taken possession of land, then he is entitled to remain on that land unless and until someone else can prove a better right to possession. If B takes possession, then A can recover possession as against B unless B can establish that A's right to bring an action against him has been statute barred. It is quite irrelevant that B can prove that A had no right to possession in the first place and that C was entitled to possession. As the person who was in possession A has a better right to the land than B. In general terms, proof that a third party has a better right to the land is irrelevant. The only time that such a plea will be relevant is if C is in possession of land and D, who has not been in prior occupation, seeks to recover the land from C. In that case, it is open to C to prove that D has no right to the land because E is entitled to it. In truth, such an instance is simply a further illustration of the general principle of relativity of title. As between C and D, D, as the person in possession, has the better right to possess the land than C.

THE RATIONALE OF LIMITATION

The general effect of a right to possession becoming barred is that the person who was previously entitled to possess the land is no longer able to pursue this action.

As it is unlikely that anyone else will be able to prove a better right to possession than the erstwhile trespasser, the upshot is that that person becomes, in effect, the owner of the land. Before

---

[3] *ibid.* at p. 25.

examining this process in more detail, it is as well, at the outset, to consider the justification for what some people may equate with theft; by an initially wrongful act of trespass, the trespasser acquires rights of ownership over the land.[4]

There are two principal reasons. The first is common to all forms of limitation. This is that the law, in general, discourages stale claims. The second relates to security of title. Given the complexity of land law, it is quite possible that a mistake may have been made in the past in terms of the devolution of title. Related to this, there may have existed uncertainty as to the location of boundaries between different plots of land. The existence of limitation periods may have a curative effect. If a conveyancing mistake had occurred in the past, this may have gone undetected for a considerable period of time. If, in consequence of this error, people have been in wrongful possession of the land for a considerable period, the effect of the limitation period is that their title, which was once challengeable, has now become immune from attack. Conveyancing errors can, in time, become of historical interest and, as a result, the land will become marketable and a purchaser need not be concerned about a technical defect in title which may otherwise have led to his right to possession of the land being challenged in the future by some, as yet unidentified person.[5] Similarly, it may happen that there is uncertainty as to where, precisely, a boundary between two properties should be. This uncertainty can be resolved if the disputed area has been in the possession of one of the parties for the requisite period. In this case, it will not be necessary to resolve the dispute as to where the boundary should, technically, have been drawn. The result of prolonged possession will be that party who has enclosed the disputed strip will have acquired title to it, regardless of where the boundary was originally sited. The effect of limitation can, therefore, be to prevent stale litigation and to cause greater security of title.

ADVERSE POSSESSION

In determining whether the rights of the owner of the paper title to the land have become statute barred, two principal issues arise. The first issue is the length of time which must elapse before a right becomes barred. The second, related, matter is to determine when, for the purpose of limitation, time begins to run.

---

[4] See, generally, M. Dockray [1985] Conv. 272.
[5] See *Re Atkinson and Horsell's Contract* [1912] 2 Ch. 1.

1. The limitation period. It is provided by section 15 of the
Limitation Act 1980, that no action shall be brought by any
person to recover any land after the expiration of 12 years from
the date on which the right of action accrued to him, or if it first
accrued to some person through whom he claims, to that
person.

For most cases, therefore, the limitation period is set at 12
years. There are some exceptions to this. In the case of Crown
land and a charitable corporation sole, the limitation period is
set at 10 years.[6] In the case of foreshore owned by the Crown,
the period is 60 years.[7]

2. The running of time. Section 15 of and Schedule 1 to the
Limitation Act 1980 govern when time begins to run for the
purpose of the limitation period. There are two main requirements. These are:

   (i)   The owner of the land who is entitled in possession has
       been dispossessed or has discontinued his possession;
       and

  (ii)   some other person has gone into adverse possession of
       the land.

1. Dispossession or discontinuance. The Act refers to the
owner of land who is entitled to possession. In cases where
there exist future interests in the land, such as where land is
limited to A for life, remainder to B, time will not begin to run
against B until he is entitled to possession. Special provisions
govern this situation.[8] Similarly, when there is a lease, time will
not run against the landlord while the original lease continues to
subsist. This situation will be considered more fully below.

The Act gives as alternatives, the dispossession of the owner
of the land and the discontinuance of possession by him. The
latter is more common and amounts to effective abandonment
of the land. Neither dispossession nor discontinuance is, by
itself, sufficient to start time running. In addition, it is necessary
that a person has gone into adverse possession of the land. It is
this element of the law of limitation which has given rise to
most difficulty.

2. Adverse possession. The concept of adverse possession
involves two issues. First, the person who is claiming that time

---

[6] Limitation Act 1980, s.1(1), Sched. 1, para. 10.
[7] *ibid.*, para. 11.
[8] See Megarry, *Manual of the Law of Real Property* (7th ed.), p. 497.

has run in his favour, normally termed the squatter, has, as a matter of fact taken possession of the land. In addition to being in possession, as a matter of fact, he must also have the requisite intention to possess. Secondly, the possession must be adverse to the owner of the land. This last requirement has given rise to particular difficulty when the owner of the land has some future use for that land, which is not inconvenienced by the occupation of the squatter.

(1) Possession. To establish possession as a fact, the squatter must show an appropriate degree of physical control of the property.[9] The clearest method of exercising the requisite degree of physical control is to enclose the land by fencing.[10] Alone, even this may not be sufficient. If the fencing has been done to protect a right of way, then this will not amount to possession of the land.[11] Trivial acts of possession are usually insufficient to amount to the taking possession of the land.[12]

(2) Possession must be adverse. The requirement that, before time will run in favour of the squatter, there must be adverse possession has occasioned considerable difficulty; much of that difficulty being caused by a lack of clarity as to whose intention with regard to the land was most important: the squatter or the owner of the paper title.

The essence of adverse possession was stated by Slade L.J., in *Buckingham C.C. v. Moran.*[13] He said:

"Possession is never 'adverse' within the meaning of the Act of 1980 if it is enjoyed by lawful title. If, therefore, a person occupies or uses land by licence of the owner with the paper title and his licence has not been duly determined, he cannot be treated as having been in 'adverse possession' as against the owner of the paper title."

The general idea is clear. If the squatter is on the land with the permission of the paper owner of the land, the possession cannot be adverse. In cases of express permission, this is not problematic. A question which arose was the situation where an implied, or imputed, permission was in issue. The source of this difficulty was a dictum in *Leigh v. Jack.*[14]

---

[9] *Powell v. McFarlane* (1979) 38 P. & C.R. 452 at 470, *per* Slade L.J.

[10] *Seddon v. Smith* (1877) 36 L.T. 168.

[11] *Littledale v. Liverpool College* [1900] 2 Ch. 19; *George Wimpey & Co. Ltd v. Sohn* [1967] Ch. 487.

[12] See *Williams Bros. District Suppliers Ltd v. Raftery* [1958] 1 Q.B. 159; *Tecbild Ltd v. Chamberlain* (1969) 20 P. & C.R. 633.

[13] [1990] Ch. 623 at 626.

[14] (1879) 5 Ex.D. 264.

In this case, the issue was whether there had been adverse possession of a strip of land. The paper owner had the future intention of constructing a street on the strip. The person claiming adverse possession had stored materials from his factory on the strip, thereby preventing its use by pedestrians, and had erected fences at each end. This was held not to amount to adverse possession. Bramwell L.J., in a much quoted passage, said:

". . . in order to defeat a title by dispossessing the former owner, acts must be done which are inconsistent with his enjoyment of the soil for the purposes which he intended to use it: that is not the case here, where it is the intention of the plaintiff and her predecessors in title not either to build upon or cultivate the land, but to devote it at some time to public purposes."[15]

The meaning of this dictum is not clear. It can be taken to mean that, if the paper owner has some future use for the land, and that future use is not precluded by the activities of the squatter, then his possession cannot be adverse. If that is the meaning of what was said, a further question arose as to what the basis of this rule was. Alternatively, it may be taken to mean that, in these circumstances, it is merely more difficult for the squatter to establish the requisite intention for his possession to be considered to be adverse. Various interpretations were proffered in the controversial case of *Wallis & Cayton Bay Holiday Camp Ltd* v. *Shell Mex Ltd & B.P. Ltd*.[16]

In this case, the squatter had performed extensive acts on the disputed land which was owned by a petrol company. The company intended, at a later date to construct a road and a garage on the land, although the latter plan was subsequently abandoned. After 12 years, the squatter claimed to be entitled to the land. The majority of the Court of Appeal rejected the claim. Lord Denning M.R., after referring to authorities including *Leigh v. Jack*, explained them in this way. He said

"The reasons behind the decisions is because it does not lie in that other person's mouth to assert that he used the land of his own wrong as a trespasser. Rather his user is to be ascribed to the licence or permission of the true owner."[17]

This reason was clearly heretical in that the whole basis of adverse possession is that the squatter acts as a trespasser. What

---

[15] *ibid.* at p. 273.
[16] [1975] Q.B. 94.
[17] *ibid.* at p. 103.

was less clear, however, was whether this was the introduction of a wholly new, and unjustified, rule or whether it was simply an unorthodox way of summing up the effect of *Leigh v. Jack*; a decision which could be interpreted as establishing that, if the paper title owner has some future use for the land in question, then, unless the acts of the squatter are prejudicial to that plan, the possession is not adverse.[18]

This issue became important owing to the legislative repeal of Lord Denning's theory. Paragraph 8(4) of Schedule 1 to the Limitation Act 1980 provides that it shall not be assumed that [the squatter's] occupation is by permission of the person entitled to the land merely by virtue of the fact that it is not inconsistent with the latter's present or future enjoyment of the land. Clearly this provision consigned Lord Denning's reasoning to oblivion; rather less clear was the status to be afforded to the dictum of Bramwell in *Leigh v. Jack*.

This issue was fully ventilated in the leading case of *Buckingham C.C. v. Moran*.[19] In this case, land, owned by the council, had been encroached upon for over 12 years by an adjoining landowner and his predecessor in title. Extensive use had been made of the plot and access to it was only possible from the defendant's house. The council, who intended to use the land in the future for a proposed road diversion, argued that the defendant had not established adverse possession. This was rejected by the Court of Appeal. It was held that the crucial issue in establishing adverse possession was the intention of the squatter. What must be established is the intention to possess the land, in the sense of excluding others. It is not necessary for there to be an intention to own the land. If the paper owner has some future use planned for the land, then this may make this intention harder to establish. If, however, that intention is established, then there is no special rule to the effect that the possession is not adverse if it is not inconsistent with a planned future use of the property.

(3) Use must be open. For time to begin to run there is a requirement, in effect, that the use of the land by the squatter is open. If the squatter has acted fraudulently, or any relevant act has been deliberately concealed, then time does not begin to run against the person entitled to the land until such time as he could, with reasonable diligence, have discovered the position.[20] The running of time will not be postponed against a purchaser

---

[18] See *Trealor v. Nute* [1976] 1 W.L.R. 1295.
[19] [1990] Ch. 623.
[20] Limitation Act 1980, s.32.

for value from the squatter who did not know, or have reason to know, of the fraud or concealment.[21]

(4) Interruption of time. Once time has begun to run in favour of a squatter, it does not matter, so far as the paper owner is concerned, if the original squatter is replaced by another. The two periods will be aggregated and once 12 years has elapsed, the title of the paper owner will be extinguished. What will stop the clock running is if there is either a signed acknowledgment of the owner's title or a part payment of principal or interest.[22] These events do not suspend the running of time. Any further claim to adverse possession must be based upon a further 12 years. A possession order will, also stop time running[23] but the mere claim for possession will not.[24]

(5) Leaseholds. Where property is subject to a lease, the effect of adverse possession depends upon whom the claim is against. If the tenant is ousted from the property, then time will begin to run as against the tenant but will not run against the landlord until the expiry of the original lease. Until then, he is not entitled to possession. If, however, the tenant pays rent to a person other than the landlord for 12 years, then the person in receipt of the rent will bar the landlord's title.[25]

A tenant cannot usually establish adverse possession as against his landlord even he remains in prolonged occupation without paying rent. This applies to fixed term tenancies. In the case of a written periodic tenancy, time begins to run from the determination of the tenancy. Where there is no written lease but a periodic tenancy has been created orally, or by implication, time begins to run from the end of the first period or the last receipt of rent.[26] In the case of a tenancy at will, time begins to run from the determination of the tenancy.[27]

Although the tenant cannot usually establish adverse possession against his landlord, he can, of course, do so against other landowners. If, however, he occupies adjoining land owned by a third party, there is a rebuttable presumption that he does so on behalf of the landlord as well as himself.[28] If he occupies adjoining land owned by the landlord, there is a similar rebutt-

[21] *ibid.*, s.32(3).
[22] *ibid.*, s.29.
[23] *B.P. Properties Ltd v. Buckler* (1987) 55 P. & C.R. 337.
[24] *Mount Carmel Investments Ltd v. Peter Thurlow Ltd* (1988) 57 P. & C.R. 396.
[25] Limitation Act 1980, Sched. 1, para. 6.
[26] *ibid.*, Sched. 1, para. 5(1)(2).
[27] *ibid.*, Sched. 1, para. 4.
[28] *King v. Smith* [1950] 1 All E.R. 554.

able presumption, the effect of which is that it is presumed that this land is subject to the terms of the original lease.[29]

THE EFFECT OF ADVERSE POSSESSION

Adverse possession is not like prescription. When one acquires an easement by prescription the law rests on the presumption that it was granted at some time in the past and so the exercise of the right was done as a matter of right. In the case of adverse possession, what is claimed is wrongful user over the prescribed period.[30] One consequence of this is that the effect of adverse possession is negative in nature; the title of the paper owner to the land is extinguished and will not be revived by a later acknowledgment of the owner's title,[31] although if that does happen, it is possible that estoppel rights may arise in favour of the owner of the paper title.[32]

What this means is that the squatter establishes a title independent from that of the paper owner whom he dispossessed. Certainly, in so far as unregistered land is concerned, the effect of adverse possession is not to effect a "Parliamentary conveyance" of the paper owner's title.[33]

1. Unregistered land.   Where title is unregistered, the squatter acquires an independent fee simple in the property. He is not, however, a purchaser for value. This means he will not only be bound by legal rights affecting the land, as these rights bind the world, but also be bound by equitable rights, irrespective of whether or not he has notice of them.[34]

(i) Leasehold property.   In the case of leasehold property, because there is no assignment of the lease from the dispossessed tenant to the squatter, there is no privity of estate between him and the landlord. The squatter is not, therefore, liable on the covenants in the lease.[35] The covenants can be enforced indirectly, however. This is because the original tenant remains liable under the covenants and, if they are unperformed, the lease can be forfeited and the landlord, therefore, entitled to possession. The squatter is not entitled to apply for relief against forfeiture.[36]

---

[29] *J.F. Perrott & Co. Ltd v. Cohen* [1958] 1 K.B. 705.
[30] See *Buckinghamshire C.C. v. Moran* [1990] Ch. 623 at 649, *per* Nourse L.J.
[31] Limitation Act 1980, s.17.
[32] *Colchester B.C. v. Smith* [1992] Ch. 421. For cogent criticism, see A.H.R. Brierly [1991] Conv. 397.
[33] *Tichborne v. Weir* (1892) 67 L.T. 735 at 737.
[34] See *Re Nisbet and Pott's Contract* [1906] 1 Ch. 306.
[35] *Tichborne v. Weir, supra.*
[36] *Tickner v. Buzzacott* [1965] Ch. 426.

A separate problem with regard to a squatter having extinguished the tenant's title concerns the surrender of the lease. The question arose in *Fairweather v. St Marylebone Property Co. Ltd*[37] as to whether a tenant, whose title had been barred by a squatter, could surrender the lease to the landlord, thereby allowing the landlord to obtain possession as against the squatter. By a majority, the House of Lords held that this was possible.

This has been plausibly criticised on the basis that, as the tenant could not evict the squatter after the limitation period had expired, he should not be able to confer this right upon any body else: *nemo dat quod non habet*.[38] On the other hand, the decision is supportable on the basis that, although the Act refers to the owner's title being extinguished, it is clear that it is not extinguished for all purposes and, in particular, continues to subsist *vis à vis* the landlord. Were this not the case, the landlord would be entitled to possession as soon as the tenant's lease had been statute barred and the tenant would not continue to be liable upon the covenants in the lease. The effect of the decision is, however, that the landlord and tenant can collude and defeat the rights of the squatter, in circumstances when neither part, acting alone, could do so.

2. Registered land.[39] Where title is registered, the title of the registered proprietor cannot be extinguished without some alteration of the position on the register. This is provided for by section 75 of the Land Registration Act 1925, which provides that the proprietor holds the estate upon trust for the squatter. Until the squatter applies for registration with a possessory title, his interest in the property takes effect as an overriding interest.[40]

Where title is leasehold, the leasehold estate is, again, held upon trust for the squatter pending application for registration. When the squatter has been registered as proprietor, then the tenant cannot surrender the lease to the landlord.[41] If the tenant purports to surrender the lease to the landlord, prior to the squatter's title being registered, it is thought that the landlord would not be entitled to possession. The tenant would hold the lease upon trust for the squatter and that interest would appear to be binding upon the landlord as an overriding interest. It would seem that the position is different, in this regard, between registered and unregistered land.

---

[37] [1963] A.C. 510.
[38] H.W.R. Wade (1962) 78 L.Q.R. 33.
[39] For a valuable discussion, see E. Cooke (1994) 14 L.S. 1.
[40] L.R.A. 1925, s.70(1)(f). See, also, *Bridges v. Mees* [1957] Ch. 475.
[41] *Spectrum Investment Co. v. Holmes* [1981[1 W.L.R. 221.

INDEX